On Broadway

On Broadway

Art and Commerce on the Great White Way

Steven Adler

Southern Illinois University Press / Carbondale

Library of Congress Cataloging-in-Publication Data
Adler, Steven, [date]
On Broadway : art and commerce on the great white
way / Steven Adler.
    p. cm.
Includes bibliographical references (p.) and index.
1. Musicals—New York (State)—New York—History
and criticism. 2. Musical theater—Economic aspects—
New York (State)—New York. 3. Broadway (New York,
N.Y.). 4. Theater—New York (State)—New York—
History—20th century. I. Title.
ML1711.8N3A35 2004
792.6'09747'1—dc22   2004010467
ISBN 0-8093-2592-6 (cloth : alk. paper)
IBSN 0-8093-2593-4 (pbk : alk. paper)

FOR NORA AND TIGER, MY TWO MUSES

Contents

Preface

They say the neon lights are bright on Broadway,
They say there's always magic in the air.
   —Barry Mann, Cynthia Weil, Jerry Leiber, and Mike Stoller, "On Broadway," as
   sung by the Drifters

The lights of Broadway, neon and otherwise, are brighter than ever. The renovation of the theatre district in the 1990s resulted in an extravagant nightly advertising barrage, an overwhelming sensory assault. The magic in the air is palpably different, too, occasioned by the arrival of both corporate and not-for-profit producing organizations, escalating costs, changing audience demographics and theatrical tastes, and the competitive muscularity of Off-Broadway and regional theatres.

It is tempting, when writing about the state of Broadway, to decry the commercialization of the district and the work seen on its stages. But historically, Broadway has been primarily a commercial enterprise, demonstrating for decades that the profit motive could support vibrant artistic expression. Broadway today, rather, must be examined in light of numerous artistic and economic currents that have changed greatly the way in which professional theatre in America is conceived, produced, marketed, and presented. Broadway, once the prime generator of American theatre, is now just one element—albeit a critical one—in the theatrical equation.

I began research for this project with an enthusiasm that stemmed from a potent desire to return to my roots. Growing up in Brooklyn, I romantically viewed Broadway as the pinnacle of theatrical achievement. When I began my theatre studies in college, however, I was exposed to the radically different world of experimental theatre. I soon adopted the prevailing attitude that scorned Broadway as an anachronistic, creaking memento; the exciting work was to be found elsewhere in New York and around the country. In many ways, that disdain was more than just hip snobbery; Broadway in the early seventies was stuck in amber. Except for a handful of daring new works and imports from England, Broadway was decidedly out of step with the cultural wildfire that had swept across the nation. Broadway was a commercial mainstream bastion, rarely inclined to risk artistic innovation.

My subsequent work in the professional theatre afforded me a more considered view. In 1981 I stage-managed my first Broadway musical, a revival of *Camelot* at the Winter Garden Theatre. As much as I regarded the production itself as merely workmanlike, my cynicism about Broadway dissipated in the palpable energy of opening night. As I gave the cues to dim the houselights and start the overture, I experienced the unexpected but not unpleasant awareness that I was now organically connected to a legacy that in many ways defined American theatre. I could appreciate, from the panoramic perspective of theatrical process of a stage manager, the extraordinary effort involved in mounting a Broadway show. I could better understand, too, the complex nexus of art and commerce that created Broadway theatre. Six years later, when I left New York for a position in academe, I had witnessed the beginning of a startling metamorphosis, both physical and artistic, in my neighborhood. I would continue to monitor the evolution of Broadway, but from a continent away.

In 2000 I began to explore the changes that had been wrought on Broadway. Generous travel grants from the University of California, San Diego, enabled me to visit my old haunts and reconnect with former colleagues, who in turn graciously introduced me to many others in the Broadway community. Over the next thirty months, I interviewed more than sixty people and attended many productions. The professionals whose voices are heard in this book come from all theatrical endeavors: they are playwrights, composers, lyricists, directors, designers, actors, musical directors, stage managers, stagehands, theatre owners, independent producers, corporate producers, general managers, press agents, advertising representatives, union leaders, city planners, theatre critics, and attorneys.

I discovered conflicting perspectives on what Broadway theatre is and should be. There was much disagreement about the germinal issues at play, as well as a wide spectrum of opinions about the future of Broadway. Fundamentally, I realized that Broadway is at a crossroads, beyond the physical one of Times Square. Its practitioners wrestle with complex forces that have begun to change profoundly the face and the nature of theatre—on Broadway, across the nation, and around the world.

Acknowledgments

This book, like Broadway itself, reflects the participation of a wide cross section of people, all of whom were extremely supportive of this project and generous with their time and insight.

Several interviewees are old friends and colleagues who assisted me not only in seeing the terrain with greater acuity but also in networking, a critical task. Many of those whom I met for the first time while researching this book were extraordinarily helpful, too, putting me in touch with their colleagues and friends, and so the circle quickly grew.

Three people, themselves subjects, deserve special gratitude. Frank Rich, the dean of modern Broadway theatre criticism, was invaluable not only in framing the critical issues but also in providing the necessary introduction to so many of the practitioners with whom I spoke. Alan Levey of Disney, a friend and colleague for years, patiently explained much and consistently pointed me in the right direction. Seth Gelblum, attorney extraordinaire, gave me a one-man tutorial in producing and arranged several interviews. Tom Aberger, Danny Burstein, Judith Dolan, Terrence Dwyer, Rebecca Luker, Des McAnuff, William Parry, Jim Pentecost, Daryl Roth, Jim Sullivan, and Dianne Trulock, gracious subjects all, provided essential introductions to so many others.

My good pals Barbara Pitts and John Vivian opened several doors that would have remained shut without their intercession. Roy Somlyo, past president of the American Theatre Wing, generously provided me with a comprehensive set of videotapes that handsomely chronicle the various aspects of working in the professional theatre. Karita Burbank of Disney Theatrical, Don Hill at Actors' Equity Association, Aaron Levin at Disney Theatrical, Allison Matera at Manhattan Theatre Club, Gloria McCormick at the American Federation of Musicians Local 802, Sandra Nance at Theatre Communications Group, Ted Pappas at the Society of Stage Directors and Choreographers, Jeremy Simon at the National Arts Journalism Program at Columbia University, Yseult Taylor at the International Society for the Performing Arts, Amy Tripodi at La Jolla Playhouse, and Zenovia Varelis at the League of American Theatres and Producers provided essential materials or explanations, or assisted with the complexities of interview scheduling and access.

My colleagues in San Diego, friends all, supplied essential succor. Julia Fulton, as before, exhorted and supported. Allan Havis offered valuable insight into the playwright's world. Walt Jones gave me institutional sustenance and personal guidance. Marianne McDonald, eternally generous and insightful, was a powerful one-woman cheering section. Jonathan Saville provided focus and clarity just when I had lost it.

Jerry James remained a good-natured touchstone for all theatrical wisdom and trivia and never failed to assist me when I needed his help. Paul Pinegar has been an invaluable mentor for years.

Nan Daugherty and Peggy Ryan deserve a standing ovation for transcribing hundreds of hours of taped interviews. Without their patience, keen ears, and practiced fingers, I would have given up long ago. Steve Cohen and Mary Lee, my brother- and sister-in-law, and Jon Schmidt all saved my neck, technologically speaking, countless times.

The indefatigable and wise staff at Southern Illinois University Press—Karl Kageff, Carol Burns, Barb Martin, Liz Brymer, and Wayne Larsen—offered unwavering support from the project's inception.

My brother Jerry and sister-in-law Beth Lebowitz, formidable chefs both, housed and fed me on my trips back home to New York. My terrific in-laws, Stan and Fimi Cohen, likewise offered a comforting oasis in the asphalt jungle. My dear mom, Hilda, took me to my first Broadway show. Thanks, too, to the rest of the gang in Brooklyn, Manhattan, Buffalo, San Francisco, Minneapolis, Los Angeles, Boulder, Seattle, San Diego, and elsewhere.

Tiger was my personal Mehitabel; his calm presence and beatific, furry countenance never failed to soothe my nerves when I hit a writing roadblock.

My soul mate, Nora Cohen—also, conveniently, my wife—was and is a never-ending source of inspiration and joy. She was with me, literally and spiritually, every step of the way.

Of course, the greatest thanks are owed to the sixty-six people who generously participated in interviews: Tom Aberger, Gerard Alessandrini, Marty Bell, Jed Bernstein, Robert Billig, John Breglio, Barry Brown, Danny Burstein, Michael Bush, Nancy Coyne, Edward Dennison, Judith Dolan, Terrence Dwyer, Alan Eisenberg, Rick Elice, Josh Ellis, Richard Frankel, Valentina Fratti, Roy Gabay, Seth Gelblum, Bernard Gersten, Randy Graff,

Barry Grove, Todd Haimes, Jane Harmon, Sheldon Harnick, Frank Harten-stein, Barbara Hauptman, Nina Keneally, Gregory A. Kotis, Rocco Lan-desman, Arthur Laurents, Peter Lawrence, Ronald Lee, Wendy Leventer, Alan Levey, Robert Longbottom, Rebecca Luker, Martin Markinson, Des McAnuff, Chase Mishkin, William Moriarty, James L. Nederlander, Wil-liam Parry, James Pentecost, Frank Rich, Daryl Roth, Jordan Roth, Nick Scandalios, Peter Schneider, Thomas Schumacher, Harriet Slaughter, Philip J. Smith, Roy Somlyo, Stephen Sondheim, Edward Strong, James Sullivan, Dianne Trulock, Hank Unger, Jack Viertel, Robin Wagner, John Weidman, Barry Weissler, Frank Wildhorn, Miles Wilkin, and Scott Zeiger. Their gracious cooperation and willingness to talk frankly about the is-sues were critical to the success of this project.

Thanks to Sue Pashko at Envision for her help with the cover photo, beautifully shot by Bart Barlow. Lyrics from "On Broadway," words and music by Barry Mann, Cynthia Weil, Mike Stoller, and Jerry Leiber (© 1962, 1963 [renewed 1990, 1991] Screen Gems–EMI Music Inc.; all rights re-served; international copyright secured), were used by permission.

On Broadway

1 The Terrain

Broadway is a very, very nice place to showcase the best of what's being done. But it's no longer a place where people are creating it anymore.
—Josh Ellis, former press agent

With shows running as long as they do, I don't think there's any real worry about Broadway not existing.
—Sheldon Harnick, lyricist and composer

When Broadway is dull, business is terrible.
—Martin Markinson, theatre owner

It's important that we make theatre seem accessible and seem nonelitist.
—Jed Bernstein, president, League of American Theatres and Producers

For more than a century, Broadway has been the marquee showplace of American theatrical production. It occupies a special corner in the American cultural landscape, emblematic throughout the world of the best of American theatre. As an entertainment mecca, Broadway has maintained a steady grip on the American imagination for years. Its larger-than-life stature has been secured by a seemingly endless parade of indelible iconography that reflects some crucial element of the cultural zeitgeist, from Ethel Merman's brassy renditions of Cole Porter in *Anything Goes* to Harvey Fierstein's exaggerated and exuberant drag performance in *Hairspray,* from the *Cotton Blossom* docking at the levee in *Show Boat* to the helicopter landing on the embassy roof in *Miss Saigon,* from Marlon Brando's signature cry of "Stella!" in *A Streetcar Named Desire* to Vanessa Redgrave's hallucinating matriarch in *Long Day's Journey into Night.* These images loom large because they so generously cater to our notion of theatrical abundance and because they display an endless flair for both substance and style. Broadway has always been the place where theatrical imagination and artistry powerfully collide with—and are often eclipsed by—the performance of extravagance.

Although much of the truly significant innovation in dramatic literature and theatrical production has occurred in other geographical arenas for at least forty years, Broadway remains the epicenter of theatrical razz-matazz, located as it is at the curious confluence of art and commerce. But in its current urban shopping mall setting, there are only faint signs of the pulse of the snake-oil salesmen who infused Broadway with their particular brand of seductive, sleazily exuberant showmanship and sold us gaudily packaged, neon-lit nostrums. Today those salesmen are often executives of international corporations that have gained a significant toehold in the bedrock of midtown Manhattan. The spirit of the previous generation of theatrical incubi is gleefully and campily channeled in the larger-than-stage-life presence of the überproducer, Max Bialystock, in Mel Brooks's paean to unabashed theatrical hucksterism, *The Producers*. Today's producers may still have a colorful streak or two of the showman in them—Broadway would wither if that were to fade entirely into corporate gray flannel—but the changing times have occasioned a remarkable shift in the nature of making theatre on Broadway.

In size and spectacle, sustained star power, and international presence, Broadway remains unsurpassed. It falters, it lurches forward, it reinvents itself, but the Fabulous Invalid continues as a legendary character of the American theatrical scene. The nickname reveals the ironic vision of Broadway conjured by its own practitioners, at once self-pitying and grandly dramatic, Bernhardt as Camille dying beautifully and tragically. Broadway has always enjoyed perpetuating the myth that it is gasping for both financial and artistic breath. For decades, alarmists have brandished pages of statistics to support their claims that Broadway's demise is imminent. James Pentecost, a former producer for the corporate giant Clear Channel as well as a former associate artistic director of the not-for-profit Manhattan Theatre Club, noted wryly that "ever since I got to New York, the theatre has been dying. It feels like it's been dying since the Greeks, and yet it doesn't die. It keeps going. The need for people to connect, in a theatre with other people, watching the same live experience at the same time, seems to be pretty primal."[1] That is empirically the case, as a quick examination of box office grosses will prove. However, Broadway is no longer the sole birthplace of the great works of dramatic and musical theatre, and that change marks a significant departure from Broadway's salad days in the first half of the twentieth century.

Many have accused Broadway of willfully abdicating its pride of place as the generator of serious work, and continue to rail against it for deferring to the sure thing rather than the great experiment. Broadway, in truth, has been a hotbed of theatrical experimentation only occasionally, and rarely since World War II, when other venues, notably Off-Broadway and the burgeoning regional theatre movement, began to earn reputations for such work. Yet Broadway is still a critical component of the cultural landscape, and not just because of the brightness of its fabled lights. It provides an essential boost to the financial health of New York City. When production costs, theatre expenses, and visitor spending have been factored in, Broadway's theatrical enterprises bring in approximately $4.4 billion to New York's economy.[2]

For years, Broadway was the source of all serious theatrical production in America, both musical and dramatic, the center of the complex hub-and-spoke mechanism that supplied pre–World War II America with the lion's share of theatrical activity. Shows were assembled in New York City and, after some glaring deficiencies were addressed in a pre-Broadway road tryout, were brought back to Broadway, where if successful, they would enjoy a healthy run of several months or longer. Runs of double-digit years were unheard of until the late twentieth century. Shows that enjoyed even a modicum of success spawned national tours that crisscrossed the country, offering a significant, vigorous slice of theatrical endeavor to the rest of the nation. Since productions were considerably less expensive then, relative to inflation, than they are today, shows did not need to earn blockbuster status to make a profit.

But in a matter of a relatively few years after World War II, Cold War conservatism and the advent of television occasioned a change in the theatrical scene, first in New York City and then around the nation. Broadway, like the rest of the country, grew more cautious in its cultural diet. Television siphoned off a sizable portion of both talent and audience alike in a way that radio and film had not. In the fifties, serious new works by major playwrights—Miller, Williams, Inge—and occasional newcomers would still garner critical attention and box office revenue. And musical writers and composers—Lerner, Loewe, Rodgers, Hammerstein, Burrows, Loesser, Bernstein, Sondheim, Laurents, Styne, Willson, Bock, Harnick—would establish or burnish their reputations and catapult the musical from its prewar anything-goes giddiness to a more sophisticated, sometimes even contemplative state. But at the same time, a not-so-quiet groundswell of theatrical innovation that eschewed Broadway formulas as artistically stultifying was beginning in New York and around the nation. By 1963, when Tyrone Guthrie opened his repertory company in Minneapolis, American theatre bore little resemblance to its prewar predecessor.

As the experimental theatre scene of the sixties began to reflect a stunning and radical shift in the aesthetics of performance, Broadway seemed to many to be a faded anachronism. A few new writers and productions dazzled, but formulaic musicals and ersatz television sitcom fare were staples of the Broadway diet. Much of the challenging and exciting work that was seen on Broadway at the time was imported, usually from England and invariably for a limited run. Escalating postwar costs meant that fewer producers could afford to take risks, even if they were temperamentally inclined to do so. Expensive as musicals were to mount, they were always a more popular genre and earned greater profits than straight plays could. Large-cast dramas like *Inherit the Wind* and *The Crucible* were no longer financially viable, so most playwrights stopped writing them. The artistically daring were discovering that their voices were more welcome in alternative venues like Off-Broadway, Off-Off-Broadway, and the regional theatre movement.[3] Although Broadway would continue as the showplace for American musicals, the landscape for straight plays was now dramatically different.

Different, too, was Broadway's diminishing production output. In the 1924–25 season, an astounding 230 works (plays, musicals, revues, and revivals) opened on Broadway. A decade later, in the throes of the Depression, the total was down to 138. Another decade of Depression and war brought the number considerably lower, to seventy-nine. It would keep decreasing steadily in each succeeding decade, reaching a dismal thirty-two in 1985–86, and would rebound only slightly over the next decade. The cost of producing on Broadway, occasioned by a multitude of factors, has never been higher, as will be examined below. Crafting a production for the Broadway stage is a labor-intensive, time-consuming process that must be invented anew for each production, and it involves a cadre of workers who must be paid a decent wage in a very expensive city. As one Broadway wag put it, "It takes a village to put on a musical." And the cost of feeding that village is not insignificant.

But Broadway itself is no longer a village, an isolated enclave of theatrical activity whose only connection to the rest of the nation is as a purveyor of goods. It is now inextricably linked to the network of American theatrical production that barely resembles its earlier incarnation of a few decades past. Broadway is now not just a seller but a buyer of goods. As regional and not-for-profit New York theatres flourished, Broadway producers soon realized that these institutions were generating some heady work that offered the prospect of longevity beyond the limited run in their home theatre. Beginning with the Broadway transfer of Howard Sackler's *The Great White Hope* from the not-for-profit Arena Stage in Washington DC in 1968, a long line of plays and musicals has made its way from theatres around the nation to Broadway. Producers today now frequently turn to these institutions to help them develop new works.

In the seventies, one of the most significant productions of the musical stage, *A Chorus Line,* was developed and nurtured at a not-for-profit Off-Broadway venue, Joseph Papp's Public Theatre, where *Hair* was born the previous decade. *A Chorus Line* emphatically signaled that a straightforward narrative was no longer a sine qua non for an artistically compelling and entertaining musical. Peter Schneider, a former head of Disney Theatrical, believes that the show occasioned "a seismic shift on Broadway." *A Chorus Line* proved that shows could be developed inhouse, from conception to performance, in a relatively sheltered environment, and then transferred to a commercial Broadway run, thus avoiding the expensive and cumbersome process of trying out a show on the road. The rush was on to find alternative venues in which to develop new work to move to Broadway.[4]

By the eighties, most of the blockbuster musicals playing on Broadway were London émigrés. The press dubbed this phenomenon the British Invasion and publicly derided what they perceived as the end of American musical hegemony. These so-called megamusicals, opulent and visually splendid as they were, lacked the idiosyncrasy and unique personality of some of the great American musicals of preceding decades. Their crowd-pleasing combination of easy-listening, pop-rock music imbued with operatic overtones, a steady barrage of scenic splendors, and accessible, earnest sentimentality proved a formidable formula that attracted audiences by the millions. But these shows lacked that brash American insouciance and irony, and the use of dance as an expressive means of exploring character and furthering the plot was marginalized. Although the nineties saw a return to a larger number of homegrown American works, the relationship with the British musical stage became a vital lifeline to a moribund Broadway and sustained it economically for a number of years. Audiences clamored to see these easy-to-digest, unabashedly romantic spectacles. Producers, in turn, learned that shows that lacked the visual scope of the British imports would fail to lure audiences. These productions also caused a noticeable ripple effect in the national touring circuit, whose fortunes are inextricably linked with those of Broadway. The road houses' Broadway subscription series exploded due to the extraordinary popularity of these productions. The box office rush for season subscriptions that were necessary to secure tickets to *The Phantom of the Opera* rendered local presenters more than willing to spend large amounts for the physical overhaul of the backstage facilities that such shows required. That expense was, in turn, handed over to the New York producers, who had to demand a much higher weekly guarantee from the local presenter to cover the amortized costs of rebuilding the stages. Road shows were now more expensive to produce, which made it more difficult for them to turn a profit.

The cost of making theatre on Broadway inhibits many producers from doing their most daring work there. Some of them prefer to produce these pieces in the slightly less risk-averse arena of Off-Broadway. Josh Ellis, who was a leading Broadway press agent in the seventies and eighties, observed that producers consciously strive to make Broadway shows safe for popular consumption. A few decades ago, when theatre tickets were much less expensive (adjusted for inflation), it was financially feasible to see a handful of shows in one weekend. Today, he said,

> People will go to see one show, and make an educated, slow decision on what that one is going to be. And the things that were marginal in the midsixties aren't even being produced anymore. There's a whole genre of light, fluffy comedies that don't exist on Broadway anymore. People now go to the one show, and before they choose it, they ask, "Why should we see it? Who's in it? How much does it cost? Who wrote it?—I never heard of that person before!" It becomes a much larger discussion, and it's not spontaneous anymore.

While the occasional straight play or quirky musical can succeed on Broadway, like the adaptation of Ovid's *Metamorphoses* and the musical *Urinetown,* it is unusual for wildly experimental works to find a home; those few that do rarely originate there. Musicals that attempt to explore darker terrain have of late failed to find an audience. *Parade, Thou Shalt Not, Marie Christine*—based, respectively, on the early-twentieth-century lynching of Leo Frank, Zola's darkly naturalistic morality tale *Thérèse Racquin,* and one of the most primal of Greek tragedies, *Medea*—are three examples of recent musicals that plumbed the depths of human experience yet failed to find an audience. Although the work of Stephen Sondheim is rarely noted for its unbridled glee, his extraordinary musical talents and great name recognition have generally allowed him the opportunity to exploit the colors of his sophisticated palette in ways that would sound the death knell for other composers. But Sondheim's works have rarely made a large profit.

Producers often gravitate to the safety net of revivals, which have formed a critical portion of Broadway fare since the early twentieth century. But in earlier decades, revivals formed a smaller percentage of the total number of productions mounted in a given season than they do today. In the current Broadway environment, it is not unusual for revivals to account for a quarter or more of the shows mounted in a given season. According to Tony Award–winning director Des McAnuff, who has staged both new musicals *(Big River, The Who's Tommy)* and revivals *(How to Succeed in Business Without Really Trying),* "It has got to be a temptation for a producer to latch on to the tried and true, given the outrageous expense of mounting one of these shows now." This temptation has led many to worry that Broadway is in danger of becoming a theatre ossuary, no different from Madame Tussaud's wax museum on West Forty-second Street. Given the attractiveness of revivals for producers, who cannot resist the sure thing, and audiences, who enjoy revisiting the tried and true, the one refreshing trend is new interpretations of classics by innovative directors. Some producers resist the lure of the traditional and far easier approach of mounting a star-driven, mothball-redolent package that closely hews to the original production. Instead, they hire directors and writers who are willing to reimagine these works according to their own, singular vision, a creative approach that sounds one encouraging note in the general revival frenzy.

There is no question as to the validity of reinvigorating the classics in this fashion, providing a new means for audiences to reexamine great works. But an increase in the production of revivals of any stripe means fewer available houses for new works. Producers gravitate to revivals because of the greater likelihood of their success, but in the eighties and nineties, they were responding to a dearth of viable new works for mainstream audiences. The AIDS epidemic decimated a generation of theatre artists, and many insiders today point to that loss as a significant factor in the falloff of successful new plays and musicals in that period.

For years, critics of the current state of professional theatre in America have pointed to the flight of playwrights to Hollywood and composers to the recording industry as evidence that Broadway can no longer provide sufficient remuneration for its creative artists. While several factors account for the decline of exciting material on Broadway, other venues can often provide an opportunity to make better money than is possible on Broadway, except in the rare event of a hit musical. In partial response to the concerns of writers and composers who worry that Broadway is growing increasingly economically inhospitable, recent legislation was pioneered by the Dramatists Guild. The Guild, representing playwrights, composers, and lyricists, worked with legislators to introduce in Congress a bill that would remove the antitrust laws that present a barrier to collective bargaining and the resultant opportunity to structure better financial deals with producers. According to the Dramatists Guild announcement on their Web site in fall 2002,

> Several lower court decisions issued more than 50 years ago have brought into question the ability of America's playwrights to bargain collectively with producers because playwrights—unlike other theatrical groups—are not covered by the National Labor Relations Act. As a result, playwrights frequently find themselves being offered "take it or leave it" contracts that force them to accept terrible terms just to get their plays produced. Forced to negotiate individual deals without the benefit of a standard contract to use as a starting point, playwrights are being forced to accept a steadily smaller percentage of revenues, pushing many out of the theater altogether. Increasingly, authors who would write for the theater are moving to television or the movies, where writers enjoy legal protection and economic equity.

In Hollywood the studio that produces a work usually purchases the rights from the author. In theatre the writers continue to control the rights to their plays, even when they enter into a contractual agreement with producers for a specific production. If this new legislation is enacted, it remains to be seen how it will affect the climate for writers and composers. But all the writers interviewed for this book agreed that the current contracts, developed to facilitate quicker payback to investors, present obstacles to reasonable remuneration. The attempt to broker a respectable financial deal between producers and writers will be explored in greater detail in later chapters.

Broadway composers once performed double duty, in a sense, as for years many show tunes made the journey from the stage to the airwaves. Broadway is no longer dynamically connected to the pulse of American popular music; with rare exceptions, Broadway does not generate songs that enter the mainstream musical vernacular, as was the case before rock ripped popular music away from its Tin Pan Alley moorings. Now the reverse obtains, as music already made popular in other media makes its way to Broadway in productions such as *Contact, Mamma Mia!, Movin' Out,* and *Saturday Night Fever.* The use of rock and pop song cycles, interpolated songs, or music recycled from a previous cinematic incarnation makes it increasingly difficult for new voices to flourish. No matter how artfully the show is conceived and presented, it bodes ill when the musical stage is no longer a forum for composers and lyricists.

The lifeblood of Broadway is its audience, and the main arteries are the major thoroughfares of Broadway and West Forty-second Street. After World War II, a series of changes in the urban landscape occasioned Times Square's slow and inexorable spiral into a grotesque American version of a Felliniesque inferno. Although the area remained a center of theatrical activity, it was no longer an inviting one. The deplorable conditions in the subway stations and the difficulty in finding a cab after a show, along with higher ticket prices and other factors, made many New Yorkers avoid Broadway altogether or view it as a special-occasion destination rather than as an integral part of their cultural lives. John Willis, the longtime editor of *Theatre World,* the illustrated annual that chronicles the professional theatre in America, wrote in the 1975–76 season edition, "In November, because of the unsavory atmosphere surrounding the Times Square area, producers, theatre owners, and performers began a concerted effort to eradicate the midtown peep shows, massage parlors, topless bars, loitering, and soliciting. The League of New York Theatre Owners and Producers voted a levy on all New York and touring companies to promote this worthwhile project."[5]

In the last decade, a sea change has occurred in Times Square, the result of considerable jockeying by the various state, city, and corporate forces with interests in the health of the district. The porn shops and massage parlors have been banished, and the detritus of street life has been largely swept away by the tidal wave of new office towers, chain retail shops and food outlets, multiscreen cinemas, Madame Tussaud's wax museum, the World Wrestling Foundation, and MTV studios. Deteriorating action or porn film houses were converted into renovated theatres and rehearsal studios. Disney's commitment, in 1995, to renovate the decrepit New Amsterdam Theatre, once the home of the *Ziegfeld Follies,* provided a substantial amount of momentum for the area's redevelopment. Today, Forty-second Street, which was bereft of any legitimate Broadway theatres for several decades, now houses four. Peter Schneider, the former Disney head, noted,

In some sense, I liken it to a jigsaw puzzle. People had been working forever on the edges, on the middle of the pieces. And along comes the jerk who says, "Oh, look, I found a piece, I'll put it in. Look, it's finished!" So in some sense, we were the last piece of the puzzle. We were not the first piece, we were not the driving force of the pieces. People have for twenty-five years been making Times Square and Forty-second Street work. A lot of things happened when Disney said yes. Did Disney give other people the courage to say yes? Yes. Did people have more confidence in the real estate development if Disney was going to redo the theatre? But fundamentally, we were the last piece of the puzzle. And we get a lot of credit, because we were the first big name company to stand up and say "We're on Forty-second Street." We were the last piece—an extremely important piece, an extremely visible piece, an extremely powerful financial piece—but we were not the drivers.

This remarkable transformation, which will be explored in chapter 7, has effectively rendered Broadway safe once more for audiences of all stripes. But many vocal critics, especially within the theatrical community, have serious reservations about the ultimate cost of such a radical makeover. Forty-second Street's high-tech look reflects a bland, corporate mall atmosphere that is, some opine, anathema to individualistic, artistic innovation. The color has been bleached from the once vibrant fabric of Broadway, they say, the inevitable result of an influx of corporate funding needed to revitalize the neighborhood. Others enthusiastically embrace the makeover and extol the pleasures of a clean, safe, well-lighted, and family-friendly environment. For the first time in half a century, Broadway is flooded daily with crowds so large that casual strolling is no longer possible. The arrival of these new Broadway denizens—day tourist, office worker, and the native New Yorker who feels it is safe to return to the neighborhood—is a force with which producers must reckon when they consider the type of material most suited to Broadway theatres.

Some practitioners believe that Broadway is now attracting an audience whose makeup is considerably more "middle-American," a term that none too subtly implies a lack of sophistication. While there is no evidence that New Yorkers are more sophisticated than theatregoers from other states, it is true that there has been a marked shift in audience demographics in recent decades. Edward Strong, a partner in the influential producing organization Dodger Theatricals, said, "It's much more a middle-of-the-road audience, much less elite [than it was in the eighties]. I think it's much more common now to see shows that we call 'four-ticket attractions'; you're not looking to sell a pair to an upper East Side couple for a night out but to a family who would come see it. And you see on Broadway many more shows that are overtly for family audiences." Roy Somlyo, a former producer and general manager and a recent president of the American Theatre Wing, agreed that theatregoers often now have a different reason for attending shows.

> It's regrettably become a special event to go to the theatre. . . . People want to go to the hit show, or the show that appears to be a hit because it is so expensive, and they go less for the sheer entertainment than they do for the prestige of being there, and they want to leave a *Playbill* on the coffee table for their friends and neighbors when they come in. And when they come in from out of town, they want to recite the list of hit shows they've seen while they were here. That creates a shrinking theatre, but that's a fact.

But Peter Schneider argued that the nature of Broadway's appeal is that it is malleable within its essential, commercial framework.

> Broadway has always been about making money. The not-for-profit theatres sprang up in response to that—it's not enough to make money; one must also develop playwrights and make good art. And we see today that Broadway is now able to do both. It can do good art and be very populist. And nothing's wrong with that. Middle-America is who goes to the theatre, middle-America is who runs this country. Now if, like with *The Lion King*, we can bring some sophistication to the process, fantastic.

This show married an exceedingly popular tale, told first in a feature animation film, with an exuberantly creative staging by Julie Taymor, previously known for her unique experimentation in the not-for-profit world.

If ticket prices cause a large segment of the potential audience to view Broadway as outside the mainstream of their cultural life—a destination, an occasion, rather than a habit—there is a growing drive to counter that perception. Jed Bernstein, president of the League of American Theatres and Producers—the organization of Broadway and national commercial theatre owners, producers, general managers, and touring presenters, known as the League—believes that the theatre community's efforts to make theatre more accessible will never succeed if ticket prices continue to spiral upward. No matter how mainstream the work itself, exorbitant prices will prevent most theatregoers, New Yorkers included, from considering Broadway as part of their regular cultural consumption. Accessibility of material, however, is currently not the sticking point. There is very little today that ventures beyond traditional theatrical parameters. Aside from departures from the stylistic norm, like the introduction of song-cycle musicals or productions that use dance as a primary idiom, Broadway has maintained a markedly conservative bent for many years. Some cultural pundits interpret this trend as the triumph of mainstream Americana in an elitist sector; others, as the dumbing down of Broadway.

In 1980 about 60 percent of Broadway audiences came from the New York metropolitan area; by 2000 that number had decreased to about 44 percent. The reduction is explained in part by a rise in the total number of theatregoers during that period, up almost two million in twenty years to twelve million audience members in 2000–2001; the actual number of metropolitan area attendees decreased over that period from about six million to 5.2 million.[6] This trend might result from the League's efforts to cast a wider marketing net. It may also represent a shift in the demographics of New York City's general population, which has seen a dramatic growth in its nonwhite population since the sixties. Broadway continues to attract largely white audiences, about 80 percent of the total, with more middle-aged white women attending than any other gender-age group. Additionally, the percentage of Broadway patrons who are younger than eighteen has almost tripled during that time.[7] To attract younger audiences, who initially might resist the relatively low-tech charms of theatre, the League has had to develop strategies that compete with more easily accessible forms of entertainment. The willingness of producers to mount stage adaptations of successful movies-with-music, like *Footloose,* represents an unfortunate effort to troll for younger audiences, as these shows offer little in the way of theatrical inventiveness. Hank Unger, a partner in the Araca Group, which produced *Urinetown* and the revival of *Frankie and Johnny in the Claire de Lune,* believes that one of the greatest hurdles faced by today's producers is being able to produce works of quality in a cultural environment that seems to seek out and embrace the mediocre.

> The biggest challenge is the level of banality in entertainment, and how banality seems to be the most desirable flavor for the mass populace.

The fact is that we live in a very large marketplace called the United States, and that seems to drive a lowest-common-denominator factor. Maybe that's always been true, the Christians being eaten by the lions *was* mass entertainment. Was it banal? Maybe it was exciting. . . . The dumbing down of the consumer is challenging. But then, wonderful stuff can pop out and become a huge hit amongst all that. I sometimes fret because I don't understand how some things, which are so immensely popular, are not particularly good, kind of middle-of-the-road. But that doesn't seem to matter, especially to a lot of business people. And that's a challenge.

Will producers find ways of attracting a more diverse audience to more challenging works? Has the presence of Disney—committed as it is to presenting family fare—contributed to this influx of younger theatregoers in significant fashion, or is Disney merely wisely serving the new demographic mix? In a League study, the number of theatregoers who cited more family-oriented entertainment as a significant incentive that would encourage them to attend Broadway more often decreased by more than half between 1997–98 and 2000–2001.[8] This reduction, coupled with a rise in younger audiences, reflects the actual increase in family-oriented shows during that period.

Some Broadway professionals worry that the presence of Disney and other corporations that actively produce on Broadway has deleteriously affected the nature of the work by presenting generic, bland material, although Julie Taymor's inventive staging of *The Lion King,* considered by many a stunning coup de théâtre, is usually cited as an exception. Individual producers, some artists and managers agree, possess the personal touch needed to discover and nurture vital and idiosyncratic theatre, which, they forcefully add, cannot be duplicated by corporations. Frank Rich, the former lead theatre critic for the *New York Times,* observed that "the corporatization of theatre has obviously made it much more difficult in the commercial arena than it ever was for idiosyncratic, and what I call 'noncommercial,' voices to be heard. It's almost by definition that a corporation cannot create truly individualistic art, because it's by nature that corporations act as committees and water down things to please a bunch of constituencies and also to get the lowest common denominator." Opinions differ, depending on the constituency. Peter Schneider disagreed, articulating another popular belief that corporate producers leave plenty of room for their independent colleagues. "I don't think you're seeing [a decrease in independent producers]. I think people are getting smarter about how they raise money, but I don't see that the corporations per se are hurting anybody in terms of their money. I think that times on Broadway are changing. I think that's the excitement of Broadway."

Others are less dyspeptic about the corporate presence or view it as a positive addition to the Broadway scene. At Disney Theatrical, the developmental process is supervised by a handful of people who originally came not from Hollywood but from the not-for-profit theatre movement and thus brought a mature theatrical sensibility to Disney's work. As Jack Viertel, an executive at Jujamcyn Theatres, observed after the success of *Beauty and the Beast,* which was developed in the theme park division and then transferred to Broadway, "[Disney] then turned around and hired the best and the brightest, basically, with lots of theatrical experience, to do *[The Lion King],* including a director who all of us thought was way too uncommercial for us to ever take a risk on. . . . I thought, well, this is great, this is a corporation that is actually paying attention, reassessing what they did before. Not too proud to say, 'We can do better.'" Peter Schneider added that when Disney made its first foray on Broadway with *Beauty and the Beast,* they were roundly dismissed by the establishment for producing in an overpriced and overhyped fashion.

> Our entire approach was that you cannot judge us until you see the content of what we can do. And that when you see the renovation of the New Amsterdam Theatre, when you see what we're doing with *The Lion King,* you would then say, "Oh, they actually know what they're doing," because on *Beauty and the Beast* [Disney] didn't know what it was doing—that was the general perception—and it was a huge hit!
> . . . So we aggressively tried to change the perception of what Disney meant on Broadway, and part of hiring Julie Taymor to direct *Lion King* was that particular impetus.

An often-asked question is whether family-oriented entertainment creates the possibility of a lifetime of theatregoing or is merely another item on a checklist for a trip to New York. James Pentecost observed,

> Yes, there is a certain type of audience that they are catering to, but they are providing a base of people to get excited, seeing something they like and taking a risk. You want to hook somebody to say, "I want to try this again," so if you go to *The Lion King* as a kid, and you get excited about the theatre, who knows what dividend that will pay in

five or ten years. And you've created an audience. The fear that you're only creating an audience for that kind of entertainment I'm not sure is valid. Because they will want to explore other things.

Unfortunately, no study points definitively to the relationship between occasional theatregoing on Broadway as a child and the development of a lifetime habit of such attendance.

Disney's success, as well as its commitment to future productions, has allowed Thomas Schumacher, president of Disney Theatrical, to fund the long-term development of several projects simultaneously by a number of formidably talented writers, directors, and designers. This process is a significant innovation for Broadway. It is doubtful that such a plan could be implemented by individual producers, who typically cannot afford to subsidize a number of shows in development, thus not earning income, at the same time. But Disney, on the other hand, is unlikely to produce a serious, adult straight play or even an adult-oriented musical, given its target audience, and those types of fare remain in the bailiwick of independent producers. "There's nothing that meshes with what Disney's mission or motives are. Disney is really about extending the life of their own properties and creating new family entertainments. The straight play is really the work of an author, it's the bastion of control by that individual author, and that's the way it should be," said Peter Schneider. But Disney is rapidly establishing itself as much more than just a niche presenter of staged versions of feature animation hits. *Aida* was not originally an animated work, although there was a time when it was being considered for such, nor was the Alan Menken and Tim Rice oratorio *King David*, which has yet to be staged as a regular Broadway attraction, although it was presented as a special event concert at the New Amsterdam Theatre in 1997.

Broadway was traditionally an insular community; the twenty or so square blocks of midtown Manhattan that are home to all but one of the approximately forty theatres in the Broadway catchment area formed a bastion of theatrical activity that largely ignored the work going on in the rest of the world.[9] In the last few decades, that insularity has been replaced by a growing interdependence between Broadway and the rest of the professional theatre scene in America. This, most Broadway practitioners acknowledge, is a healthy development. It is the peculiar relationship between the commercial and not-for-profit arenas that has generated some of the most provocative debate in American theatre in decades.

As production costs have escalated on Broadway, far outstripping inflation, producers have sought less expensive ways to develop works for the
Broadway stage. *Oklahoma!* was produced in 1943 for about $180,000
(about $1.86 million in 2003 dollars). In the early years of the twenty-first
century, a large musical is likely to cost at least ten or twelve million dollars.[10] The costs of producing continue to increase annually at alarming
rates, and money, especially in the weak economy after September 11,
2001, is generally more difficult to raise. New paradigms for producing
had to be explored, and the not-for-profit theatres provided a welcome
arena for Broadway producers.

For several years, producers have found it necessary to look beyond
the traditional formula for developing plays and musicals. This custom
usually entailed trying out a production in commercial road houses in a
few cities—Boston, New Haven, Philadelphia, Washington DC, Balti-
more, and Wilmington being regular destinations—before bringing the
show in to Broadway. That procedure has grown untenable as the costs
of transport and labor have escalated to prohibitive levels. Only a few
shows still take that route to Broadway, usually those whose producers
feel sanguine about the chance for success in New York. According to
Richard Frankel, one of the producers and general managers of *The Producers,* the pre-Broadway Chicago run of the musical cost more than two
million dollars.

In decades past, a commercial producer might regard an exciting original work at a not-for-profit theatre as a worthy investment for transfer
to Broadway. While this practice still occurs, it is increasingly common
for commercial producers to seek out partnerships with not-for-profit
theatres at the point of conception of a new play or musical to develop
works more economically in front of discriminating audiences. Similarly,
as private and government subsidies have eroded not-for-profits' funding, some institutional theatres that regularly produce new works now
cultivate relationships with commercial producers to help defray the costs
of production.

The commitment of a million dollars of enhancement money to a not-
for-profit theatre is a considerable investment but less than the cost of a
road tryout. The producers can evaluate the production during a run of
several weeks, during which time the creative staff can continue to re-
write and restage the piece. When the theatre is far from New York, there
is a psychological advantage to be gained by virtue of a greater distance
from the prying eyes of Broadway insiders. The benefits for the not-for-

profit theatre can be substantial. The possibility of a steady income stream from a successful Broadway run, the chance to share in subsidiary rights, and the enhanced reputation and cachet in the local community derived from a presence on the national stage are seductive.

This approach to producing is so popular that a current snapshot of thirty Broadway productions reveals that eleven were transferred from not-for-profit theatres in the United States or Britain. In addition, three highly respected not-for-profit theatres—Manhattan Theatre Club, Roundabout Theatre Company, and Lincoln Center Theater—now maintain an ongoing presence on Broadway in the mortar-and-bricks sense, as they own or permanently occupy theatres whose productions are eligible for Tony Awards. The institutional advantages enjoyed by these theatres are a source of irritation to some commercial producers. They resent that the companies benefit from the prestige of a Broadway address and Tony eligibility while enjoying a not-for-profit status that reduces their financial risk.

The relationship of once strange bedfellows, which will be examined in chapter 4, is not the only recent important evolution in the methodology of producing on Broadway. The advent of large groups of producers collaborating on one show is a phenomenon that demands considerable scrutiny. Escalating production costs have made it more difficult for producers to pay back investors in timely fashion, thus creating greater obstacles to the raising of money. As approximately 85 percent of shows produced on Broadway lose some or all of the money it takes to mount them, a longer time for recoupment is a serious disincentive for many investors. Thus Broadway has seen a tectonic shift in the nature of producing. Gone are the days of the impresario producer, in the mold of Florenz Ziegfeld, Rodgers and Hammerstein, Kermit Bloomgarden, or David Merrick. With the possible exception of Cameron Mackintosh, whose last hit was *Miss Saigon* in 1991, few independent producers are able to go it alone. The list of producers of a Broadway musical may occupy several lines in an advertisement. The producer credits of *The Producers* read as follows: "Rocco Landesman, SFX Theatrical Group, The Frankel-Baruch-Viertel-Routh Group, Bob Weinstein, Harvey Weinstein, Rick Steiner, Robert F. X. Sillerman and Mel Brooks; Associate Producer: Frederic H. Mayerson, Rhoda Mayerson and Lynn Landis; Produced in association with James D. Stern and Douglas L. Meyer."

An ironic contrast can be seen between two Tony Awards ceremonies. When the corporate-produced *Lion King* won the Tony award for best musical in 1998, Peter Schneider and Thomas Schumacher accepted the prize. In 2001, when *The Producers* took the award, the people lined up across the stage to receive the award could not fit into the camera shot. A few decades ago, it was not too difficult to entice individuals to participate in the excitement of producing; with an investment of a few thousand dollars, they could "go along for the ride," as several producers put it. It was a much smaller financial commitment for the individual investor, who in 1980 could commit twenty thousand dollars for a percentage of a one-million-dollar musical. In 2003 money that show would cost about $4.35 million, which is less than half the final price tag for an equivalent-sized show today. A musical that now costs ten million dollars requires a considerably larger investment pool or, more typical, a smaller number of very wealthy investors. This change has forced producers to form partnerships to raise funds. Some producers have rejected entirely the more tedious route of pursuing small investors and now sell only to "accredited" (read "wealthy") investors, for whom a sizable commitment is less of a financial burden.

While most of the people who receive billing are investors and not active producers, it can be difficult for an artist to navigate the production process when so many are at the titular helm. Robin Wagner, one of the most accomplished scenic designers of the last thirty years, whose credits range from the original *Great White Hope* through *A Chorus Line* to *The Producers,* believes that the decentralization of producing control has led to a dilution of the vision so critical to the most successful producers. Central artistic oversight has frequently devolved to the directors. "I now have ten or twelve people to answer to. They each would like to have control. So it's like running a retail business. It's not about theatre."

It is more expensive not only to produce shows today but also to keep shows running each week. Roy Somlyo said, "In the fifties and sixties you could run a show at 50 percent capacity and keep a show alive. But you can't do that any longer because you're geared to 75 percent or more of capacity." As an illustration, two impressive hits of their times, both elaborate, large-cast productions—*My Fair Lady* in 1956, and *The Phantom of the Opera* in 1988—recouped their initial investments, but while it took thirteen weeks for the Lerner and Loewe musical to do so, the Lloyd Webber show took over two years. One distinguishing factor is that *My Fair Lady,* sumptuous though it was, relied on conventional theatre technology of its time. *Phantom* spent large sums to excavate the basement and modify the infrastructure of the Majestic Theatre to accommodate spectacles like the rowboat gliding through the sewers of Paris, candelabras that magically appeared through the stage floor, and the now famous crashing chandelier.

Today, competing interest groups on Broadway variously attribute soaring production costs to union featherbedding, theatre owner avarice, producer inexperience, exorbitant advertising rates, skyrocketing real estate costs, and similar expensive budgetary line items. Some, like the price of materials, are the result of a host of economic factors outside the control of the theatre community. While there is general agreement that costs need to decrease to encourage more production and generate more profit, the "who will flinch first?" staring match of most League-union negotiation processes has occasioned an environment in which no major concessions can be reached. Another link in the vicious circle is forged when audiences clamor for more spectacle and producers, designers, and directors cater to those demands. As Disney's Thomas Schumacher noted,

> Survival in today's marketplace presents specific challenges and demands more novel solutions. Tourism, an essential mainstay for our business, is down, due to the economic landscape at home and abroad, and anxiety about travel in general. Also, the proliferation of media outlets has created much more noise in the marketplace. Given the number of television, radio, cable, Internet, magazine, newspaper, and billboard options, and the vast sums of advertising dollars spent each week by literally thousands of products, each yelling for our attention, how can a Broadway show cut through all that clutter without breaking the bank? While the seventy-five to one hundred thousand dollars that shows spend on average each week may be a tiny fraction of McDonald's weekly budget, it's still wildly expensive for us.

According to some producers interviewed for this book, the current top ticket price of one hundred dollars is barely enough to keep productions afloat unless they play at or near capacity. This situation, in turn, makes it more difficult for shows to recoup. One statistic producers frequently quote is that production costs have risen at about twice the rate of ticket prices over the last fifty years. Today, they say, tickets for musicals should cost $150 for a show to recoup in a reasonable amount of time. When ticket prices actually do break through the one-hundred-dollar ceiling, there will be public outrage, but it will probably not stem the rising tide of expenses. Producer and general manager Roy Gabay offered that the actual prices people pay for tickets are going down. "We're now pricing things to be discounted. . . . We've instilled the mentality that you can get theatre tickets for a discount. It's not even how much of a discount or that people can't afford the full price; it's the concept of 'why should I pay retail, why should I pay full price?' We may have dug ourselves into that hole too deeply." At current full prices, which most hit shows can command, audiences tend to avoid any inclination toward experimentation and prefer the safety of the must-see hit. As Rocco Landesman, first a successful independent producer and now president of the Jujamcyn theatre chain put it, "People want to see hits. They tend to want to see a safer show, a revival or a show that's been certified as a hit. They want a show with a certain reputation. They're not likely to come in and take a chance on something new. I think the tourist audiences tend to make safer choices than a traditional New York audience."

The League and the unions have wrestled with making Broadway more accessible to the general public. There have been many promotional campaigns, including Kids Night on Broadway and educational discount prices for tickets to certain shows, but none of these tactics has had significant impact. Some efforts, like the Broadway Alliance, which was a plan to cap costs on the production of certain new straight plays, fell by the wayside due to lack of foresight and heartfelt industry cooperation. Under this agreement, utilized briefly in the midnineties, each of the three theatre chains designated one theatre as eligible for the production of new straight plays produced under certain budgetary guidelines. Ticket prices were similarly less expensive, but the shows produced under Alliance rules seemed, in the main, visually underproduced and would have been better served in Off-Broadway theatres.

The presence of producer consortiums and corporate producers has rattled the complacency of the older members of the community. Some Broadway independents aver that large bureaucracies cannot generate the passion and vision of the individual producer, a difference that will perforce result in standards geared to the lowest common denominator. Others admit that Disney, the most visible corporate producer, has provided a welcome injection of energy, enthusiasm, and capital. Daryl Roth, a successful independent producer, tried to knit together both perspectives.

[Producing] comes from the heart. The initial seed is "I love this play. It has to be seen. I want to do it. I can hopefully bring it there." And I think there will always be room for that, no matter how corporate Broadway becomes. But I can't imagine that the corporate world won't make a huge difference in the way things are produced. It already has. The influx of this kind of capital is very healthy. [And] as a corporate producer you are your own master in many ways. You're not beholden in other ways as independent producers might be to theatre owners, to other forces. You have a more contained organization, which is wonderful, and it makes a difference.

Clear Channel, whose theatre division not only is active on Broadway but also controls the programming in more than fifty touring venues around the country, avidly pursues producing in New York with the specific intention of developing new "product" (a term some Broadway people detest) to "feed the road." Miles Wilkin, a former CEO of SFX Theatrical and now the chairman of Clear Channel Entertainment Theatrical Worldwide (which bought SFX), simply stated his corporation's need: "We need multiple theatrical productions for the distribution system. . . . Therefore, we are constantly empowering projects to happen, with the goal of going into full production. That is the name of the game for us, and what distinguishes us from many other producers."

The national touring market generates a tantalizingly large slice of the potential income of a show. In 1999–2000, almost twelve million tickets for touring Broadway shows were sold, slightly more than the number of tickets sold on Broadway itself.[11] As the Broadway imprimatur is exceedingly helpful for marketing a show around the country, Broadway itself is in danger of becoming a factory whose primary function is generating shows for touring. In the growing touring market, many theatres offer profitable "Broadway season" subscription packages of five or six shows, a phenomenon that is in large part due to the success of tours of British musicals in the eighties. These theatres require a number of musicals each year to fill their subscription offerings and will frequently seek less expensive, sometimes nonunion tours of Broadway perennials to complement the one or two new productions from Broadway. A significant selling point for a tour is a "direct from Broadway" logo affixed to the show's ads, but often these shows were critical and artistic failures on Broadway. As Chris Jones, writing in *Variety* pointed out, "By now, there's a clear model for the post-Broadway road rehab of musicals with plenty of cash to recoup. And it's a simple recipe: Fix the problems as much as possible and hope hinterland ticket buyers never paid attention to what those snippy Gotham crix had to say."[12] A recent trend has demonstrated that tours of well-known musicals with bankable television celebrities can succeed without having played on Broadway at all in their current incarnations.

When road presenters and producers were granted the privilege to vote for the Tony Awards, there was a change in the dynamics of the internal politics of the League, long controlled by New York producers, theatre owners, and unions. At the 2002 Tony Awards ceremony, the crowd-pleasing but unabashedly formulaic *Thoroughly Modern Millie*, which garnered mixed reviews, was anointed best musical, even though the more extravagantly praised and adventurous *Urinetown* won awards for best book and best score. The prevailing wisdom was that voters from road venues viewed the latter as a hard product to sell on tour, given its title and its high irony quotient, and accordingly chose to bestow the highest accolade on the more conservative *Millie*. While awards shows are generally regarded as insignificant barometers of a production's artistic merit, they are essential in developing public perception of a show's bona fides.

Corporations are making their presence felt in more pronounced, visible fashion on Broadway. Naming a theatre was long considered a means of either honoring someone who had made a contribution to Broadway in some fashion, be it a producer, a writer, a critic, or an actor—Brooks Atkinson, Helen Hayes, Al Hirschfeld, John Golden, David Belasco, Richard Rodgers, Neil Simon—or bestowing fanciful or geographic descriptors of some sort: Imperial, Majestic, Longacre, Lyceum, Royale. Now corporations are affixing their names to marquees in exchange for contributions or investments, and it is causing some unbridled irritation within the community. There was some concern when Livent, a now defunct corporate producing entity, leased two Forty-second Street theatres that were in disrepair, the Apollo and the Lyric, and created the Ford Center in exchange for funding from the auto maker. This bit of commercialism paled in comparison, though, with the harsh and vocal response generated when the Roundabout Theatre, a not-for-profit institution that was seeking a permanent Broadway presence after it was evicted from the Criterion Center, moved into the renovated Selwyn Theatre and struck a deal with American Airlines. That sponsorship earned American the right to attach its name to the building for an initial ten-year period. Corporations have long been active sponsors of not-for-profit theatres, with their logos prominently displayed in lobbies and programs, but some critics believed that this very public display of corporate and not-for-profit symbiosis was somehow both deleterious and shameful. Todd Haimes, the artistic director of the Roundabout, tried to put it in a larger context. "[American Airlines] gave us $8.5 million to have their name on a building and not be artistically involved. Nobody complained about Mobil Masterpiece Theatre . . . and my guess, being the cynic that I am, is that five or ten years from now every single theatre will be doing this." Not too long after, the Shubert Organization accepted a contribution from Cadillac, whose name is now affixed to the venerable Winter Garden.

While Broadway traditionalists lament the presence of corporations, in truth, large companies have been investors in Broadway shows for decades. In 1956 CBS Records contributed a considerable amount to the capitalization of *My Fair Lady*, largely for the right to produce its cast album. Suntory Whiskey, ABC/Capital Cities, Universal Studios, Miramax Films, Fox Searchlight, and other prominent corporations have invested in shows in more recent times. But the current concern about the potential changes to be wrought by an active corporate presence on Broadway is similar to the discontent voiced in the world of sports. Most stadiums and arenas have been redubbed with corporate monikers, the result of enormously profitable naming-rights deals. That Wrigley Field has always been named after the large corporation that also owns the Chicago Cubs does not seem to disturb Cubs fans. The venerability of the old stadium obscures the fact that baseball has been supported by corporate money for decades. But the naming of Pro Player Stadium, 3Com Park, Petco Park, and others offends many who believe that this overt corporatization is trampling on sacred American ground. Does it matter whether a musical is presented in a theatre that is named after a long-dead producer or a current car manufacturer? The growing interdependence between the corporate world and Broadway will be examined in subsequent chapters.

For years the League of New York Theatres and Producers presented an apparently unified and harmonious public face as it negotiated with the unions and marketed its wares. As the organization grew to include road producers and presenters, and the name was changed to reflect the new membership demographics, some notable discord has had ripple effects on Broadway and beyond. For years, the major powers in the League were widely acknowledged to be Gerald Schoenfeld and Bernard Jacobs, the two lawyers who ran the Shubert Organization, the largest theatre owner on Broadway. After Jacobs's death in 1996, that power shifted to the producers themselves, and there is now less apparent harmony within the ranks. Disney chose not to join the League, believing that its corporate mandate provides sufficient differentiation from other producers to warrant its own contract with the unions, although Disney does participate in League-union negotiations. Peter Schneider observed that "the League really needs to find a direction and a point of view, and it doesn't have one at the moment." Dodger Theatricals withdrew in late 2001, alleging a lack of League initiative in negotiating on the Dodgers' behalf for critical salary concessions with the unions after the September 11 terrorist attacks, when only certain producers managed to obtain cutbacks without official League intercession. The never-ending tango within the League, and between the League and the unions, is danced on constantly shifting ground, occasionally resulting in a real crisis, like the 2003 strike by the musicians' union to stave off League demands to drastically reduce jobs in many Broadway theatres.

Of all the elements that currently shape Broadway, the most significant is, of course, the nature of the work that is produced there. While fashions may trail those in the rest of the cultural scene, they do change. In the course of just one month, *Variety* featured two articles by Robert Hofler; the first trumpeted the success of feel-good and cartoonlike musicals, and the second signaled the arrival of more shows that embraced serious themes presented in a more realistic, less caricatured style. A number of recent innovations and long-term trends contribute to the content and form of work produced.

The three theatre chains that oversee almost all the commercial Broadway houses are owned or controlled by men in their seventies and eighties. James Binger, the head of Jujamcyn, the smallest of the chains, handed the producing operations to Rocco Landesman, who is in his fifties, but both the Shubert and Nederlander organizations have at their helms men of advanced years. The power they wield is considerable, as they make the deals and select the plays that will occupy their theatres and play on the road. Several theatre people interviewed for this book questioned how generational change might affect the work that the owners choose to showcase in their theatres. The great likelihood, given the conservative nature of tourist audiences and the daunting economics of producing, is that when change does come, Broadway will continue to present crowd-pleasing fare.

The advent of rock music and electronic amplification have contributed greatly to the current state of Broadway musicals. Electronic amplification was initially difficult to control, but it eventually changed the way in which audiences heard and perceived the musical theatre event. For years, despite the success of shows like *Bye Bye Birdie, Hair,* and *Two Gentlemen of Verona,* rock music struggled to join the mainstream on

Broadway, in part because of the conservatism of audiences and in part because of the difficulties in adequately controlling the amplification and in staging with cabled microphones. The invention of wireless microphones and more sophisticated mixing boards allowed a light rock sound to flourish on Broadway. Unfortunately, many composers write in a glib, pop-pastiche, or pseudo-rock-opera style that defies any commitment to a particular musical idiom and creates, instead, a bleating, interchangeable aural wallpaper. As director Des McAnuff commented, "I'd love to see a wider array of musical genres in New York, and I still have the feeling that Broadway aims itself mainly at nine-year-old girls. Broadway's in this loop of quoting itself." Sheldon Harnick, the lyricist for such classic Broadway musicals as *Fiddler on the Roof* and *She Loves Me*, observed that today "the rhythms are different. The attention to the kind of clever lyric that was in vogue ever since the 1920s seems to have faded. Audiences still seem to respond to them, but it's not as important to many audiences. What seems to be important to audiences paying the prices they do, is that what they see is big and loud. Give them something for their money. And something that is different from the experience that they get from film and TV." He acknowledged that the occasional successful revival of a musical like *Kiss Me, Kate!* or *The Music Man* points to an audience that wants "well-crafted shows that tell their story well and have attractive music, even though the music may not be a la mode," but very few new successful shows are now written in that style.

In early 2003, during the bitter negotiations on the musicians' contract, producers threatened to use virtual orchestras—sampled electronic accompaniment—in place of live, but striking, musicians. The theatre world never had the chance to judge these orchestra replacements, as sympathy walkouts by the actors and stagehands brought a swift resolution to the strike. Should their use ever come to pass, it would signal a dreadful aesthetic milestone in the evolution of the Broadway musical, moving shows one step closer to the canned theme-park entertainments that many fear is Broadway's eventual fate. William Moriarty of Local 802 emphasized that "[w]e need to reach the theatre audience . . . and make them aware of the value of live music and the presence of live musicians. I think, especially on Broadway, there are a number of audience members who don't even realize that there's a live orchestra there."

While many composers have chosen to work in the pop-rock style, on the other side of the musical divide is a new generation of composers indelibly influenced by the work of Stephen Sondheim. Among the signal accomplishments of this influential and innovative composer is the creation of a starkly different and discrete musical world for each of his shows. Des McAnuff noted,

> The difficult thing is that Sondheim is a genius and most of us aren't. So he manages to do what he does because of this divine inspiration that he has and he's able to break all kinds of rules. . . . But people try to do what he does and they're just not quite up to it. I think there's a spirit of rebellion there, with the idea that it's not about tunes you can whistle, that it's about musical expression in perhaps a more abstract way. If you can pull it off it's a wonderful thing, but it's not so easy to achieve.

Sondheim's shows, of course, despite the extravagant and well-deserved critical praise they have often earned, have rarely been box office bonanzas. And composers who, of late, have tried to write in idiosyncratic styles that do not adhere to pop prescriptions, such as Michael John LaChiusa, Adam Guettel, Jason Robert Brown, Andrew Lippa, Skip Kennon, and others, have found it difficult to enter the Broadway mainstream. In the wake of September 11, audiences seemed to gravitate to feel-good works that provided respite from fears about terrorist attacks, a war with Iraq, and the Washington DC snipers. The darker themes and subject matter chosen by these composers have demonstrated little appeal to the average Broadway theatregoer.

Regardless of their stripe, musicals are the popular mainstay of Broadway. They offer the greatest opportunity for spectacle, easy entertainment, touring sales, and ancillary income from souvenir programs and cast albums. Straight plays have been a tougher sell on Broadway for several years, and even the few unbridled successes typically run for much shorter periods than hit musicals. Large-cast straight plays, once exceedingly popular, are not producible today except in limited runs, and smaller-cast shows often lack the visual stimulation audiences seem to crave. Straight plays are also difficult to market on the road, making them less desirable to many producers. As producer Chase Mishkin, whose straight play credits include the hit Irish import *The Beauty Queen of Leenane,* noted, "If you have a straight play and you run on Broadway for a year, you're a huge hit. If you've got a musical, you can run for multiple years. Because tourists from foreign countries come and see you. They don't come to see straight plays when their English isn't perfect." International tourists accounted for 2.7 percent of straight plays' audiences in 2000–2001, while they made up about 9.8 percent of musicals' audiences.[13]

For several years, the prognosticators have assured us that the death of the straight play was all but guaranteed, but such shows are still produced, and occasionally, there is a surprising small swell of straight works presented. As Frank Rich accurately noted, however, most straight Broadway plays are made from one of two basic molds. "I'm paraphrasing William Goldman [from his 1969 book, *The Season*], but basically, he said that there is room for one snob hit, which means a British play, or a very intellectual American play, and one Neil Simon kind of hit. That's it for any season on Broadway. And that still holds." The snob hit may be an excellent theatrical work, but according to Goldman, whose gleefully scabrous take on the Broadway of more than thirty years ago was not only extraordinarily funny but filled with deadly accurate observations that still hold true today, it had to be either British or at least a little unintelligible. "The audience that goes to the Snob Hit," Goldman wrote, "must be convinced that the 'average' theatregoer wouldn't understand it. Or . . . like it."[14] An examination of the plays presented in the last few seasons proves that Goldman's dictum is still generally applicable. The straight play has found its true home in the regional and Off-Broadway theatres.

In the 2001–2 Broadway season, nineteen straight plays (excluding one- or two-person shows) opened on Broadway in both commercial and not-for-profit theatres. This is a relatively healthy number, bolstered in part by works mounted at the not-for-profit theatres. Of those nineteen, ten were revivals, and only two, Edward Albee's *The Goat* and Neil Simon's *45 Seconds from Broadway*, were produced initially for Broadway, with the other seven transferring from not-for-profit venues around America and England. By contrast, nine musicals opened that season, and six of these were new works, although only two, *Thou Shalt Not* and *Sweet Smell of Success* opened on Broadway without prior success in other arenas. While musicals are usually more profitable than straight plays, their higher costs mean that fewer musicals than straight plays will open each year.

The Broadway community always wishes for an increase in the number of productions mounted annually, but while that may generate more employment, it might not generate more good works. The 1920s saw several Broadway seasons in which over two hundred productions opened, a staggering number by any reckoning. The overwhelming majority quickly faded into obscurity. For every bland, banal, or misconceived play or musical of recent years, countless analogs may be found in the past. The majority of Broadway productions over the years have been little more than disposable entertainments devised for quick, popular consumption and lack the artistic heft and complexity of some of the enduring classics. This disposability speaks to the central issue, which is that Broadway has always been a center for popular entertainment. Can forty theatres consistently house artistically invigorating works? But the critical question remains: are the forces that shape Broadway conspiring of late to create a theatrical world of retreads, movie and cartoon adaptations, and rock music concept shows?

When popular entertainment and artistry marry, Broadway audiences are graced with exceptional productions. Broadway can survive economically on a diet of mostly populist fare, whereas its chances for financial solvency are minimal if it were to present only artistically challenging but inaccessible shows. As William Goldman pointed out, there is room for only one or two snob hits a year. But Broadway's economic survival would be a Pyrrhic victory of sorts if artistic invention is slowly leached out in an attempt to make the Great White Way a New York outpost of the theme park–ing of America. Several of the Broadway practitioners interviewed for this book lamented that Broadway was already well on that road and has been for some years. Others endorsed the view that in a market-driven theatre community, there is little wrong with giving the people what they want. The dismaying subtext is that if the production values are unimpeachable, content matters little.

The 2002–3 season was a typical one, comprising a mix of musicals, straight plays, revivals, and one-person shows. The only certified blockbuster that season, and the only one since *The Producers* sent Broadway spinning on its ear in 2001, was the musical *Hairspray,* which opened in August 2002 and recouped its investment eight months later. A few other musicals did brisk, if not monumental, business. It is a surprise to many that Broadway was able to fare this well. The flurry of punches that assaulted Broadway—the terrorist attack of September 11, 2001, the nation's economic downturn, the cold and stormy winter of 2003, a short-lived but potentially disastrous musicians' strike, and the war with Iraq in spring 2003—all contributed significant obstacles to the health of the industry. Still, at the end of the 2002–3 season, Broadway had set a new box office record for gross receipts, more than $720 million, up 12 percent from the previous season, which included the terrorist attacks. The numbers must be considered in context, however. Rising ticket prices distort the true meaning of the receipts, as attendance was down about five hundred thousand from the 2000–2001 season. But in light of the assaults it has weathered, Broadway is maintaining a relatively steady financial course.

The Fabulous Invalid was never in greater peril of expiring than in the days that followed September 11. That it survived underscores the tenacity of the Broadway community. It sometimes displays an inflated sense of its own importance. It is a world with its own argot, rituals, behavioral quirks, and bizarre superstitions. It runs on a curious mixture of gossip and rumor, character assassination and consummate professionalism, oversized narcissism and petty sniping, cutthroat competition and occasional gestures of true generosity. It has produced some of the most stultifyingly banal and egregiously misguided productions in the history of theatre. Yet it has also generated countless enduring works of theatrical genius and stunning feats of artistic prestidigitation. It attracts impressively creative talents and the sharpest business minds eager to make their artistic and financial fortunes, as well as charlatans, misanthropes, and misguided souls seeking to bask in the reflected glow of theatrical accomplishment.

Broadway's evolution must be understood in the context of artistic and economic forces that play out in a global arena. But as James Pentecost pointed out, "Broadway should change. It should continue to evolve. It shouldn't be what it was in the twenties. The desire for people to express themselves, and the desire for people to see people who express themselves, that's a constant. What evolves is the specific entertainment. And it's our job as producers to shape that." It is that shape of things that is at the heart of the matter. In subsequent chapters, this book will explore the ways and means of making theatre on the precipitous terrain of Broadway.

2 The Producers

Hope springs eternal, and that's the way we are in this game; we're always optimists.
—Richard Frankel, producer and general manager

Individual producers are a very important part of this equation to keep the theatre interesting and vital and vibrant, and I think fewer of them think of it as "product" in the same way the corporations have to.
   —Nina Keneally, producer

You still can make a big difference as an individual producer.
   —Daryl Roth, producer

The best way to become a millionaire producer is to start off with a billion dollars.
   —attributed by Edgar Dobie, producer, to James M. Nederlander, theatre owner and producer

There are no real producers on Broadway anymore.
   —Heard far and wide for a number of years from countless sources in every walk of theatrical life

In June 2001, *The Producers* opened on Broadway to wildly enthusiastic reviews and an enormous box office advance. The Mel Brooks musical lavishly and savagely satirizes the world of producing in the persona of the down-on-his-luck impresario Max Bialystock, whose scam to rescale the heights of his former Broadway glory involves finding the worst play ever written—a loving musical tribute to Adolf Hitler—capitalizing it at 25,000 percent of its real costs, hiring the worst·"talent" available to ensure its spectacular one-night demise, and absconding with the leftover millions to Rio. Despite their worst intentions, Bialystock and his hapless partner, Leo Bloom, unwittingly engineer a camp blockbuster of mammoth proportions and are faced with the impossible task of paying back all the little old ladies who entrusted them with their money.

A few days after the show swept the Tony Awards, the *New York Times* ran a piece in which some *real* Broadway producers told a few jokes on themselves. Emanuel Azenberg, long-time producer of Neil Simon's work, captured a few truths about his profession.

This treatment is long overdue, but the truth is devastating. The public is laughing, but the churches and the synagogues are crowded with producers who are lamenting their fate. The reason producers get condemned is, 1) they deserve it, and 2) they deserve it. Keep in mind, however, that they're being condemned by the creators, and we'll get them back: we producers are getting together to write a musical to improve our image. Except we can't raise the money.[1]

For good or ill, Broadway would not function without producers. Jokes and stories—some with more than a kernel of truth—abound about their greed and avarice, lack of taste, and brutal tactics, but without them, playwrights and composers would never be able to bring their works to a commercial forum. Despite the overwhelming odds against success on Broadway, the possibility of hitting it big, like a siren's song, lures players, some with little understanding of the craft, to dash themselves on the rocks of Forty-second Street. But those who succeed over time generally display a great passion for the theatre that is married to commercial and financial acumen. Roy Gabay, a producer and general manager, said, "In producing and managing, you're in control of everything. Yes, you need to raise the money, you need people to give you the product, but that aside, your fingers are in every aspect of the show, everything. You see how it all comes together, like a giant puzzle."

Evidently, the previous generation of producers—the name Kermit Bloomgarden is almost reverentially invoked, as is Robert Whitehead's and, with a mixture of horror and glee, David Merrick's—was able to put those pieces together more effectively to capture the hearts and minds of the Broadway community and theatregoers. Dozens of Broadway veterans frequently lamented the passing of these giants of the industry, whose idiosyncratic and instinctual approach to theatre flew in the face of contemporary methodologies, replete with sophisticated marketing schemes, focus groups, and corporate imperatives. One industry insider, a former producer himself, observed "I go to a production meeting, and a show is trying to find a path, to improve, and people are afraid of their shows, because they have to answer to some mysterious board that isn't even in the room." That is a far cry from the swaggering savvy of a David Merrick or the meticulous attention to detail of a Robert Whitehead.

In the mid-twentieth century, a producer was fairly easy to identify: a solo entrepreneur with a few shows in the pipeline. He—and except for a few stalwarts like Cheryl Crawford, Theresa Helburn, the infamous Adela Holzer, and a handful of others, a producer was invariably a man—ran a cottage industry, with little more than a desk, a phone, a file cabinet, a list of willing investors, and ideally, remarkably well developed contacts within the creative arena of theatre. His relationships with writers, composers, directors, designers, theatre owners, and agents were key to his success. He might work alone, like David Merrick, for whom sharing any sliver of power was unthinkable, or he might join in a long-term, fruitful partnership, like Cy Feuer and Ernest Martin. Business was often conducted on the fly, in the lobbies of theatres, in front of rehearsal halls, or over Danish and coffee at the "Polish Tea Room" and similar Broadway eateries.

The routes by which most Broadway shows traveled were remarkably similar in certain respects, regardless of the origin of the material. A producer found a property—either brought to his attention or developed from his office—and optioned it, raised money, hired an artistic team, rented a theatre, cast the show, rehearsed it, took it out of town to work it into shape, and then "came in" and opened on Broadway. Today, the role of the Broadway producer is infinitely harder to define. While the basic building blocks of the production process remain comfortingly unchanged, the rest of the particulars have grown geometrically in complexity. Indeed, *Broadway producer* is a term ascribed no longer only to individuals but also to consortiums, corporations, and not-for-profit theatres. Producers' work is often transparent to the public, who might be only dimly aware that it has something to do with the financing of a production, but in truth the involvement of producers is essential and overarching. The exigencies of bringing a play from page to stage are such that careful and constant shepherding of the work is needed. It takes years to bring a show to Broadway.

As in any field of commercial endeavor, some of the players are rapacious, others, with limited vision, are little more than functionaries, but the best make an essential and critical contribution to the theatrical process. At times they even provide the initial spark of conception of a project. They offer the long-term guidance and support without which a show would be stillborn. That support is manifested most concretely and immediately in the financing of the production but is also seen in the constant decision making that is essential in the life of a production.

It is accompanied by a muscular boosterism necessary to propel the artists over the inevitable bumps in the process and to generate a strong word-of-mouth response to the play even before it opens. It also involves a considerable amount of theatrical wisdom, both practical and aesthetic, as well as an understanding of what audiences want or will accept. Rocco Landesman noted, "The most successful producers have been those, like Cameron Mackintosh, whose own tastes have reflected a wide popular taste. You have to have a taste that is not too esoteric but still have the intelligence to be able to discern quality."[2] But taste alone is insufficient to succeed. Producing attracts many dilettantes, often wealthy dabblers, who figure that success is only a matter of a checkbook and a narcissistic overappraisal of their own theatrical insight. After a failure or two, they usually move on to another endeavor.

Contemporary producers can trace their lineage back some twenty-five hundred years to the Greek theatre, where a *choregus,* a wealthy patron citizen of Athens, sponsored the dramatic festivals that spawned the great comedies and tragedies. Over the centuries, that role was assumed first by the church and then by municipal authorities and guilds. By the eighteenth century, leading British performers began to form their own theatrical companies, often selling shares in them to raise money, and for many years the actor-manager was the working paradigm in both Britain and America. In the late nineteenth century and the early part of the twentieth, as Broadway became the center of American theatre, men from disparate backgrounds gravitated to the cutthroat world of producing. The most successful producers were also theatre real estate magnates, and in the early twentieth century, the two roles often went hand in hand. The marriage of the control of the physical space and the work performed inside would continue to evolve over the decades and generate a bloc of omnipotent theatre czars. Aside from a few people with theatrical backgrounds, such as David Belasco, a noted director and writer, most Broadway producers in the early years were shrewd businessmen, many of them immigrants or first-generation German or Eastern European Jews with no experience in or particular talent for theatre. But they all saw the potential for huge profits in the world of entertainment, which included a lucrative national touring circuit, and they waged intense internecine battles for supremacy in the early years of the twentieth century. By 1905 the Syndicate, the imperious and often unscrupulous controlling force within the national theatre community, was supplanted by the Shubert family, led by brothers Lee and J.J. The Shuberts themselves ruthlessly extended their power and soon owned and controlled more than a hundred theatres in New York and around the nation. Although a 1950 anti-trust ruling stripped the Shuberts of many of their theatres and diminished much of their national presence, their power is still formidable in New York, where they control the lion's share of theatres on Broadway.[3]

In 1972, after Lee and J.J. had died and other members of the Shubert family proved unable to provide strong leadership, control was transferred to the organization's attorneys, Bernard Jacobs and Gerald Schoenfeld. These two proved to the Broadway community that despite their legal background, they could successfully oversee the artistic and business fortunes of the most powerful theatrical organization on Broadway. Individual theatre owners soon discovered that competition with the Shuberts was difficult, and the financial demands of running one or two theatres were daunting. By the 1970s, when Broadway had entered a fallow artistic period and fewer theatres were occupied, owners began to sell their properties to real estate developers who clamored for more midtown space, allowed them to go derelict, or sold them to one of the other two theatre chains, the Nederlander Organization and Jujamcyn Theatres. The Nederlander group began its theatrical legacy in 1912, when its founder, David T. Nederlander, purchased the Detroit Opera House. Now in its third generation of control by family members headed by James M. Nederlander, the group has nine Broadway theatres in its portfolio and controls programming in several more around the country and in England. Jujamcyn Theatres is owned by James Binger and his Minneapolis clan. Binger's wife, Virginia, after whom a Broadway theatre is named, was heiress to the 3M fortune. (*Jujamcyn* is an acronym of their children's names: Judith, James, and Cynthia.) The couple, with a deep commitment to the arts, was given two Broadway theatres by her father, William L. McKnight, who had purchased them in the 1970s. The Bingers never exercised direct oversight of the theatrical activity in their theatres, preferring to hire experts in the field. This smallest Broadway theatre chain, which controls five houses, is overseen by president Rocco Landesman, a former independent producer whose pre-Broadway credits included a stint as a professor of theatre criticism at Yale School of Drama.

The critical relationship between owner and producer has gone through several permutations, as will be seen in this chapter and in others. At times, owners have taken up the reins of producing to keep their houses filled. Frequently, though, owners have preferred to let others assume the responsibility and liability of putting a show together and have been content to earn their rent as landlords only.

In recent years, the economics of Broadway and, to some lesser degree, the success of Disney's feature animation films, have occasioned the advent of corporations as producers. While Disney is the only significant corporate player producing shows from the ground up without partners, the corporate presence has caused many independent producers, despite their enthusiastic public espousals that "the more players there are, the better the business," to glance more than once over their shoulders. Roy Gabay voiced his concern that the independent producer would be rendered obsolete by corporations. "In fifteen or twenty years, I can't imagine there will be independent producers. Costs will be too high. We'll need big corporations to raise money." This sentiment was echoed by a number of independents. But Disney's Thomas Schumacher believes that the playing field is wide enough to accommodate producers of all stripes. He pointed out that Disney's mandate does not currently include producing straight plays, leaving considerable room for producers who work in that arena. (Of course, some worry that straight plays are an endangered species on Broadway.) As for musicals, he noted that there is still considerable independent activity, not just by established impresarios like Cameron Mackintosh, with whom Disney is coproducing a stage-musical version of the books and film *Mary Poppins,* but by newer producers as well. Schumacher did, however, correctly distinguish between producers who "actively pursue artists, go after material, develop it and shape it and frame it, then bring a show to New York, or abandon a project because, for a variety of reasons, it's not worthy of Broadway," and the newer style of producer now seen more frequently on Broadway, who is more of a presenter or glorified investor. Schumacher also noted that Disney Theatrical's decision-making process is overseen by a small group of experienced theatre people who approach the process of producing much the same as any individual producer.

Others who believe that independents are being edged out of their former pride of place on Broadway acknowledge that corporations are not the only competition and point to the growing stature and power of the not-for-profit Broadway theatres. A few decades ago, these institutions, like corporations, were not a significant factor in the world of commercial producing except as spawning grounds for works that an independent producer might transfer to a commercial production. There were notable exceptions, though. When the New York Shakespeare Festival's production of *Two Gentlemen of Verona* moved from Central Park to Broadway in 1971, no commercial money was involved. Bernard Gersten, currently the executive producer of Lincoln Center Theater, was Joseph Papp's right hand at the Shakespeare Festival in the seventies and an associate producer for *Two Gents*. Commercial producers approached him and Papp about transferring the show to Broadway. "At one point, Joe and I turned to each other and said, 'Why do we need anybody to produce the play? We've already produced it. All we need is somebody who knows a little bit about Broadway business.'" They received the necessary $250,000 from their board chairman, LuEsther Mertz. "That was how the first not-for-profit production made its move to Broadway, totally capitalized with an earmarked gift from a donor, and became a 100-percent-owned transfer from the not-for-profit sector to Broadway." The Public Theatre enjoyed all the profits from the production and never had to disburse payments to investors.

While competition grew in the not-for-profit sector, the independent producer still led the pack on Broadway in the seventies and eighties. A leading theatrical attorney, John Breglio, succinctly described the old breed. "Producers were individuals, whether they were working through a corporation or not, whose calling card was their talent in raising money, bringing artists together, and identifying great work." But even the most successful producer has committed more than one egregious blunder, which can take the shape of choosing the wrong material, hiring the wrong creative team, or misjudging the audience zeitgeist. According to Thomas Schumacher, an effective producer must possess a number of key attributes.

> You have to be able to make both—the Apollonian and Dionysian factors eternally at odds—feel comfortable, so that the work can proceed in a productive and timely way. Those who deal with the commerce and the physical production and the producing details must feel that a producer has a very sure hand and will partner with them to deliver all of that responsibly. And ideally, a producer should have the same relationship with the creative team. A producer will share a vocabulary and an understanding and a passion for what the production actually is. A good producer is able to enable both sides of the process. And if you can move fluidly between them, and honor both sides, and foster both sides, and embrace both sides, I think you have a good chance for success. If you can add to that a sense of the popular, and

simultaneously, a diverse range of interests in things that probably aren't popular; if you can add a dash of art history, and a little bit of panache, and of course, as Kipling instructs, "If you can keep your head while all about you are losing theirs," I think these, ultimately, are the signs of good producers.

Today, when fewer new works are attempted on Broadway, producers face challenges different from those in the past, when the greatest risk was the mounting of new work, sight unseen. Years ago, producers' wisdom and instincts about the prospects for a new piece often defined their success, but this talent has largely been rendered moot. Now, especially in the world of straight plays, producers frequently either mount revivals or transfer successful works from not-for-profit venues. According to James Pentecost,

> Your risk in doing a revival of *Death of a Salesman* today is, can you make a great production out of it, can you entice people to come see it if you get good reviews? It's not any longer a question of, "Is Arthur Miller's play a good play?" So the challenge of this kind of producing is packaging it or finding stars or directors who reinterpret the work in a persuasive way that is going to get people into the theatre. It's a far cry from Kermit Bloomgarden taking the play from a playwright who had one flop and one quasi-sort-of-hit, and getting Elia Kazan interested, and casting Lee J. Cobb. Who knew that would be a success? But again, it probably cost a lot less in 1949 than it would now.

Roy Gabay, who gained the commercial rights to produce the successful *Metamorphoses* during its initial Off-Broadway run at the not-for-profit Second Stage, added, "It's such a misnomer when we say that we're producing these shows. It's what it was when it was at Second Stage. I think it's better at Circle in the Square [its Broadway house]; the physical space helps it out. But did I say to [director and playwright] Mary Zimmerman, 'Well, if you make the Midas myth like *this*. . . .' No, I didn't do that. It's not my place to do that. We moved the production, we moved her vision. In a way, that's what commercial producing in New York has become." He added, however, that on the shows that he produced from their inception, his artistic involvement was considerable. In part, because so many Broadway shows are now developed in other venues, producers often lack that all-encompassing oversight that their predecessors enjoyed.

Often producers organically connect with a genre or style or writer. Some, like Cameron Mackintosh, are associated with large, sumptuous musicals, and others, like David Richenthal, are known for their work on straight plays and revivals. But several will work on a cross section of shows. "[I produce] what turns me on. What speaks to me. That which I feel passionate about. I can't just say, 'I want old-fashioned musicals.' . . . I love to tell a good story. I like it to be simple, I like it to be straight, I like it to be strongly in the audience's lap," said Barry Weissler, producer of such recent hits as the revivals of *Chicago* and *Annie Get Your Gun.* Intuition is important, but without a personal connection to the work, the tortuous gestation of a show would prove daunting to even the most intrepid producer.

In point of fact, however, not all producers are suited to every work that comes along. A sense of one's own taste and proclivities is essential. The eminent producer and director Harold Prince, in his 1974 autobiographical work *Contradictions,* underscored this point when writing about the failure of his 1960 musical *Tenderloin:* "Clearly, we were the wrong producers for *Tenderloin.* The whole notion of wrong and right producers is in discard today, the personality of a producer's work, his identity is missing, and it seems to me therein lies one of the sicknesses of Broadway."[4] But playwright John Weidman commented that many producers are not creatively inclined.

> Certainly on Broadway, I think they're businessmen before they are artists. I think that if a man wants to be a businessman, there's a lot of things he can make, from shoes to tires to spandex. But I think that guys who decide to become businessmen in the theatre should be, and in the old days they were more likely to be, guys who are driven by more complicated impulses. Yes, to make money, but also to make art. To say, "I've *got* to put this play in front of people. I love this playwright. I want to produce everything that Wendy Wasserstein writes. I need to make it perfect, I need to find the perfect set designer, the perfect director."

Hank Unger, who coproduced *Urinetown,* observed that producing "is shepherding an idea and a project through its hopefully successful run and watching audiences love what you thought was a good idea on paper. And it's everything that happens in between—the struggles, the fights, the challenges, the ups and downs . . . seeing that from beginning to end. It's a lot more creative than a lot of fields, and it's that use of our creativity that's really terrific. It really nourishes something deep within all of us." Roy Somlyo paraphrased the legendary producer Kermit Bloomgarden, whose credits included Arthur Miller's *Death of a Salesman* and *The Music Man*. "Years ago, I remember a lecture Bloomgarden had given. The one thing I took away from that lecture was, 'If you people want to be producers, the only standard that you should use is: Is this something I like? Don't sit back and say, "This is something I could sell them." Just do it if you like it.'"

A producer's intuition will not always result in a popular work. The multiyear time frame for producing a show often precludes the chance to cash in on the taste of the moment. Instinct, while it may occasionally pay handsome dividends, can still result in a bomb. Yet most producers stress that topicality must be subordinate to personal connection to the work. Rocco Landesman produced three successful musicals—*Big River, Into the Woods,* and *The Secret Garden*—before taking up his current position as president of Jujamcyn Theatres. "I have a literary orientation. I love story, narrative, and great literature. If you look at the three shows I personally had a hand in producing, all had literary underpinnings. I've also always been interested as a producer in the story element onstage. Others are interested in the theatricality of the theatre—what theatre can do scenically or theatrically. My interest has always been more literary."

Landesman's particular background is unusual; several successful producers, as noted earlier, were either lawyers or investors first. But a strong grooming in the practice and aesthetics of theatre can be an invaluable asset. In discussing the work of the Araca Group—whose hit musical *Urinetown* was initially viewed in the Broadway community as a likely disaster—Hank Unger added,

> We like to pride ourselves on understanding both the business side . . . and the artistic side of producing a show. We try to weigh and evaluate both sides, but if the show isn't any good, or if the show is not something people want to see, then the business side is not important. I think it's very important to understand the business side, but to understand why an actor is good for a role, or why they're not good for a role, or why these two people could have chemistry, or what it is about a play that is going to capture a Broadway audience's imagination . . . that's the subjective, gut call that we make all the time and pride ourselves on, because we started off in that background, acting in plays,

directing plays, even producing plays on an amateur level. That's where we came from; we didn't really come from a business background. We spend less time doing business and more time doing the art side of theatre. The business side we figured out.

For most producers, the ultimate reward is not just fiscal but artistic. Daryl Roth, who has produced both musicals and straight plays such as *Proof* and *The Tale of the Allergist's Wife,* acknowledged that "the best thing for me has been getting to know new young playwrights and having a relationship with them as they grow so I can help them get their work out there." Jane Harmon and Nina Keneally produced *The Last Night of Ballyhoo.* Harmon noted that "if we feel it is well written, and we make the judgment that other people feel that way, then we'll go for it. I think we all enjoy the creative developmental process, with the writers and directors and the technical people. That's the favorite part of our business." Keneally added, "One of our strengths is also being personally involved in all aspects of the production. It's no fun to sit in an office and just write checks."

The job of producing is to some extent fluid, but certain aspects remain inescapable. A producer can generate the idea for a production and hire a writer or, in the case of a musical, writers and composer, to create the work. He may elect to premiere an original work that he discovers through a literary agent or other submission process. He may also transfer a work from another venue or produce a revival. Marty Bell, whose most recent projects were *A Class Act* and *Sweet Smell of Success,* as well as overseeing *Ragtime* for Livent, remarked that "most of the great musicals in history were originated by producers and not by writers. . . . In the great years of Broadway, which is '27 *[Show Boat]* to '75 *[A Chorus Line],* the shows were producer-driven." David Merrick, for example, the larger-than-life autocrat famous for unpredictable, flamboyant, and sometimes hateful shenanigans, had the germ of an idea and the determination to develop *Gypsy* and *Hello, Dolly!* Bell went on to explain that "then [Broadway] got into a period where the cost escalated. Instead of career producers we started having teams of producers because you need that many people to raise the money. . . . We needed the people—it's an industry—but they didn't have the skills or the background to originate shows the way the great producers from the previous era had originated shows. And I think theatre lost something. So my goal was to always get back to that."

As most musicals are adaptations of previously existing works, those producers who follow Bell's dictum must often doggedly pursue the rights to the underlying material. Barry Brown, who produced *La Cage aux Folles* and successful revivals of *Gypsy,* related how he developed the idea to turn Friedrich Dürrenmatt's dark comedy *The Visit* into a musical. (The show, written by John Kander and Fred Ebb, received a not-for-profit production in Chicago and awaits a Broadway production.) Brown had seen a small production of the original play in Los Angeles in the early nineties and was intrigued by its potential as a musical.

I went to try to get the rights from ICM, who represents the [Dürrenmatt] estate. And the agent said, "I don't really think it's such a great idea for a musical, so I don't know that I can recommend it for them. But you know, there's a German opera [version] coming to New York. Why don't we go to the opera together, and then we'll talk about it." We went to the opera, we stood up at the end when the curtain came down, and she turned to me and said, "Well, I'm certainly glad we did this because this convinces me more than ever that it should *not* be a musical." And I said, "Are you nuts? This convinces me more than ever that it *has* to be a musical." And I hounded her and hounded her. I must have called her three times a week for six or seven months. And I think finally, just to get me off her back, she said okay. So I got the rights to it.

Without a producer's vision and oversight, the disparate strands of theatrical production would never coalesce to form a viable theatrical event. Although artists offer differing opinions about the degree to which they believe a producer should be involved in a production's artistic process, the best producers know how, and when, to offer a critical contribution. Hank Unger likened it to being the CEO of a company.

You need to know if the director is doing a good job, you need to know if the designer is doing a good job. Not just on opening night, but being able to take the pulse of the show on an ongoing basis. . . . It's ultimately your responsibility for what's going on onstage. You need to be able to communicate with the director, to be able to say, "The play ends three times. We need to have one denouement, and get out as quickly as possible because the show loses steam at that point." . . . It's being able to speak the language of everyone you've hired—that's the most important skill on the artistic side.

The producer is responsible for assiduously pursuing the best creative team for a particular work. The most successful relationships develop when producers forge strong ties to one or more writers and continue to support their work over the course of their careers, as Harold Prince did with Stephen Sondheim.

Marty Bell discussed his process in overseeing the creation of *Ragtime*. Bell first convinced Livent's chief, Garth Drabinsky, of the worth of adapting the E. L. Doctorow novel into a musical and then began to assemble the creative team.

> The first person we went to was Terrence McNally, to write the book. He wrote a fifty-page treatment for the show. And what happens in treatments is you often end up using very little that's in the treatment in the show, but it gets everybody started. . . . I don't think I [would] do [this] again, but we gave money to ten different composers and had them each write four sample songs. . . . And E. L. Doctorow and Garth Drabinsky and I sat and listened to the songs without [me] letting them know [who had written which songs], and that's how Lynn Ahrens and Stephen Flaherty were selected.

That process is unusual, Bell admits, but not unheard of.

After the rights are secured by the payment of options and advance fees, the producer must raise the initial capitalization costs for the production. These can range from over one million dollars for a small-cast straight play to more than twelve million for a musical. These funds are earmarked for all expenses necessary to arrive at opening night. Aside from a small contingency reserve from those funds, the show lives or dies by its weekly box office receipts. For some producers today, raising money can be the most frustrating aspect of their job. Sometimes the producer's record is enough to lure investors; at other times it is the material, or even the director, that is most appealing. Investors carefully examine both the time it has taken the producer's other shows to recoup, as well as recoupment projections for the new show. Jane Harmon observed, "We aren't going to keep investors around if we don't give them a good shot at returning their investment and making a profit. I don't think people put money in commercial theatre because they're charitable. There are plenty of other places to be charitable." Frequently the producer invests his own money in the show, sometimes only a token amount as a good-faith move to attract investors, sometimes considerably more. As Chase Mishkin noted, "When I make a commitment to a play, the guys I work with know

I'm going to do it. And they also know that if I can't raise half of my commitment, I'll probably come up with it myself. But that's not the idea. The idea is I put up a dollar for every dollar I raise." Barry Brown added, "I don't think I can ask somebody else to put their hard-earned money into something if I don't." This demonstrates confidence to potential investors and decreases the amount necessary to raise; producers who invest in their productions will make greater earnings if the show recoups. Some, however, view their creative and administrative contributions as sufficient, and prefer to treat the production with a degree of dispassion that is possible only when one's own money is not involved.

The producer hires the creative and production staff, often with the assistance of the general manager, the producer's right hand, who oversees the day-to-day aspects of the operation. Some producers function as their own general managers to consolidate power and save money. He participates in casting; strikes a rental agreement with a theatre owner; sets ticket prices; hires legal, insurance, marketing, advertising, and group sales representatives; and negotiates contracts. It is also a producer's task to mediate artistic disagreements within the creative team. One potential flaw in the current producing paradigm is that without a strong lead producer, multiple voices in a consortium can create discord or diffuse focus. The former theatre critic Frank Rich believed that "if there is someone with the muscle and the vision, an auteur, it can work. . . If someone is playing that role, then maybe it doesn't matter if eight people put up the money and all have their names billed above the title if all they're doing is throwing opening night parties and giving out house seats."

By opening night, the show's fate will have been determined largely by two factors: the reviews that were written a few days before and the box office advance. The wise producer can make critical decisions to best exploit the show's future by determining marketing strategy, deciding how far in advance to sell tickets, managing subsidiary rights, and attending to a range of other daily problems. The goals are to maximize the show's longevity, pay back investors quickly, exploit ancillary and subsidiary rights, and keep the show on an even keel. Harold Prince, in a published interview in 2001, remarked,

> I discerned that the first thing you had to do to be a good producer was possess enough artistic taste to know when to say no and when to say yes. If you deny an artist the money to support his vision, you have to know as an artist that he's throwing money away. I knew. I also

knew where money would work. Sometimes it seemed as if I was being very indulgent, but I felt that the artist had a hook on something amazing and it was worth the extra ten thousand dollars to provide it. And other times I thought, "He's going to change his mind tomorrow. I will have blown ten thousand dollars and he'll say, 'Sorry, wrong muse.'" . . . So I knew when to say yes, and I knew more specifically when to say no and be responsible about it. I hated throwing money away. It is hard to find.[5]

The playwright and director Arthur Laurents, whose career on Broadway and in films spans almost sixty years and whose credits include writing the books to *West Side Story* and *Gypsy* and directing *La Cage aux Folles,* offered that "the producer's function is to stand back and look at [the work]. And then say to the director and the author, 'Is this what you meant? I see *this*.' To point out what is on stage. Because when you're working on a production you go blind. And that's his important function. Objectivity." He added that the best producer is one "who has conviction. Who has courage. I don't care if his taste is terrible, let him have conviction. And the conviction should not be, 'Is this going to be a success at the box office?' When you go that way, it's suicide. No one knows what will be a commercial success. Not even applauding audiences at previews or out of town or the by now customary standing ovations. The goal is to make it as good as it can be. Commercial success is then gravy."

Composer and lyricist Stephen Sondheim agreed with Laurents. In discussing his long-term relationship with Harold Prince and Robert Griffith, his first Broadway producers, Sondheim observed that "what was good about them was that they let the writers do the work. They didn't interfere. That's what a good producer does." As far as a producer's contribution to the artistic process is concerned, "I think an intelligent producer can, like an intelligent agent or an intelligent lawyer or an intelligent friend, look at a show, once it's up there, in a run-through, and make some cogent remarks. But I don't like working by committee. I think writing is writing. What you want, primarily, is a producer who loves the piece." Director and choreographer Robert Longbottom, whose credits include *Side Show* and the revival of *The Flower Drum Song,* added that producers must be joined at the hip with the piece, echoing Sondheim's sentiments. "You need the producer to love the show. It is very important for them to be passionate about what's going on. To really believe in what's happening on that stage. Stubbornness is helpful, especially when confronted with money people saying 'no' or 'maybe,' or hedging their investment. Then, in spite of all those challenges, that no matter what, they're going to see it through to opening night and beyond."

Actor Danny Burstein underscored the need for producer tenacity. Burstein, who has appeared in a number of Broadway shows, discussed the contribution made by the producers of *A Class Act*, in which he understudied the leading role. The musical, which married the songs of the late Ed Kleban, best known as the lyricist of *A Chorus Line*, to a new book about his life in the theatre, originated at Musical Theatre Works and then played successfully at Manhattan Theatre Club. Its producers, including Marty Bell and Chase Mishkin, decided to move it to Broadway, where, despite mostly positive reviews, it failed to find an audience. Still, the producers did not give up on the show. "I've never seen more dedicated or intrepid people," said Burstein. "They tried every angle they could to make the show work, and did it because they so loved the piece. And they had influence over what went on in the show. Artistically, they put their two cents in. It was not just a monetary thing. They were not idly throwing money into it. They really cared about the piece." He elaborated on how the producers shepherded the show from its initial incarnation at Musical Theatre Works to Broadway.

The producers oversaw years of readings and workshops until Manhattan Theatre Club agreed to produce it Off-Broadway. Marty [Bell], Arielle [Tepper], and Chase [Mishkin] knew that with decent reviews and good word of mouth they could eventually move the show to a Broadway house. [Authors] Lonny Price and Linda Kline were very interested in their input. They would listen, discuss options, and go to work. Often, the changes came immediately or the very next day. The trick was to try and make Ed Kleban, who was an enigma in many ways, the focus of a Broadway musical. He's not your usual protagonist: a human thornbush who happened to be a songwriting genius. How to introduce him honestly and ask the audience to spend the next two hours watching him create gorgeous music, while spinning out of control? As usual, getting the first fifteen minutes of the show moving properly seemed to be the most difficult. The problem was marrying the right amount of drama without getting bogged down in exposition. We tried an endless array of openings with different songs, opening monologues, scenes, et cetera, until finally, I think, a perfect mixture was discovered. Every decision was discussed in production meetings and then with the cast. It was quite an amazing process. Don't get me wrong, there were disagreements, but everyone wanted the same thing. And being on the same page throughout this difficult creative process is proof of an excellent production team and director.

Although many producers interact with actors to a lesser extent than they do with the creative team, some do try to develop relationships with their casts beyond the initial contract negotiations. Rebecca Luker, who was nominated for Tony Awards for her performances as Magnolia in the Livent revival of *Show Boat* and as Marian in the revival of *The Music Man,* agreed that it is difficult for producers to negotiate with a cast of actors whose agents demand similar considerations. The best producers adopt an honest approach to negotiating—but some do not. "Somehow, the actor and the agent always find out when the producer is lying. And it always becomes a big mess. It's unusual to find a straightforward producer who is not afraid to say, 'Look, we can't do this for you, and yes, we're doing it for them. But we'll do it for you next month.' And one that keeps in touch with his company, and visits from time to time. And tells you how the show is doing."

Randy Graff, a Tony winner for her role in *City of Angels* and a nominee for *A Class Act,* observed that many producers pretend to court actors but very few of them actually understand the theatrical process or provide the nurturing essential to a show's development. "Relationships with producers are one of the things I loved about working with Marty Bell [on *A Class Act*]. He's a real hands-on producer. He takes good care of his actors. And you really feel like you have a personal relationship with your producer. If there's a problem, you can go to him. I'm very comfortable with that kind of relationship, that kind of dynamic." Producers have a stake in their actors' happiness, especially leading actors. Disgruntled performers who feel they are not being treated properly are more apt to leave a production when their contracts expire. The time and energy spent in replacing an actor, coupled with the potential for the loss of income if a star departs, can prove a drain on the production.

One of the most salient relationships a producer can cultivate is with the theatre owners. Roy Gabay stated it baldly. "There's a fallacy that commercial producers dictate what people see on stages. It's not [true]. It's theatre owners, because they choose what goes into their venue." As noted earlier, there have been times when owners have actively engaged in producing, usually as partners with lead creative producers. During the seventies, a decade with a dearth of good new shows on Broadway, the owners discovered that the chain that was willing to invest in a show would usually land that show for its theatre. Rocco Landesman, who became president of Jujamcyn in 1987, hired Jack Viertel, the dramaturg at the Mark Taper Forum in Los Angeles, as Jujamcyn's creative director. At the time, three of the company's five houses were empty. Viertel recalled that "because Jujamcyn was the smallest of the three theatre owner chains, and because they did not have the most prestigious theatres, and because they did not have the great relationships built up over the years with the Andrew Lloyd Webbers and Cameron Mackintoshes, the only way we were going to make a success out of this company would be to create our own shows." Landesman and Viertel set out to bring in a handful of independent producers and support their efforts. But owner-as-producer is a cyclical phenomenon, Viertel pointed out. Attorney John Breglio elaborated.

> When the theatre business was in bad shape in the seventies, the theatre owners stepped up and became more active as producers. They didn't have the product, and they had to fill their theatres. So they stepped into the breach. As more and more plays were produced, and musicals ran longer and longer, filling their theatres for five, ten, fifteen years, they stepped back from producing somewhat. Why should a theatre owner risk capital when he can sit there and get 6 or 7 percent of the gross for rent for every week the theatre is filled?

Marty Bell agreed that the owners were in a position of considerable power in the seventies and eighties, exhibiting tight control over the fortunes of the League and, in turn, independent producers.

> The theatre owners were producing a lot more and putting a lot more money into shows, so they had a lot more to say over how shows were done. I think some of the organizations thought they could produce everything, and the era of the independent producer was over. And there are very different interests when you are on the real estate side than when you're on the producing side. And I think the interests of the real estate side at that point became the dominant theme of the industry, as opposed to the interests of the producer.

In the mideighties, Bell was a founding member of the breakaway Producers Group, which was intended to give independent producers a greater voice in the League's operations. One of the founders was Rocco

Landesman, and when he joined Jujamcyn, Bell felt that the theatre chains' control began to ease. "I think independent producers had a lot of successful shows, and the theatre owners needed them more. The theatre owners didn't want to put as much money into shows as they were doing, and maybe the [owners] learned that they can't produce as much, and so I think that there was a necessary balance that was struck." Each of the chains maintains a cadre of artistic advisers to guide them in making producing, investing, and booking decisions. The power of the theatre owners is especially strong when all desirable theatres are occupied and there is a backlog of shows waiting for spaces. The owners are then able to exercise greater discretion in their selection of shows and to demand more lucrative rental deals.

When independent producers began to assert themselves with a stronger voice in the League, several participants in negotiations with the theatrical unions noted that the producers adopted a tougher stance at the bargaining table. Frank Hartenstein, a long-time production stage manager on Broadway and a member of the Actors' Equity Association's contract negotiating team, said,

> The producers really began to do their homework, and they came to the table with a lot of requests. Up until that point, negotiations were pretty much a situation where Equity would go in and say, "This is what we want," and the League would say okay to one thing, no to another, and compromise on yet another. But the producers came in with lists of demands upon the unions, which had never happened up to that point. It became a much more interesting negotiation, because you really were hammering out problems. The producers were much more knowledgeable about theatre practice than the owners were.

At the same time, a long-standing rift was healed between the Shubert and Nederlander organizations. Nederlander executive vice president Nick Scandalios pointed out that despite the ill will that had existed between the two largest chains, they still coproduced shows during that time. The feud was common knowledge, so much so that in the early eighties, the Off-Broadway musical revue *Forbidden Broadway* featured a parody song, "All the Shuberts and the Nederlanders Should Be Friends," sung to the tune of "The Farmer and the Cowman," from *Oklahoma!* Scandalios attributed the current rapprochement to a robust theatrical environment in which most theatres are lit, many with long-running productions. The peaceful relations also led to instances in which the-

atre chains produced in theatres that they did not own. In 2000 the Nederlander Organization coproduced *Copenhagen* in the Royale Theatre, a
Shubert house, and the Shuberts produced *Dirty Blonde* in the independently owned Helen Hayes.

Rocco Landesman acknowledged that his position as president of
Jujamcyn gave him "a bigger canvas to paint on. I could get involved in
more shows, have a bigger impact on theatre. . . . If I wanted to produce
a show, as happened with *The Secret Garden,* for instance, I had much
greater resources through which to do that." Landesman explained that
the shows he pursues for his theatres are sometimes rather different from
the ones he would choose to produce independently. "We have to book
our theatres, we have to make money. We have a responsibility to fill our
theatres . . . but we'll do a certain number of shows simply because they
have to be done, rather than [out of] some financial necessity. *Angels in
America* is a good example of that." Landesman was also instrumental
in negotiating a strong relationship with PACE, Clear Channel's predecessor, earning Jujamcyn a steady income stream from subsequent tours
of shows playing in PACE markets. "Their support of a show can be decisive because they can deliver [many] markets with one phone call."

There is another practical advantage enjoyed by theatre owners who
produce. Vertical integration, adopted from Hollywood, allows a company to control the fortunes of a production from top to bottom—a concept propounded by Garth Drabinsky. In the ideal model of vertical integration, a producer would own and control the rights to the show, own
the theatre, own the shops that build the physical production, and control the distribution of the show on the road, as well as subsidiary and
ancillary rights. Although no producer currently enjoys such unilateral
oversight, it is a paradigm of producing that is attractive to many, especially corporate producers. The benefits are obvious from a financial
perspective, although the lack of cross-pollination flies in the face of standard theatrical practice. Vertical integration will be examined in greater
detail in chapter 3.

Do producers deserve the unfavorable press they have received over
the years? Before the founding of Actors' Equity Association early in the
twentieth century,[6] many producers treated actors like cattle, and it was
not uncommon for a producer to strand a company of actors on the road
and make off with the show's receipts. Adela Holzer, a producer of several hit Broadway shows in the sixties and seventies, was convicted of and
served a prison term for stealing money from investors. In 1998 Garth

Drabinsky, whose productions included *Kiss of the Spider Woman* and *Ragtime* and who was heralded as a brash new type of showman capable of redefining Broadway, was indicted for allegedly maintaining two sets of books at Livent, and awaits trial in both New York and Toronto. These are egregious and widely publicized examples of producer malfeasance. It takes a considerable amount of financial skullduggery to bypass monitoring by outside government agencies.

But a producer occasionally does succumb to the temptation to swindle his investors. In one recent and unusual instance, a producer deposited distribution checks made out to certain investors into his own account, and then wrote new checks in smaller amounts to the investors—or no checks at all. The general manager was unaware of any impropriety, since the bookkeeper, who had no reason to investigate whether the original checks were endorsed properly, was able to inform him only that the checks had been cashed. The scheme was discovered when a major investor, who was a theatre professional, noticed that his check was incorrect. The incident was settled without criminal charges being filed, but word of such behavior is hard to contain and such actions can quickly and irreparably tarnish a producer's reputation.

The unions and guilds frequently characterize producers as bloated theatrical plutocrats and do so most vocally just before contract negotiations commence. While there is nothing unique to Broadway about the chasm between management and labor, the theatrical flourishes inherent in the Broadway negotiating process often yield intriguing scenarios and dramatic posturing. The negotiations are frequently accompanied by chest-thumping and brinksmanship, with jeremiads on how inequities will destroy Broadway as we know it.

The tension between the producers, for whom it is essential to pay back investors quickly, and the writers, who demand a consistent royalty for their work, occasioned the birth of the Dramatists Guild Approved Production Contract. Antitrust legislation has for years prevented writers—who are not considered employees of a production—from forming a united front, although current legislation before Congress may change that. Under the earlier Minimum Broadway Production Contract, the writers received a specified weekly royalty as a percentage of the gross receipts, regardless of whether the show made a profit after its weekly operating costs. Investors, however, would receive a reimbursement only in weeks when there was money left in the till once the operating expenses, including the writers' royalties, had been paid. It was possible, in theory and in practice, for marginal shows hovering at the edge of the black from week to week to run for long periods. There was little if any money left to pay back the investors, although the writers continued to earn their royalty. This situation grew untenable for producers, while the writers were understandably satisfied with the formula. As production and weekly running costs increased, though, investors more frequently found themselves without reimbursement. Chase Mishkin mentioned that when she produced a revival of *Moon for the Misbegotten,* "an investor I had brought in said it was the first time he ever got a check back. I thought he meant that it was the first time he'd been with a play that recouped. He meant that he'd never had a check back *from anything he'd been in,* which I had to laugh about. I asked him, 'Why do you keep doing it?' It was really a little crazy. And he said, 'It's fun.'" Under the older contract, fewer investors had fun waiting for their investment to be returned.

As weekly operating expenses crept upward, producers encountered a shrinking pool of willing investors, so the League lobbied for a different contractual formula to stem the tide of plays that could run for years without recouping. Most notable at that time was *Woman of the Year,* whose two-year run in the early eighties is frequently cited as a catalyst of significant change in the way contracts are structured, because its investors never recouped in the course of the run.

In effect since the mideighties, the Approved Production Contract suggests, in nonbinding guidelines, the creation of a royalty pool comprising the writers, other royalty-earning members of the creative team, the stars, underlying rights holders, and the producers. The pool shares in a reduced royalty until the investors earn back their money, and subsequently receive a higher royalty.[7] The contract created a more hospitable environment for investors, although it did not provide an industry-wide panacea. Alan Levey of Disney Theatrical characterized the royalty pool as a device to protect the health of the production in bad times and to improve the return to the creative team and royalty participants in good cycles. "It's one of the most significant changes in the last twenty-five years affecting the financial structure of the commercial theatre. It's flexible enough to adjust to the financial cycles of a production over the long run, making it possible for these productions to weather the really dark times. It's a very valuable and irreplaceable financial device." But Roy Gabay indicated that royalty pool participants, including the producers and general managers, continue to find ways to adjust the accounting methods so that recoupment is still more difficult than is necessary. "Before anything gets passed along to the investors, so many people are pulling at it. We need to come up with a better model." Still, royalty pools offer producers the flexibility to survive financial dips. Hank Unger contrasted the formulas that can be employed in crafting a royalty pool, citing his group's productions of a successful revival of *Frankie and Johnny* and the Off-Broadway musical *Debbie Does Dallas*. The royalty pool

> encourages recoupment. It can be structured in different ways. It depends on the clout of the staff. A project like *Frankie and Johnny* has an enormous pedigree in the creatives . . . and *Debbie Does Dallas* has a lot of people under thirty. So you're able to structure it in a way so that if the show is successful, they do better and better, but they can't demand as much up front. But the people in *Debbie Does Dallas* aren't selling tickets. Edie [Falco] and Stanley [Tucci] and Terrence McNally *are* selling tickets based on their name and their pedigree. So you reward that. What's selling tickets in *Debbie Does Dallas* is the concept and the title. . . . What are the assets somebody brings to the table?

The royalty pool can be beneficial for the pool members. A reduction in the weekly royalty can keep marginal shows running longer in the hope that stronger box office weeks, and thus higher royalties, lie ahead, but at first it greatly dissatisfied those who had been used to receiving royalties based on the gross receipts.

Other producer-union negotiating issues have proved divisive and controversial. Producers have frequently accused the unions, most often the musicians and stagehands, of featherbedding and have struggled to relax some of the rigid rules about the minimum numbers of employees on a show. For years the American Federation of Musicians, Local 802, was the beneficiary of an antiquated contractual rule that mandated a minimum number of musicians for every Broadway house, regardless of whether that theatre housed a musical. The producers struggled without success for years to eliminate the minimum. David Merrick was notorious for railing against this practice, and the apocryphal tale has it that he demanded that the musicians required for one of his straight plays spend the preshow and intermission serenading the audience from the men's and women's lounges. It took decades for the League to finally win the critical point that the entire concept of minimums for straight plays was nonsensical, and the rule was eventually phased out in 1993. In exchange, the musicians gained higher salaries for musicals.

The League, however, continued to press its grievances with the union.

It was also successful in the more crucial battle to redefine the number of musicians to be employed on a musical. Producers argued that the minimum of twenty-five musicians for the biggest musical houses could easily be reduced by as many as ten or more without compromising the sound of the show. With the advent of computer-generated music, the prototypical pit orchestra was no longer a necessity, they claimed. As the use of synthesizers and samplers has propagated in recent years, producers can now aver that aesthetics, rather than economics, are the driving force behind their move to reduce the size of orchestras. Minimums were devised to insure job security but were also based on the premise that a larger house required more musicians to fill the theatre with an appropriate sound. The advent of amplification and rock scores largely mooted the need for minimums, said the producers, although a Rodgers and Hammerstein revival or a new musical by Sondheim might very well demand the full complement. Was there a reason for *Rent*, performing in the Nederlander Theatre, to employ the contractually mandated sixteen musicians? The producers won their point at an arbitration hearing (a mechanism devised in the 1993 negotiations) and were allowed, instead, to employ a band of five. Had they been required to use sixteen musicians, the sound of the show would have differed considerably from that intended by composer Jonathan Larson and would have cost the producers several thousand dollars extra each week.

In 2000, Local 802 president William Moriarty looked ahead to the next contract negotiation and predicted,

> I don't know what is going to happen in 2003, but I think [the producers] are going to come after [minimums] pretty hard. We argue with management that when they want creative freedom, they're not talking about aesthetic creative freedom, but the creative freedom to lower the payroll. . . . If you are free to decide whatever orchestra you're going to choose, [then it will be] the absolute lowest-size orchestra that you can get away with. And we don't think that's good for either our own interests on Broadway or the interests of musical theatre on Broadway in the long run.

But the producers believed otherwise and prepared for a potential costly battle with the union as they began the next round of negotiations in early 2003.

After expensive publicity campaigns were waged by both camps, the musicians threatened another strike. It was an intimidating prospect for producers, who were already enduring the downturn occasioned by a weak economy. Many recalled 1975, when a walkout by musicians shuttered Broadway shows for twenty-two days and forced several shows to close. But a large faction in the League insisted that minimums were now unwarranted and untenable, and they vowed to weather a strike. Producers threatened a potent retaliation, the use of "virtual orchestras," which are sophisticated preprogrammed computers that can mimic an entire orchestra. The musicians did strike, but the producers never had the opportunity to test the new technology in front of audiences. The stagehands and actors decided at the last minute to honor the picket lines (an unexpected development, as the musicians had never been perceived as particularly supportive of Equity's problems with the League). The League's hand was forced, and after a few days during which all but a few shows not working under the 802 contract were shuttered, an accord was reached. The settlement, brokered at the strong urging of Mayor Michael Bloomberg, greatly reduced but did not eliminate the minimums. The League had won a sizable victory without a long, crippling strike. Despite the union's public avowal that a united front had preserved the integrity of the sound of Broadway musicals, most insiders acknowledged that this very integrity was compromised. Most producers, given the choice, would opt for the minimum rather than employing the additional musicians that a composer or orchestrator might request.

Other conflicts between unions and producers continue to affect the health of commercial theatre on Broadway and beyond. A successful production can lead to one or more potentially lucrative national tours that allow investors to recoup. Until the early 1980s, it seemed that successful tours could generate impressive revenue for producers, local presenters, and union membership. But increased costs, ranging from trucking and salaries to per diems and marketing, threaten the health of the touring industry. For some producers, the only financially viable recourse now is to produce nonunion tours. Dodger Theatricals, under the aegis of their nonunion touring division, Big League Theatricals, sent out a nonunion tour of *The Music Man* in 2001. Actors' Equity Association spent considerable time and money attempting to derail the production, picketing and leafleting at each venue and vociferously decrying the caliber of talent onstage and the union-busting tactics of the producers. Their efforts, however, did not result in the show's closing or in any notable loss of revenue. Other producers have chosen to work in similar fashion, and Cameron Mackintosh, one of Broadway's most respected producers, announced that he would lease his touring rights for *Oklahoma!* to a nonunion producer.

The unions well understand that if they can be marginalized or rendered obsolete on tour, Broadway itself will stand a greater risk of following suit. Despite public proclamations about the poor quality of the tours, Equity officials privately acknowledge that the production values are respectable. The success of several nonunion tours gave Broadway producers the upper hand in negotiating sizable contractual concessions for the national tour of *42nd Street*, which was greeted with considerable alarm by many Equity members.

For this production, Equity's agreement to drastically cut salaries and per diems for a cast of over fifty enabled the production to travel more economically than under a traditional touring contract. Most actors earned slightly less than half the standard minimum salary of thirteen hundred dollars, saving the producers more than thirty thousand dollars a week. The producers were not required to contribute to the actors' 401(k) funds, and per diems were similarly lowered for additional savings. For years, actors viewed tours as one of the few potentially lucrative opportunities in theatre. They would often sublet or rent out their homes in the New York area, use the eight hundred dollars a week of per diem to cover housing and food expenses, and subsequently save much or all of their salaries. This windfall was seen as compensation for their frequent periods of unemployment: about 85 percent of Equity membership is without work at any given time. But producers argued that road revenues had failed to keep pace with expenses and noted that tours can cost as much as two hundred thousand dollars more a week to run than the equivalent show on Broadway. Cutbacks were the only means, they claimed, to preserve union employment on *42nd Street* and other shows. Many actors interpreted this assertion as an unsubtle means of preserving the producers' and road presenters' own sizable income stream.

The producers held a trump card. While audiences, particularly in the smaller markets, clamor for a degree of visual spectacle, they are less apt to perceive a difference between the talents of union and nonunion performers. After a long and discordant negotiation, Equity agreed to many concessions for *42nd Street*. To allow actors the chance to recoup some of their lost salary, a contractual mechanism was established for potential profit sharing of 7.5 percent of the producer's share of profits, after the producer's weekly guarantee was deducted from the gross, expenses were settled, and royalty holders and investors were paid. Although some in Equity viewed the concessions as necessary to preserve the primacy of union contracts, others perceived it as a major capitulation. Producers and investors, they said, are the speculators, and the risks should be borne by them, not by actors. This argument was articulated in a compelling letter printed in *Equity News,* the union newsletter, in which a *42nd Street* cast member expressed his frustration that actors were being paid twenty-three dollars a day for food, grossly insufficient when eating in restaurants. When they did earn money from the percentage mechanism, they were paid less than two hundred dollars each for four weeks of performances.[8]

Other touring producers were encouraged by this critical concession and queued up to demand similar dispensations from the union. Equity's executive director, Alan Eisenberg, responded that an exception was granted because of the unusual size of the *42nd Street* cast but that subsequent musical tours would be sent out at full contractual compensation. Subsequent wrangling has not produced a mutually acceptable contract for touring. The union's great fear is that a road presenter such as Clear Channel, which controls the majority of markets in the nation, could decide to book only nonunion tours, as there is a strong corporate relationship between Clear Channel and one of the largest nonunion tour producers. According to producer Hal Luftig, who sought concessions for the touring production of the Tony Award–winning musical *Thoroughly Modern Millie,* further reductions need to be brokered across the board. "We need to find a way to make this work, however, or the road will cease to exist. You will have megahits and non-Equity productions."[9]

Producers identify rising costs and the raising of money as their greatest hurdles. With the advent of royalty pools, producers are less likely to make an early killing on a show, although investors can now be repaid in a more timely fashion. Barry Brown admitted that "what's changed most [about producing] is that it's become much more about money-raising than about putting a show together" and acknowledged that it is difficult to work as a producer "unless you have some outside source of income." Martin Markinson, who owns the Helen Hayes Theatre and also produces, agreed. "When I started in the business and you went into a producer's office, he had a show running, a show in rehearsal, and perhaps a show on the road. It was always revolving. But today, producing is not a business unless you have another source of income." Richard Frankel, who is both a producer and the general manager for many shows, including the current hits *Hairspray* and *The Producers,* concurred and noted that "almost all producers have another source of income . . . even if the source is general managing. Virtually every other producer has personal wealth, family wealth, a real estate business."

Although the majority of investors are passive partners, ceding control and decision making to the producer, ethical producers realize that they have an obligation to safeguard the investors' money. According to Barry Brown, "My friends have always said, 'You're so lucky. You don't have a boss and can work for yourself, you can do what you want.' I don't think that's true. I think that all my investors are my bosses, and I'm not a publicly traded company. You know, if it were all my money, I could go out and do whatever I pleased, but if I'm spending someone else's money, I need to be careful." Most producers agree that locating investment capital has grown more difficult in the wake of post–September 11 anxiety and a national economic downturn. To create a more hospitable environment for investors and producers, attorney John Breglio, who is also the chairman of the Theatre Development Fund, proposed a tax credit for investors of new productions.

> We would seek to designate the commercial New York theatre as an empowerment zone, which, on the basis of the number of people hired and their salaries, translates into a tax credit on the investors' return. So, in the most simple-minded way, if you have a ten-million-dollar production, and an investor put up a million dollars, and the show failed, in addition to a write-off for the investment, the investor would get a one-hundred-thousand-dollar credit on his tax return. This is a significant incentive for the investors, but not costly to the government.

While the producing community endorsed the plan, the 2001 economic recovery package never made it through Congress, and according to Breglio, in December 2002, there were no further plans for a similar initiative. While it appears initially to be a form of government subsidy to the arts, it is no different from other tax breaks for any number of financially challenged industries.

Producers have begun discussing the creation of new approaches to the traditional money-raising methodologies in which they seek investments for one production at a time. David Richenthal, Clear Channel, and Jujamcyn have discussed the development of a number of productions at once, with investors putting money into the entire lot, much like a mutual fund. Although producers are intrigued by the greater flexibility that it would afford them, the idea has not caught on, as most investors prefer to aim at one known commodity rather than a series of risky ventures. "It is the rare producer who has such a reliable track record that investors wouldn't prefer to invest on a show-by-show basis and make their own decisions, rather than rely on a producer to make the decisions for them," offered attorney Seth Gelblum. Garth Drabinsky, at Livent, demonstrated a capacity for multiproduction development, but alleged improprieties caused the corporation to fold. Only Disney, which does not need to raise investment money at the Broadway level, has evidenced any real ability to fund several shows at once. According to Thomas Schumacher,

> Everyone thinks that someone is doing what we do, but of course, no one is. There is no other institution like the Walt Disney Company currently producing a consistent portfolio of theatre on Broadway—and not necessarily just for Broadway, because we're now exploring projects that would primarily tour. Clear Channel isn't really doing it; they are more in the business of presenting than producing. Garth Drabinsky of Livent was the closest model. He was essentially a one-man institution who would sit down and say, "I have an idea. I'm going to get the rights to that idea, then I'm going to commission artists to work on it, and if I like what they do, I'm going to continue in that direction. If it's not working for me, I'm going to change direction," all at the will of a sole producer, which is the institution. That's the model that we use at Disney, and it's also the model that closely resembles how regional theatres operate. Some people see this as a general producing trend for Broadway, but frankly, I don't see anyone else doing it.

Schumacher characterized other film studios' occasional forays into producing as one-time deals. Clear Channel's theatre arm is active in coproducing many shows but rarely takes on the role of primary, nurturing producer. Disney's particular developmental process will be further examined in the next chapter.

Perhaps investors' reluctance to engage in the mutual fund approach stems in part from the gambler's desire to let it all ride on one particular horse. Investors enjoy the perks of associating, even peripherally, with the production process; they can enjoy the parties, the excitement of watching a show churn its way through rehearsals, the frisson of opening night jitters, and the potential for a windfall afterwards. The titillation and romance of show business are more seductive in a one-horse race, it seems, than in an open field. While investment in a portfolio of shows might eventually prove more lucrative in some instances than the current mode of involvement in one show at a time, it lacks the concentrated electricity of the old-fashioned method. Thomas Schumacher observed, "You only invest for three reasons. Either you actually believe in the work. Or, it may serve your interests to lose some money. Or, you want to be in the club, go to parties, be part of it, have a blast, and maybe make some money. There's no other reason to do it. But let's just assume that you're doing it because you want a return on your investment. It's the producer's responsibility to do the kind of work that stands a chance of generating that return." Sometimes, investors will back an artistically worthy show, knowing it will fail, and will take the tax write-off as compensation for having participated in something they believed in. Roy Gabay said, "I think there was a sense that *Metamorphoses* was not going to work commercially. It was a noble effort, everyone felt that it was important to do, but it did not have a commercial expectation. A lot of the people that we raised money from honestly gave [it] because they felt it was an important and worthy piece, not necessarily because they thought they were going to make it back. So when we were able to return it all, it was a great feeling." *Metamorphoses*, a relatively inexpensive straight play, took little more than three months to recoup.

Many producers prefer to minimize the effort and the time to raise several million dollars. They choose instead to attract a handful of accredited investors, bypassing a number of restrictive government regulations regarding the raising of money. This method is favored by producers who transfer a work in performance at another venue, as they cannot afford the time to raise money from multiple, smaller sources. A few producers, though, notably Richard Frankel and his partners, Marc Routh, Steve Baruch, and Thomas Viertel, prefer to cast a wider net, seeking a large pool of investors who contribute smaller amounts of money, usually around ten thousand dollars. Their list of potential investors is about five hundred names long. They often raise from two to two and a half million dollars—usually their partnership's portion of a musical's capitalization—from two hundred or more investors. "It gives us a lot of independence," said Frankel. "We aren't dependent on the one or two or three high rollers to whom [you] have to go begging for half a million dollars, and when they back out, you have problems. . . . The difficulty does lie, however, in the fact that there's not much you can do for two and a half million dollars anymore. So whereas we're not dependent on the big investor . . . we still are dependent upon partners." The struc-

ture he employs makes it financially viable for small investors to participate in the process. "If they invest ten thousand dollars and the show pays
back 80 percent, they've lost two thousand dollars, half of which is a tax
deduction. So they've lost a thousand dollars and they were part of a
memorable theatrical experience. Nobody is betting rent money on this."
To protect unwitting investors from unscrupulous producers, monitoring agencies began to require the inclusion of boilerplates in offering
circulars to underscore the potential risk of backing a Broadway show.
A typical caveat emptor found in an offering circular reminds the investor that

> in such ventures the risk of loss is especially high in comparison with
> the prospects for any profit, and that therefore investment in the Com-
> pany is suitable for persons of substantial means who do not require
> liquidity in this investment; this is an entirely new and speculative
> venture and it is impossible to project or predict whether any Produc-
> tion will actually be produced or, if it is, if the Production will result
> in a gain or loss to investors, and that therefore THESE INTERESTS SHOULD
> NOT BE PURCHASED UNLESS THE INVESTOR IS PREPARED FOR THE POSSIBILITY OF
> TOTAL LOSS OF THE INVESTMENT.

Additional wording, the investment version of "Abandon all hope, ye
who enter here," reads, "There can be no guarantee that any such Production will provide any return of the Investor Members' investment,"
and is followed by the inevitable disclaimer about the viability of this
particular form of investment. "Most live theatrical productions have to
run for several months at close to capacity houses to recover the initial
investments of investors. The production of theatrical productions [sic]
is a highly competitive business, and the vast majority of plays produced,
for example, for Broadway in the most recent theatrical season failed to
run this long. Of those which did, very few played to capacity audiences."
Producer Jane Harmon added her personal credo about raising money.
"I think the first thing you have to say to an investor, and I don't care if
they give you five dollars or a half a million dollars, is, 'You have to be
prepared to lose this money, and I don't want a dime unless you can afford to lose this money.'"

But many investors who commit sizable sums want more than just
financial remuneration; they want billing, especially those who may be
attempting to develop credentials as possible lead producers themselves.
According to an article in *Variety*, an investment of sixty thousand dol-

lars "got you a producing credit on (the 2002 revival) of *The Crucible*, with *Hairspray* being more costly at five hundred thousand dollars for an 'in association with (your name)' credit."[10] This titular inflation now makes it difficult for an outsider to discern who is the creative lead. Seth Gelblum acknowledged that many of those listed are strictly financiers. "Even if there are only one or two general [producing] partners, you see many people above the title because you have to raise ten million dollars for a musical, [so] you are going to be getting large chunks of it from some other people, and people who put up a large chunk will get their names above the title as a producer." Chase Mishkin noted, "If we need a lot of extra money and if [someone] comes in with a big enough chunk of money, I've been known to give a producer's credit to someone, but you don't give them a voting right. I don't mind credits in exchange for money. I don't think there's anything wrong with it." Martin Markinson agreed. "If you get someone who says, 'Okay, I'm going to write you a check, but I want my name to appear above the title, because I want to be called producer,' you didn't have that years ago. Today I call them 'check-writers.' I don't really call them producers. I don't mean that derogatorily, [it's] just that they're really not in the game of producing and they don't do this for a living."

In a recent *New Yorker* profile of successful producer Daryl Roth, the author, Ian Parker, described a meeting of Roth, her producing colleagues, and advertising agents the morning after the March 2002 opening of Edward Albee's play, *The Goat, or Who Is Sylvia?* Parker reiterated the distinction between the working producers and those investors who are completely ignorant of the craft. Parker described a woman among the latter group "with bright blond hair and an unnervingly dark tan, who had arrived in a fur coat. . . . [S]he was struck by the idea that theatre tickets could be sold on what she called 'the webnet.' She seemed put out to learn that someone had already thought of this."[11] This anecdote may represent one of the more humorous examples of investor vacuousness, but it speaks to the issue in subtler fashion as well. Ronald Lee owns Group Sales, the leading Broadway group sales agency. His Broadway career began in the fifties as a teenage dancer in *The King and I, Peter Pan, West Side Story,* and *Mr. Wonderful.* He has also produced, both on Broadway and in the West End. He observed that the trend to court backers as coproducers "started when you needed money and you would approach people who said, 'Oh, I love the theatre. Yes, I go to the theatre all the time!' That doesn't mean they know what they're doing. You take a check

and it bestows instant legitimacy on somebody. [On one show], we had two people as coproducers, or associate producers, who didn't know [anything] about the theatre. The only thing they had done in the theatre was sit in a seat."

Producing partnerships have developed to take advantage of the variety of strengths and network of relationships that a group can offer; one producer may have strong connections to accredited investors, another may have excellent dealings with a theatre owner, yet another may have previously coproduced with a regional or Off-Broadway theatre that might provide a home for a new piece. Hank Unger, whose Araca Group partnered with Dodger Theatricals in a fifty-fifty arrangement on *Urinetown*, said, "We seem to see eye to eye, and artistically we seem to have the same opinions. Our styles are a little different, but we've learned to appreciate each other's styles and communicate. It's like a marriage—nothing's ever perfect, but you figure it out. But we all have the same goals for the show. When we disagree, we're not *afraid* to disagree and hash it out, and figure out why, and see what we can do. And there have been compromises on both sides." He noted that not only did the Dodgers have many years of Broadway experience, they also "had a fantastic relationship with the owner of the Henry Miller theatre." However, not all producing partnerships work out so happily. When expectations for a hugely successful run of a recent musical were crushed by mediocre reviews and a weak box office, the two lead producers blamed each other for obstructionism and lack of vision.

Daryl Roth acknowledged that she is careful to safeguard her own vision of a show but admitted that there are advantages, in some instances, to having a strong relationship with a partner or two. "Over time, you realize whom you are compatible with, whom your strengths dovetail with. It's nice to be able to talk to somebody about issues and problems, even if it is as simple as 'Do you think this advertising campaign is as strong as it should be?' You have somebody to bounce it around with. [But] the most important thing in finding a coproducer to work with is that you have a shared vision for the piece. And if you don't, and you can't seem to get that into place, it will be problematic down the line."

Corporations can offer institutional support for a project that far outstrips the abilities of many independent producers. Not-for-profit theatres have also gained greater prominence as Broadway producing organizations and compete with commercial producers for audiences. Peter Lawrence, a production supervisor who for many years oversaw shows for producers Emmanuel Azenberg and Cameron Mackintosh, commented that "there are only a few hands-on producers anymore. It's mostly a corporate thing. The corporations now put up the money, or a consortium of people put up the money and call themselves producers. And the general manager is more or less responsible for the day-to-day decisions that a producer used to be responsible for, including artistic positions. So it becomes less of a personal taste than about being responsible to the money itself." Many artists offer that the erosion of the power of individual producers and the dilution of that overarching vision contribute to the diminution of artistically challenging new works on Broadway. Marty Bell said, "There has to be one person that has a creative vision of the show, and everybody else falls into place and respects that creative vision and supports it. If anything, shows over the last twenty years have been hurt by compromise. . . . As soon as you dilute [the producing process] with more people, you start to compromise to please people," said Bell. David Richenthal, a producer whose successes included the revival of *Death of a Salesman*, with Brian Dennehy, agreed with Bell. He commented in a *New York Times* article, "There are times when those of us who truly are there, stepping on the grapes 12 hours a day, find the work we do seeming to be diluted by that."[12]

Richard Frankel acknowledged the potential drawbacks in working with groups but questioned how else producers might approach the daunting task of raising money.

> When there is criticism in the press of all the names over the title, I react with wonderment. What planet are they on? Don't they understand what is going on these days? They decry all the names over the title and at the same time decry the corporate producers. I would propose that there is no other way to raise ten and a half million dollars other than by having Disney as the sole producer or by having four or five or six or seven producers get together to raise that kind of money. Herman Levin [who produced *My Fair Lady*] never had to raise eleven million dollars. Nor was the number equivalent. It isn't fair to say, well, *My Fair Lady* cost three hundred thousand dollars in 1956, and that was an equivalent amount.

Frankel is correct in his assessment. In 2002 dollars, that amount would equal a bit less than two million dollars, and the opulence and size of that production, if mounted with today's standards for spectacle, would easily cost more than ten million dollars. "So we have worked out collegial, reasonable ways of decision making and of meeting and of sharing information, and of dealing with multiple partners."

Nick Scandalios, executive vice president of the Nederlander Organization, affirmed that at times all the titular producers, regardless of their degree of experience, want a say in the proceedings. "Producers seem more actively engaged in the day-to-day creative workings of the show. If you are raising that kind of money, you don't want to stand there and say, 'I didn't know that was happening.'" But this can cause confusion and delay the decision-making process. "We all go to advertising meetings where there are seven people who all could be doing something else, but they're all there because everyone wants to chat about it. I suppose it's good that we all care." Roy Gabay added that although the many opinions offered often have little impact on the major artistic decisions, they can be a drag on the day-to-day running of the show. Mundane discussions can take on epic proportions, like the design of the opening night invitations or the color of the poster. "They are writing a bigger check or raising a bigger amount of money and want to have input." Some producers negotiate in advance with big investors to limit the number of production meetings they can attend. Nancy Coyne, head of the advertising agency Serino Coyne, which handles the campaigns for many Broadway shows, agreed that the numbers can be unwieldy. "There are more people in [advertising] meetings than ever before. When I first moved into this office space, the people who built the conference room put in a table for twenty-two people, and we laughed. Well, not only are there twenty-two people sitting at that table frequently, but I have extra chairs and that room is frequently two deep in people. That's insane, but that's the way it is."

Set designer Robin Wagner lamented the advent of multiple producing partners, attributing what he perceives as the mediocrity of many of today's offerings to the fact that artists are now the servant of many masters. "You've got twenty-five producers on every show and they all want to see what's going on. If you do a set model, you have to show it to them in groups, because you can't fit them all into one room. And they all insist on seeing it. Because they all think of themselves as instrumental at every turn. And a lot of the time they simply don't know what they're looking at." Attorney John Breglio lent credence to Wagner's concern. "I have clients who are writers who say, 'You know what? I know I can't stop this trend of thirty-three producers and six corporations above the title of a show, but I want you to write it in the contract that I only have to listen to or take notes from X and Y.'" Director Des McAnuff drafts his contracts with a clear understanding of the importance of the director-producer relationship. "I don't care how many opinions there are from the producers. When they are presented to me, I want unity and I want to hear it from one or possibly two people, but no more than that." But composer Frank Wildhorn, whose productions of *Jekyll and Hyde, The Scarlet Pimpernel,* and *The Civil War* have been handled by different groups of producers, enjoyed his work on each one. "The most any artist can ask for is not just an opportunity to be heard, but to be heard in the right way, with dignity and the support you need, and I've had that."

Nina Keneally recounted the old-school response to the new trend in producing. When she was a company manager on *Sophisticated Ladies* in the early eighties, "there were five producers. After one meeting, Joe Harris, the general manager, walked out shaking his head, and said, 'The only thing that five people should do together is play basketball.'" But today, some argue persuasively that it is no longer the producer who is the driving force—the sheer number of them has occasioned a shift in power to the director. Frank Rich added,

> I used to take the point of view that the greater number of names above a title had a negative effect, even given that half those producers are just rich people with enough money that their name is up there, and they've absolutely nothing to do with producing the show. I guess I feel more and more that you have to take it on a case-by-case basis. Yes, I do think there's a lot to be said for the days of a Merrick or a Max Gordon or a Flo Ziegfeld or a Hal Prince or a Kermit Bloomgarden, who had a vision and did it. But in the case of *The Producers,* probably the real muscle was [director-choreographer] Susan Stroman. It could not have been done without her. She made it work, and although Rocco [Landesman] and Mel Brooks are obviously very powerful figures, I have a feeling, without having been there, that what she said, went. And so it doesn't really matter that there were eleven producers.

Marty Bell suggested that the antidote to multiple-producer madness was the presence of one strong leader.

> Have the producer as an active, creative part of the [collaborative] process, actually sitting there, going through the writing process and structuring the show. And planning the show. Give everybody decent advances so that they can afford to focus on your show and not have

to do six shows at once. Give them deadlines and schedule readings and workshops on those deadlines so they have to finish because a group of actors is going to be in a room. . . . A good producer has a vision of where the show is going. [And] the patience to get it there.

This hands-on approach is very much the order of the day at Disney. David Merrick was notorious for his involvement in every aspect of his productions. But some producers today delegate the decision making to general managers, which underscores Peter Lawrence's concern about the lack of a guiding vision.

Despite the public displays of League unity, producing is still a hardscrabble, competitive industry. One prominent producer, who requested anonymity, expressed his concern about the nature of that competition. "There is an enormous desire to see other people fail as well as to see yourself succeed. I think it was David Merrick who first said that. And I think he was really right. I think it is more true than in other industries . . . and I don't know what that comes from. I don't know if it comes from the type of people it attracts, or maybe the incredible competitiveness of this tiny boutique industry, and the struggling . . . everybody is always so negative about everything. And I think it's sad." While several producers indicated that they welcome additional competition, and expressed a generous bonhomie when discussing the advent of corporate producers, the intense competition for ticket sales can generate remarkable bitterness in an industry with such poor odds for success.

In each producer beats the heart of an inveterate gambler, who thrills at the thought of defying those odds. Most producers enjoy quoting the old saw, "You can make a killing in the theatre, but you can't make a living in it." But there is an additional, critical ingredient that is perhaps the driving force for each of them. As Seth Gelblum put it, "Even the most ruthlessly mercantile producers love the theatre." The infrequent but fortuitous combination of that passion, a finely honed artistic sensibility, and an acute understanding of theatre management and finances is the best hope for a healthy Broadway, but it is currently under fire from other sources.

3 Broadway, Inc.

The big change [on Broadway] has without question been the corporatization of commercial theatre producing.
—Frank Rich, former theatre critic for the *New York Times*

The good side [to corporate producers] is that independent producers, no matter how bright and wonderful they were, if they didn't have millions behind them, never knew whether or not they could raise the money. For major corporations, if they say they are going to do something, there is seldom any issue about getting financing.
—John Breglio, theatrical attorney

Everyone's afraid of corporations taking over Broadway, unless they can get their idea produced by a corporation.
—Thomas Schumacher, president, Disney Theatrical

At the center of the most intense debate on Broadway in recent years is the impact of corporate producing. The presence over the last decade of Disney, Clear Channel Entertainment (and its predecessors), Stage Holding, Andrew Lloyd Webber's Really Useful Group, Madison Square Garden Productions, and the now defunct Livent has occasioned a series of prognostications that the pendulum is swinging inexorably in the direction of corporate hegemony. A new lexicon, with terms like *vertical integration, synergy, product, focus groups,* and *corporate branding,* has found its way onto the street. The entry of corporations into what was essentially a boutique industry has raised questions about the future of Broadway among not only independent producers—who would seem the most threatened by the competition—but also artists, union leaders, and other theatre practitioners.

While some independent producers gamely point out that competition, a broad spectrum of theatrical tastes, and a variety of approaches are in the best interests of a healthy Broadway, several privately concede that if for no other reason than their deeper resources on every front, corporations may eventually reign supreme. There is no way to compete with corporations, they aver, given the continued escalation of production costs, unless they form partnerships with other producers, ceding their individuality to a group that rules by consensus. There are still those producers working alone or in pairs—usually on less expensive straight plays—who have avoided teaming up with an unwieldy number of colleagues, either independent or corporate, but it is extremely rare for a solo producer, other than Cameron Mackintosh (who has indicated that he might focus on producing revivals) to attempt to mount a new large-scale musical.

Some of the more dire predictions about the corporatization of Broadway are undoubtedly born of a mix of envy and anxiety, but some of the concerns are valid: the fear of pandering to the lowest common denominator and the greater whitewashing of Broadway fare by the corporate brush—what one producer termed "corporate sameness." Although corporations currently make up a very small percentage of the active producers on Broadway, more than a dozen productions currently have visible corporate involvement, representing a third of the Broadway market. Further, because of the success enjoyed by Disney on Broadway and the more modest but still impressive gains made by Fox Searchlight, a producer of the musical *The Full Monty,* several movie studios are developing musicals based on their extant film holdings, as well as new works. In May 2003, Warner Brothers announced that it had commissioned Elton John to write a musical based on a triptych of Anne Rice vampire novels and that it was developing several other projects, including a musical version of *Batman.*

Corporate involvement in the arts was acceptable if the corporations maintained a low profile as donors or passive investors. No segment of not-for-profit artistic endeavor today could survive without corporate support, but commercial Broadway was for years viewed as a bastion of self-sufficiency, rarely looking to corporate coffers except as occasional investors. Livent was the first corporation to make a serious foray as a producer on the modern Broadway stage with *Kiss of the Spider Woman* in 1993. However, the Broadway community's response to Livent's presence was minimal compared with the impact Disney made with its first Broadway venture in 1994, *Beauty and the Beast.* When, the following year, Disney committed itself to the renovation of the New Amsterdam Theatre, traditionalists believed it was time to circle the wagons. As former Disney Theatrical head Peter Schneider observed, "There was a huge uproar, and the sense that Disney had no class, and didn't have what it took to be theatrical people. And it's a very small community, the theatre community, very small and insular, and they don't like outsiders."

Broadway's xenophobia has always been pronounced when responding to possible Hollywood incursions, but Disney was viewed with particular distaste at the outset. The studio represented not just moviemaking but theme parks, cruise ships, television, and cartoons, as well as an extraordinary amount of financing and influence that could easily tip the delicate balance of the world of producing.

The corporations' most obvious weapon is their wealth. Roy Somlyo remarked that one reason the developmental process of *The Full Monty*, which was financed largely by Fox Searchlight Pictures, proceeded so harmoniously was that the money was securely in place. "Good producers are distracted today by the funding process, and in [this] instance, they could devote their entire time to seeing that the show got to where they envisioned it to be. . . . If you are distracted about money, then maybe you can't bring all your efforts to do what it takes." Livent was notorious for committing massive sums to productions, and Disney spent at least thirty-four million dollars, perhaps much more, on the renovation of the New Amsterdam, and very likely more than twenty million dollars on *The Lion King* alone. Barbara Hauptman, president of the Society of Stage Directors and Choreographers, noted that the majority of the League's independent producers are asking for concessions and rollbacks from the unions so that they can stay afloat in a sea of corporate money. "I think any independent producer's concern at this point is that there's a lot of money being thrown around these days. It's very difficult for them to compete, and so it's painful."

Producer Nina Keneally noted that large corporations enjoy the advantage over independents in terms of name recognition. People are much more likely to recognize the Disney name over a show's title than the name of any independent producer or consortium. "We live in an age when the public, in great numbers, responds to a brand." Corporate branding—tying the sale of Broadway shows to videotapes and DVDs of feature animation films, the exploitation of other ancillary products, and the burnishing of the corporate image—provides Disney with the potential for a much larger income stream than is possible from mere box office revenue. When Disney opened a store adjacent to the New Amsterdam, audience members leaving the theatre were funneled through the shop for an opportunity to buy Simba sweatshirts and a full line of Disney merchandise. This strategy of forced consumerism prompted a fresh round of disparaging remarks about the company's overt commercialism, although producers have for decades sold apparel, cast albums, and other show-related items from stalls in theatre lobbies. Disney had the ability to do so on a grander scale.

Some observers note that corporations are much less likely to engage in artistic risk taking than independent producers, who, unfettered by a corporate imperative and a responsibility to stockholders, are inclined to generate more idiosyncratic works. In actuality, corporations have been involved in edgier works as both financiers and creators. After the critical lambasting of *Beauty and the Beast,* which was brought to Broadway under the aegis of Disney's theme park division, CEO Michael Eisner and feature animation division executives Peter Schneider and Thomas Schumacher realized that there was a tremendous potential for Disney's expansion on Broadway. *Beauty and the Beast* was making money despite poor reviews because of the immense name recognition of the cartoon movie. It spawned several tours and international productions, even while being derided as vacuous theme park entertainment. But Eisner and his colleagues realized that lasting success on Broadway—and the respect of the Broadway community—was predicated on an approach that incorporated traditional Broadway methodologies with Disney's own particular house style. They knew, too, that true producing leverage meant control over the entire project, and few Broadway houses were large enough to accommodate the shows they imagined producing. Thus Michael Eisner boldly committed to renovating the derelict New Amsterdam Theatre, once the shining jewel of the Forty-second Street theatres and home, at the beginning of the twentieth century, of *The Ziegfeld Follies.* The New Amsterdam would bestow on Disney a legitimacy and permanence on Broadway that one show, *Beauty and the Beast,* running in a Nederlander house, would not. Schneider and Schumacher, who had cut their teeth in the not-for-profit theatre world, relished the chance to prove to the community that Disney was capable of more than a one-time exploitation of theme park material. *The Lion King* demonstrated extraordinary prowess in the execution of its imaginative production concept, engineered by the most unlikely of candidates, director-designer Julie Taymor, a highly respected member of the avant-garde and a stranger to Broadway.

Livent's shows, especially *Kiss of the Spider Woman, Ragtime,* and *Parade* (the last coproduced with Lincoln Center Theater) were not considered generic family entertainment by the Broadway establishment. These productions explored complex, mature issues such as gender identity, the politics of repression, torture, racial tensions, and lynching, and were not engineered for mass audience consumption. But Garth Drabinsky, who ran Livent, made his reputation in movie theatre chain ownership and film distribution, and employed the popular cinematic device of focus groups for *Ragtime*. A focus group might be useful in the development of marketing strategies, but its formalized use is anathema to theatre artists. While some inside Livent claimed that it employed a few focus groups during the workshop phase primarily to help formulate marketing ideas, others have indicated that Drabinsky passed on considerable feedback from the groups to the creative team. Despite the slow integration of Disney and its grudging acceptance by the Broadway community, overt Hollywood style is profoundly disturbing to Broadway traditionalists because it flouts the established theatrical notion of collaboration. It is especially alarming to writers, because film scripts are owned and controlled by studios. Producers also envied the sizable marketing resources available to Livent, which were essential to sell a show that had not achieved hit status. Drabinsky was willing to spend sums far in excess of the Broadway norm for marketing and advertising to create a hit.

But Livent is no longer producing. Currently, only Disney has displayed any real staying power as a solo, creative corporate producer. Disney's theatrical sensibilities are shaped by its mandate to produce family entertainment that can be exploited via vertical integration, a mandate that differs from that of most independent producers. Disney has explained on several occasions that while the company presents family-oriented material, its aim is to present it with the greatest theatrical flair by the best talents in the business. Additionally, they note, Disney's artistic and management teams hail from the world of legitimate theatre and bring a keen regard for the collaborative artistic process.

But the corporate connection to mass-marketed, consumer-friendly goods and services disturbs many who believe that it presages the end of challenging, idiosyncratic productions. Todd Haimes, the artistic director of the not-for-profit Roundabout Theatre, however, made the trenchant observation, at a 1999 panel sponsored by the International Society for the Performing Arts entitled "When Theatre Owners Produce," that current family-oriented productions "are not dumbing down an audience. These shows are a response to an audience that's already been dumbed down by everything else in society—the education system, television. . . . To appeal to the mass number of people that a huge Broadway [production] needs to appeal to now, they have responded by giving fare that more closely resembles the mass-appeal movies than what

we consider the highest quality theatre."[1] The dumbing down to which
Haimes refers can be seen, too, in the makeover of Times Square, fes-
tooned with concrete examples of an international corporate presence.
While Disney was not by any means the sole deviser of the Times Square
redevelopment, its move to the New Amsterdam provided a welcome
impetus to the stream of chain stores, movie theatres, and conglomer-
ates suddenly clamoring for space on Forty-second Street.

Frank Rich observed that the single most significant change in theatre in the past several years has been the "corporatization" of commercial theatre producing, a force that has affected not just Broadway but the
larger arena of both commercial and not-for-profit theatre in America.

> [It's] had an effect on everything. It's had an effect on how nonprofit
> theatres work, when a company like Lincoln Center is involved with
> the now-defunct Livent, producing *Parade,* or the Alliance Theatre in
> Atlanta is involved with Disney in producing *Aida.* That's a big change
> from ... individual commercial producers [just] sweetening money
> to nonprofit theatres. And the corporatization of theatre has obviously
> made it much more difficult ... for what I have to call noncommer-
> cial, idiosyncratic voices to be heard in the Broadway theatre and,
> therefore, on the road, which is a huge component of theatre ... which
> wasn't the case not that long ago. And then, inevitably, it has a spill-
> down effect on the nonprofit theatre. Because for every George Wolf
> or Michael Greif or someone who's going to go his or her own way,
> there are unfortunately going to be plenty of other theatres where, for
> reasons of their community or whatever, are going to ... take their cues
> from commercial theatre, even while they're part of a movement that
> was formed in opposition to the commercial theatre. And in the case
> of the corporatization of the commercial theatre, there are several
> things operating that have made this happen that have nothing to do
> with the theatre per se. The first is the redevelopment of Times Square,
> in which Disney played a huge role but which ... has changed the
> whole shape of popular entertainment in New York City.... The media
> mergers ... have affected everything—from how TV news operates
> to how book publishing works—[and] have had a spillover effect in
> the theatre because it's ... given companies like Disney the idea of
> adding theatre ... to the existing product lines, along with theme parks
> and movies and TV shows and so on. But it's also ... represented by a
> company such as SFX [now Clear Channel] ... a mammoth corpora-

tion that, last time I looked, also handles . . . the preponderance of touring rock acts playing major arenas, monster truck rallies, and all the rest of it.

Some downplay the concerns voiced by Rich. Marty Bell, who was a key member of Livent, observed that aside from Disney and Clear Channel, there are currently no highly visible corporate producers, and noted "a lot of transience in the producing business. And [corporations] may be the flavor of the month. I'm not sure how long they'll be here. . . . I still think the theatre will finally be dependent on the independent producer who has to go out and raise the money dollar by dollar and put on a show. And Disney has pretty much set up their theatre division almost like an independent producing office." The more sanguine members of the Broadway community observe that in the last decade, independent producers have continued to make a go of it. They are inclined to welcome the corporations into the fold, a gesture also displayed by the major not-for-profit theatres on Broadway, who have long felt comfortable with their corporate donors. But some of the more conservative members of the community consider the corporate approach to producing a threat to the old-fashioned methods, like brokering deals over cheese blintzes at the coffee shop in the Hotel Edison. Even if corporations did not produce on Broadway, the multiple-producer model now necessary on so many shows would strain the blintz-producing capabilities of any short-order cook. Advertising executive Nancy Coyne added, "In fact, it is much harder, with disparate producers, to put on a show than with one or two people who come out of a corporation." But Rich's concerns are shared by many, artists especially, who perceive the corporations' complex agendas as constitutionally antithetical to the promulgation of unique theatrical voices.

Those who seek to reassure their colleagues point out that Disney is the only significant corporate player that operates as a from-the-ground-up producer. Clear Channel does participate in developing productions but usually does so with one or more partners who often take the creative lead. The impact of Clear Channel, which controls an impressive share of the touring market, cannot be underestimated. Both Disney and Clear Channel, according to Jujamcyn president Rocco Landesman, have agendas that reach beyond Broadway. Disney, he noted, is able to exploit a number of different sources of collateral income from its Broadway hits, and Clear Channel's interests are served by shows with great touring potential. In 1997 Jujamcyn entered into an informal producing agreement with a Clear Channel predecessor, PACE Theatrical, to capitalize on the potential for income from Broadway-generated national tours. Some viewed this development as an excellent opportunity for independent producers working with Jujamcyn and PACE to tap into substantial funding reserves, while others believed it demonstrated yet another massive entrenchment that would shut out independent producers not already in the Jujamcyn-PACE stable.

The reassuring voices point to a number of blockbuster hits engineered primarily by independents. Many of these shows, however, have received some corporate financing. Clear Channel, which often invests a minimum of one to two million dollars in shows it coproduces, is not a corporate impresario like Disney but has a significant say in the evolution of its production. Many independent producers are eager to partner with Clear Channel for their financing as well as the promise of lucrative tour bookings. Others, though, worry that partnering with them might result in Clear Channel either delaying or canceling a production if the corporation determined that it would conflict with another property of theirs in the same market.

But there is general agreement that corporations have provided a much-needed boost to Broadway by expanding the audience base and keeping shows flowing from New York onto the road. Nick Scandalios of the Nederlander Organization commented that "hits breed hits, and if people . . . can't get a ticket for *The Lion King,* and they're [in New York City], they're going to buy a ticket to something. . . . It certainly fills the houses on the road." Daryl Roth, a strong proponent of the independent producing system, believes that the influx of corporate capital is exceedingly healthy, especially if corporate producers can control their own real estate destinies. "As a corporate producer you really are your own master in many ways. You're not beholden as independent producers might be to theatre owners, to other forces that be. . . . You have a more contained organization, which is wonderful." The number of Broadway theatres remains fairly constant; the chance for a producer to control a show's destiny and avoid paying exorbitant rent is highly desirable. Currently, Clear Channel controls the Ford Center and Disney the New Amsterdam. Should any of the three theatre chains choose to sell off any of their properties, a vigorous bidding war by corporations might result.

Attorney John Breglio, who holds that great theatre is born of a passionate belief by an individual in the merits of a particular piece, presented a balanced view of the corporate presence. He pointed to personality as the key ingredient in making vital and lasting theatre. In the corporate environment, he observed,

> you lose the personality of this business to a large degree when you make it more of a corporate culture. And I think the essence of this business is collaboration among strong individual personalities. That, in my experience, is how the great shows have been produced and created. Not just by the creative team but also by the managers and producers. I may be very old-fashioned, but that's what I believe. Now, that doesn't mean that a corporate culture doesn't have a place in the theatre. But . . . the way to achieve something special is to try to meld the two cultures so that you have strong corporate backing with the financial wherewithal and powerful, creative, and intelligent individual producers who bring the authors and all the other creative elements of the production together.

Thomas Schumacher of Disney admitted that corporations often work with a different guiding precept.

> Because we're a corporation, we must invest our time and money to work [a production] for its greatest return, not just *a* return. And, therefore, smaller works, which might have a perfectly fine return, might not survive corporate scrutiny, because we need to create shows that are franchisable and large enough to justify the level of support we have to give them on a continuing basis. When I think of the portfolio of projects I would develop as an independent producer, there are many things I could never do at Disney, because they are just too small. Corporate producers will tend to do larger-scale, more commercial projects that are inherently less risky. And then, there are the finer points of risk management: It was risky to hire Julie Taymor on *The Lion King*. It was not necessarily risky to do *The Lion King*.

The need and ability to exploit a work are reasons that independent producers resent the global reach of corporate producers. Donald Frantz, who worked for Disney as an associate producer on *The Lion King,* was a panelist at the ISPA symposium "When Theatre Owners Produce" and offered this view: "The corporations that are coming in spend more to produce. It's just the nature of the beast. They have to live up to every letter of the legal model, the attorney world, the risk-management world, the consensus-building network that a corporation has. . . . And the reward they're looking for is a global market. Therefore the product that they choose has to be a product that can sell around the world."[2] The durability of Cameron Mackintosh's blockbuster productions in markets around the world provided Disney with the assurance that their model could succeed—to market a show from the outset as an international phenomenon.

Corporations have passively invested in shows for many years. While most producers were eager to accept corporate funding, a few expressed concern that corporate involvement would compromise their artistic freedom. Nancy Coyne recounted Joseph Papp's qualms about accepting corporate money for shows at the Public Theatre.

> We handled a division of AT&T that does corporate arts underwriting and sponsorship, and I was always trying to get [Papp] to take some AT&T money and do a play, and he was totally nuts on the subject. "If I take AT&T money, the next thing you know they'll be making us do a play with phones in it." I said, "Joe, nothing could be farther from the truth. They, as a corporation, behave so much more ethically than an angel." I've watched individuals who have money in shows do the most unforgivable things, suggest the most outrageous things. But people in the theatre accept it because it's coming from a backer, one person. Let that backer be a corporation and it's suddenly suspect.

Papp's concern was echoed when the Roundabout accepted its grant from American Airlines in exchange for naming rights to its new theatre. Although Papp feared that product placement might eventually result in the degradation of artistic prerogative, there have been no untoward results from American's involvement with the Roundabout. But corporate investing and lead producing are separate issues. As Frank Rich pointed out—although he acknowledges that not everyone shares his view—"a corporation cannot create truly individualistic art." Jujamcyn's Jack Viertel voiced similar sentiments. "There's always the risk with corporate producers that there isn't a single aesthetic guiding voice or principle, and so the shows tend to get built by committee, and they tend to lose their originality." He added, though, that in the thirties and forties, the heyday of the Hollywood studio system, huge corporations managed to produce some extraordinary films, and ventured that the corporate system on Broadway did not have to sound the death knell for creativity. Here Viertel identifies a critical issue: it is essential that those at the corporate helm are not only responsible to the shareholders but also dedicated to the promulgation of artistically engaging works for popular consumption.

In the early nineties the tectonic plates under Broadway began to shift. Garth Drabinsky, who had dabbled with Broadway producing in the late seventies, was the force behind the movie theatre chain Cineplex-Odeon, but his rapid expansionism occasioned his ouster in 1989. He retained control of one legitimate theatre, the Pantages in Toronto, which served as the foundation for Livent, his new theatrical producing organization. The money for Livent's start-up came largely from both rental charges and presenter fees from the Canadian production of *The Phantom of the Opera.* Livent became a publicly traded entity in 1993 and was modeled on the movie studio paradigm. Drabinsky was a latter-day mogul who controlled production, distribution, and presentation—vertical integration—a bold move at the time relative to established Broadway methodologies.[3] Drabinsky developed a reputation for hands-on producing. He employed a unilateral approach in which he owned everything, including the rights to the written material, in itself a major departure from established theatrical protocol. He demonstrated a willingness to spend money in grand fashion to create an empire on Broadway and on the road, a latter-day Shubert family of one. He brought to the organization a number of key associates in financial, technical, and artistic positions, and was able to attract top-rank artists to his projects.

Judith Dolan, who designed costumes for two of Livent's productions, both directed by Harold Prince—the revival of *Candide,* for which she won a Tony award, and *Parade*—pointed out that from an artist's perspective, Drabinsky was the best kind of producer, one who understood the needs of a production and respected the talents and visions of his artists. He was there to support his artistic staff and not simply put budgetary restraints on them in the support of a bottom line. She also noted that Drabinsky did not attempt to usurp Prince's directorial prerogative, as some producers do. "He is a producer who is interested in the art, not just the money. When he got the *Parade* sketches, he called me up to tell me how beautiful they were, and that's not normal for producers. . . . It was Hal directing, not Garth, and that's how he was supportive of the artists." She said that Drabinsky, who developed a reputation for wanton spending, did pay attention to cutting costs, but never at the expense of her designs or the integrity of the production. He owned a costume shop in Toronto, but Dolan believed that the *Parade* costumes could be executed better by a shop in Manhattan, and Drabinsky accepted her opinion. "It was not like he was padding his own Livent production site." She went on to say that "I'm sorry that he's not in business, because there are very few creative producers who thought the way he did, and very few who are willing to put their neck out on chancy, difficult pieces. He listened not just to the money side, which is of course important, but to the creative side."

In 1993 Drabinsky was the sole producer of the critically acclaimed production of the Kander-Ebb-McNally musical *Kiss of the Spider Woman*, beginning an artistically and financially profitable relationship with Harold Prince, who directed four of Livent's seven Broadway productions to considerable acclaim. Livent's successful revival of *Show Boat* debuted with a run of more than a year in Toronto before moving to Broadway in 1994 for twenty-six months and a subsequent lucrative tour. Drabinsky then brought the musical *Ragtime* to Broadway and later engineered a coproduction, with Lincoln Center Theater, of the musical *Parade*. *Ragtime* was the first original musical that Drabinsky developed from its inception, as the others were either revivals or acquired properties. And *Ragtime* would be the first production housed in Livent's brand new Ford Center for the Performing Arts, one of the magnificently renovated theatres on Forty-second Street and the first in modern times to be owned by a producing entity.[4]

Even poor financial ratings from Standard and Poor's and from Moody's, and accounting methods that were unorthodox by Broadway standards but apparently acceptable within its own corporate parameters, did not inhibit Drabinsky's ability to raise investment capital. Other producers expressed concern that Livent's extravagant budgets were raising the ante for the competition at a frightening rate, outstripping the ability of most independents to keep pace. Drabinsky, considered a maverick who chose not to join the League, was known for his generous salaries to actors and other artists, and his exorbitant advertising budgets, which engendered considerable ill will from his colleagues.[5] Chase Mishkin remembered that when *Ragtime* was about to open, "they were running double-truck ads, and they did it every week. [With] the money they spent on advertising, I could have produced a new show!" But, she added, "I watched them with awe. But then, of course, ultimately you see what happens. Livent turned out to be a total disaster." Prior to that, however, Livent's shows earned eighteen Tony awards. It seemed as though a new mogul had brazenly arrived on Broadway.

But swiftly things began to sour for Livent and Drabinsky. In April

1998, despite its critical and box office successes, rumors began to circulate about substantial red ink and the need for an infusion of significant cash. Michael Ovitz, formerly of Disney and Creative Artists Agency, moved to take over Livent by engineering an investment of twenty million dollars and relegating Drabinsky to a secondary position within the organization. Some people believed that Ovitz saw this as an opportunity to finally enter the New York arts scene as a significant player. Others said that the move was fueled in part by a fierce competition with erstwhile friend Michael Eisner, whose two Disney productions at the time were Broadway hits. Then, just a few months later, in August 1998, articles appeared about egregious financial improprieties at Livent engineered by Drabinsky and his colleague Myron Gottlieb. It appeared that they had maintained two sets of books; it was the phony accounts that had allegedly inflated Livent's profits by several million dollars and reassured Ovitz and his investment group that Livent was a viable commodity. According to Martin Peers, writing in *Variety,* "Drabinsky is believed to have shifted costs from one quarter to another and from one production to another or into Livent's real estate area, while accelerating the recognition of revenue from one quarter to another. . . . [Livent] staffers claim Drabinsky instructed them to keep the second set of books a secret."[6] Livent filed for chapter 11 bankruptcy later that year, and its assets were sold at auction in 1999, with most of them bought up by SFX (later Clear Channel). Although sixteen counts of fraud and conspiracy that covered up sixty million dollars in losses were filed against Drabinsky and Gottlieb in New York in 1999, the pair refused to appear in court and remained in Canada, where Drabinsky continued to try to vindicate his name and rebuild his Canadian entertainment empire. As recently as May 2002, he announced plans to bring a revival of Ronald Harwood's play *The Dresser* to Broadway the following season, a difficult feat given his inability to travel to the United States without risking arrest. But his legal status did not seem to deter him, and he secured the services of a prominent director and set designer. However, in fall 2002, charges were preferred against him and Gottlieb in Canada, apparently spelling the end of his Broadway resurrection.

The wonder and awe at the implosion of Livent was palpable along Broadway. Many theatre pundits had marveled at its seemingly bottomless coffers, and while rumors had floated for some time about the possibility of fiscal shenanigans, few people were prepared for the extensive battery of charges leveled against Drabinsky. Although SFX purchased most of Livent's assets, the hole left by Drabinsky's departure from the street was felt most acutely by the cadre of producers and artists who had worked with him on several shows. According to Marty Bell, who had been one of Drabinsky's main associates,

> Livent had a philosophy, and some of it worked and some of it didn't work. I said from the day I went up there that Livent was a great experiment in theatre. First of all, it was a public company. My feeling is that Wall Street and Broadway don't go together, that Wall Street is all about quarterly reporting, and that's not the cycle of theatre in any way. And in order to show decent quarterly results, we probably did a lot of shows we shouldn't have done, just to increase cash flow, and that's no reason to do shows. You have to do shows because you are passionate about them and they mean something to you, and you can't do them for any other reason. Livent had a philosophy that if everybody worked together as a team and worked under one roof, we'd have better shows and there'd be some kind of economy of production, but it's untrue. We had a staff of 150 people, and now I have a staff of three people, and we're doing as many shows here as we did under Livent.

Drabinsky's unwavering support for his artists and his willingness to underscore that support with the funds needed to realize their vision were the hallmarks of Livent's contribution to Broadway. His fall was greeted by a collective sigh, part relief at the elimination of a major competitor who threatened to eclipse the competition and part an expression of Broadway schadenfreude.

Although Livent was a corporation, it was very much one man's domain. Drabinsky's producing efforts reflected his vision, and the gap between Livent and the older Broadway world of solo producers was not insurmountable. Clear Channel, however, is an international conglomerate whose far-reaching fingers are firmly embedded in a multitude of pies. Its entertainment group operates several divisions, with oversight of concerts, family entertainment, multimedia, television, radio, and sports, as well as theatre. According to its winter 2002 Web site, the San Antonio–based Clear Channel Worldwide/Clear Channel Communications, Inc.

> [i]s a global leader in the out-of-home advertising industry with radio and television stations, outdoor displays, and entertainment venues in 66 countries around the world. Including announced transactions, Clear

Channel operates approximately 1,225 radio and 37 television stations in the United States and has equity interests in over 240 radio stations internationally. Clear Channel also operates approximately 776,000 outdoor advertising displays, including billboards, street furniture and transit panels around the world. Clear Channel Entertainment is a leading promoter, producer and marketer of live entertainment events and also owns leading athlete management and marketing companies.

Clear Channel acquired Robert F. X. Sillerman's SFX organization in a four-billion-dollar deal in 2000. Sillerman had in turn purchased both PACE Theatrical and, later, Livent. PACE began as a theatre and concert promotion and presenting organization, active especially in the South in the seventies, and by the time it was sold to SFX in 1997, it was a leading player in the national touring market as well as on Broadway; the success of *The Who's Tommy* in 1992 was in large part engineered by PACE's Scott Zeiger (now CEO of Clear Channel's North American theatrical division). In early 2003 Clear Channel was a producer or coproducer of more than a half dozen Broadway musicals, including the hits *Hairspray, The Producers,* and *Movin' Out.* Perhaps more critical, it also controls a formidable chunk of the road, with fifty-six cities in its portfolio and subscription audiences totaling close to three hundred thousand.[7] It also owns the Ford Center for the Performing Arts, acquired when it bought up most of Livent's assets, as well as fifteen theatres in the United States and more overseas. In 2000 Miles Wilkin, now the chairman of Clear Channel Theatrical Worldwide and the chairman and CEO, Europe, of Clear Channel Entertainment, described the evolution of the organization.

PACE Entertainment Corporation, a predecessor organization to Clear Channel Entertainment, was founded by Allen Becker. When I encountered them in 1979, PACE was already prominent in the music and motor sports world as an ongoing Houston-based entertainment company. I was approached [by Becker] in 1982 to start a theatrical company, because they had a number of disparate theatrical interests. Their objective was to create a plan that would grow and bring the business together as a whole. I began this endeavor with the execution of a vision: an organization that would operate Broadway subscription seasons in small U.S. cities, middle-American cities, and the operation of theatres, if and when necessary. [At an early point] we realized that there weren't enough theatrical productions to service the needs of our five burgeoning cities, in order to maintain Broadway subscription seasons. In order to fill the void, we became investors and producers of Broadway shows. The first show was *Fiddler on the Roof,* with Herschel Bernardi [in 1983]. Our history was made during these PACE years, and we became the largest theatrical organization in North America.

PACE's participation in producing national tours continued swiftly throughout the eighties. According to Wilkin, the PACE paradigm was to find an old favorite like *Fiddler,* revive it for touring with its original star or another star who would be credible in the role, and to send it on the road for as many months or years as the market would bear. PACE also invested, in a strictly financial capacity—with no artistic or controlling involvement—in new Broadway shows to secure the rights for North American tours. But, Wilkin added, the excitement and the turmoil of producing a new Broadway show from scratch was something they had not yet experienced. "I guess we never knew how easy we had it before," he joked.

Despite Clear Channel's current involvement with producing new shows for Broadway, it is their connection to the road that is most lucrative. The Broadway imprimatur is an essential ingredient in touting a tour, and it is on the road that Clear Channel is able to make significant earnings and enjoy the corporate branding and tie-ins with its media outlets. Wilkin explained that "what distinguishes us from most producers [is that] most of them produce out of a passion about a particular project they encounter or chase, and certainly that is the case when we embrace a project—we're very engaged in it. But the primary reason we create [a project], whether we do it ourselves or with partners . . . is that we need product for the distribution system, more than what normally exists. . . . We are constantly trying to empower projects to happen. That is the name of the game for us." It is essential for Clear Channel to keep their road vibrant, pulsing with productions crisscrossing its subscription cities, and that requires them to work with a spectrum of producing partners. "We don't approach these things with an 'Oh, it's mine, I've *got* to have it' [attitude]," said Wilkin. "Our idea is we want these things to get out and get done right, as many shows as possible. If that means working with other people in any capacity, that's great. We welcome that opportunity." The logistics of the road are such that fifteen to twenty shows annually are generally needed around the country, although each city might host only six to eight productions a year for one or two weeks, allowing local presenters the chance to craft their seasons on the basis of knowledge of their particular audience.

A glance at Clear Channel's production portfolio reveals very few straight plays, which are difficult to sell on the road, where cavernous performing arts centers provide inhospitable venues. Clear Channel's touring musicals are currently produced for about four million dollars, less than half the cost of mounting a Broadway production. These shows often break even at about five hundred thousand dollars weekly, and a show that sells well in large road houses with audience capacities generally in excess of twenty-five hundred can expect to recoup in forty to fifty weeks. According to Wilkin, the life cycle of a successful tour might be up to three years, producing some substantial income after the initial year spent earning its recoupment. That sort of longevity is critical to Clear Channel; the longer a show remains in the touring pipeline, the more self-perpetuating its hit status and the greater the potential income.

The first notable success PACE enjoyed as an original Broadway production was *The Who's Tommy,* which won five Tony awards in 1993. The musical, based on the rock group's groundbreaking 1969 concept album, premiered at La Jolla Playhouse, a regional theatre in San Diego, where it enjoyed enormous critical and box office success in the summer of 1992. That production, directed by Des McAnuff, with the Who's score virtually intact from the album and with a book by McAnuff and Who lead guitarist and composer Pete Townshend, moved quickly to Broadway, in time for a spring opening the following year. Engineered by Scott Zeiger, it reflected the rate of the company's growth, from regional presenter to Broadway producer in less than ten years. Zeiger had been working for PACE since 1981 and had tried for years to persuade Townshend to develop the album into a fully realized stage musical. Townshend finally agreed to a meeting with Zeiger, who carefully laid out PACE's intentions for the musical. He proposed an initial regional production, with Towshend invited but not required to participate, after which a decision would be made as to the next step. Townshend agreed, and requested that a director work with him on shaping the book. The show is sung through, and Townshend understood that its dramatic structure would need additional honing to make it a viable stage work. At that point, Zeiger sought out the production advice of the Dodgers, with whom PACE had partnered on a couple of tours.

> We were comfortable working together, and they were hip and younger than the producers that we had known. We had never produced a new musical. We had only produced revivals and tours. We had never nurtured a new property, so we thought it would be a good idea to have

someone with some experience as our partner, and we thought it would be good to have someone to help raise the capital. . . . [The Dodgers'] Michael David said, "I think that Des McAnuff would be the right guy. He's young, he's hip, he runs a regional theatre. He plays guitar. He's a rock musician." So I flew out to La Jolla and met with Des. And he had all the right sensibilities. And he had the right playhouse. He gave us a tour of the physical plant. They could build the set, props, costumes, and wigs right there. And we figured it would be a great, protected environment. He had done a similar *Big River* transfer from La Jolla Playhouse to bigger and better things. And he, too, was unsure whether [*Tommy*] was [best for] Broadway, or a tour, or an amphitheatre, or arena show. So we packed Des up and we flew him to London.

The rest of the process was remarkably smooth. According to Zeiger, McAnuff and Townshend cobbled out an outline in one afternoon. The show was a spectacular success at La Jolla Playhouse and opened in New York just five months after it closed in San Diego. Frank Rich's extravagant praise in the *New York Times,* along with other excellent press, spurred a successful Broadway run, as well as a major tour and productions in Canada, Germany, and the West End. PACE's reputation was established, and the organization began to pursue other producing ventures.

Unlike Livent, however, Clear Channel does not produce alone, nor does it invest its own money solely as its share of the capitalization costs. Zeiger explained that "a big company like ours could do [a Broadway show] by ourselves, but you want to divide up the work load. It's a lot of time and energy to produce a show." This employment of a mutual fund strategy of sorts allows Clear Channel to invest in several shows at once rather than sinking its entire capital into just a few shows. Diversity of investment allows the company a greater pick of shows for touring. Additionally, coproducing results in shared liability; if a show is a disaster, Clear Channel is not the only producer to shoulder the financial burden. Unlike Disney, which can afford to invest completely in its own shows because of its ability to radically exploit the property across its various holdings, Clear Channel has fewer options for vertical integration. But the company's share of the touring market is so broad that it easily provides the necessary opportunities for additional long-range income. Zeiger echoed Wilkin's opinion.

We need to get a product supply out there. We have a distribution network. So the motivation is really to fill the product pipeline. For a company like ours, if the total motivation was to strike pay dirt on Broadway, it's like wildcatting. That's not what we do. There is a bundle of rights that we garner when we get involved in a show. And the most important one is the territorial right to present the show in Atlanta or Fort Lauderdale or Houston . . . where we have subscriptions. . . . The really exciting properties (*a*) turn us on artistically and (*b*) feed the pipeline and all things that we need to do to keep the company properly vertically integrated.

Although Zeiger's personal theatrical taste does not gravitate to revivals, he acknowledged that they are a necessary element of the subscription environment. Important, too, are nontheatrical shows like *Tap Dogs* and *Riverdance,* since it is difficult to fill a six- or eight-play subscription season with all new Broadway fare. Occasionally, Clear Channel invests in or produces straight plays but only those it believes can be sold on the road. However, its record in that field has proved less successful. It provided funding for the 1999 David Suchet revival of *Amadeus,* which failed on Broadway after a run in Los Angeles, and coproduced, without investors, the disastrous Kelsey Grammer production of *Macbeth* in 2000. But even if a show does not recoup on Broadway, Clear Channel often realizes sizable returns from the tour. The company invested in *Swing* on Broadway, which did not recoup. "But it will have a tour and it will play in my cities," said Zeiger. "And we will present it on subscription. I will make money as a presenter. I will make money as a theatre owner in the theatres that it plays in. My company is doing the merchandising for the tour. So, I see it almost as a rights payment as much as I do an investment."

The impact of Clear Channel on the future of Broadway is uncertain, but some repercussions have already been felt. The symbiotic relationship between Broadway and the road never has been crafted so precisely; in the past, the road was strictly the beneficiary of Broadway's largesse. Now, with touring prospects factoring so heavily into the choice of material at the outset, Clear Channel's influence is considerably greater than that of other road presenters. Disney's Peter Schneider felt that Clear Channel's control of the road presented new and potentially viable ways in which producers could view the relationship between Broadway and touring. According to Schneider, "People are starting to ask, 'How can we use this to our advantage? Clear Channel needs product. Great. Let's go to them, let's do something for the road first, then go to New York; let's do it this way.'" PACE's coproduction of *Jekyll and Hyde,* the Frank Wildhorn–

Leslie Bricusse musical, followed such a path. Although it was dismissed by the New York critics when it opened in 1997, the word of mouth and press excitement generated during its long pre-Broadway tour was sufficient to catapult the show to a run of almost four years.

Critics of Clear Channel express concerns on two fronts. Some have commented that the organization has pressured road producers to take on the corporation as a producing partner, using the lucrative Clear Channel road market as a lure. Clear Channel's ownership of television and radio stations also allows the company the potential to control the advertising for shows that are not part of the Clear Channel portfolio. Of greater concern is that contemporary "middle-American" tastes, shaped so mightily by a relentless media assault, will now drive the choice of what is produced on Broadway, eliminating any vestige of sophistication once displayed there. The need to keep Clear Channel's growing distribution system awash in product may force producers to churn out shows simply to meet demand. This possibility threatens some independent producers' hopes that Broadway can combat a growing tide of mediocre, assembly-line shows.

But some practitioners are more optimistic about the corporate incursion. They believe that the infusion of cash and a growing audience will eventually prove a boon to Broadway interests. Todd Haimes of the Roundabout said,

> I have no problem with the corporate presence. I don't ultimately know whether, for a lot of corporations, it's going to prove to be the moneymaker that they might internally need. There is obviously an element of the lowest common denominator. When you're working with a company, you want to get the most people who could possibly see your show in New York and on the road, and take the lowest risk you possibly can. . . . But that's okay with me. [The] more people that come into Times Square and go to the theatre, the better. I don't think it stops people from going to the more serious theatre.

Thus far, statistics indicate that tourists, an ever-increasing component of the Broadway market, will not shift their theatregoing preferences to straight plays, even at the Off-Broadway theatres in the Times Square area. Jed Bernstein, of the League, built on Haimes's observation. "I don't think [corporations] are interested in doing a terribly different kind of work. The normal complaint is that these big corporations always take the safest route. I think they're doing what everybody else is doing, except they happen to be corporations. At the end of the day, it still comes down to one person having an idea about how you tell a story in the dark to a bunch of strangers." But Equity's Alan Eisenberg raised a concern that there is pressure to produce works specifically to fill the Clear Channel–controlled road houses, which will result in a proliferation of less expensive nonunion tours.

Another element that disturbs the old guard on Broadway about Clear Channel is the use of corporate lingo. "Feeding the road" and "creating product" may be apt descriptors, but they tend to irritate those who view making theatre as a hand-crafted process that demands individualized attention. The growing corporate pipeline, when seen in the context of the broader, jarring physical changes wrought on the Broadway landscape, is disquieting to many. The following was posted in 2003 on the Web site of Broadway Across America (broadwayacrossamerica.com), a Clear Channel subsidiary that markets its touring shows:

Take a seat, and get ready to see how theatre can work hard to meet all of your company's marketing objectives. This is the opportunity for your brand to own the experience of live theater.

You're about to have an eye-opening experience:

- Did you know . . . over 30 million people attend the theater in a year, more than Disney's Magic Kingdom and Disneyland combined?
- Did you know . . . Theater-goers index at 134 in fine jewelry ownership and 125 in women's clothing apparel purchased recently vs. the general population?

Clear Channel Entertainment's theatrical division has rapidly become the leading presenter of theatrical subscription seasons and individual presentations in North America presenting nearly 13,500 shows in 59 markets. We entertain over 17 million attendees each year. As an encore, we are a leading theatrical producer including the Tony Award winning THE PRODUCERS and the upcoming Broadway sensation, SWEET SMELL OF SUCCESS in spring 2002 starring John Lithgow.

Clear Channel Entertainment offers live properties that enable your company to tailor marketing programs that maximize your marketing efforts by placing your brand in the spotlight. Properties include

- NYC Broadway—marketing alliances with Broadway's hottest shows and Tony Award–winning talent

- Touring Productions—association with national touring Broadway shows across North America
- Broadway Across America—access to more than 275,000 Broadway Series season subscribers in 59 markets
- Venue Program—opportunity to conduct customized marketing program in 14 owned & operated venues in North America.[8]

For the purposes of marketing to a non–New York audience, Clear Channel's Broadway producing is characterized as an "encore" activity. This hard sell represents the kind of pitchmanship that irks many on Broadway, precisely because the hard sell is geared toward marketing "synergy" rather than selling the actual virtues of theatregoing. In the above copy, there is nothing to tout the pleasures of participating in an artistic or entertaining journey, nothing to underscore the importance of art in our cultural diet.

Two recent attempts by Clear Channel to nurture productions from an early phase, *Seussical* and *Sweet Smell of Success,* demonstrated the important lesson that no producer, corporate or independent, is immune to bad press and conflicting and confused artistic vision. Both musicals received readings or workshops prior to commercial out-of-town tryouts (Boston for *Seussical,* Chicago for *Sweet Smell*), and both encountered significant problems with negative publicity at the outset. The out-of-town and New York reviews were largely negative, and neither show could find its audience or establish a head of steam through word of mouth or aggressive marketing campaigns. *Seussical* managed to eke out a Broadway run of almost six months, and *Sweet Smell* barely made it through three months.

Seussical, based on several works by Dr. Seuss, seemed at the outset like a brilliant idea, and the excitement about the show's prospects was formidable, but by the time the show opened in its Boston tryout, it was apparent that the show was searching for a coherent vision. The director and costume designer were fired. By the time it opened in New York, word of mouth in the Broadway community was devastating, abetted by nasty Internet gossip columns that provided a public forum for Bostonians and New Yorkers who had made the trip north. Writer Lynn Ahrens ruefully observed, "People used to pick up the phone. Now they can broadcast across America. Nobody can be safe anymore, learning from their mistakes in private."[9] Miles Wilkin observed that "[the Internet] makes you question whether or not you would really want to do a show in Chicago and Boston. . . . I'm a bit cautious as a result of the

Seussical experience. If I were starting from scratch, I think I would probably opt more toward a regional theatre experience."

According to the *New York Times,* composer Stephen Flaherty envisioned a small-scale musical that eschewed lavish special effects in favor of a work that focused on the human element in Dr. Seuss, but pressure from the producers caused the show's design to grow. Robin Pogrebin of the *Times* wrote in July 2001 that "[a]fter *Seussical* was acquired by Clear Channel Entertainment . . . actors performed the Toronto workshop production in August 1999. It was performed on a bare stage, with the cast in everyday clothes. . . . The producers who traveled to see the performance were practically tripping over themselves to get a piece of the show."[10] The gutters of Broadway are lined with the detritus of shows that looked promising in an initial workshop, where most of the audience are friends or potential backers and thus not representative of a real audience. Producers and artists are often misled into believing that they have a surefire hit on their hands after a successful workshop.

Barry and Fran Weissler were invited by Clear Channel to join their consortium in a lead role. The *Times* article indicated that the producers, especially Barry Weissler, lobbied heavily for a larger physical production, espousing the belief that audiences paying top dollar for a show expect a certain degree of spectacle. Despite their ministrations, the musical foundered during previews and never recovered its footing. Pogrebin, in the *Times,* noted that the show, which was largely snubbed by the Tony nominating committee, was being punished by its peers and pointed to "the old guard trying to rein in the new corporate interests, namely Clear Channel."[11]

But Clear Channel still enjoyed some degree of control by virtue of its ability to exploit the show's road potential, and a retooled national tour began to earn a profit in Clear Channel cities. Clear Channel decided to address the negative press the show received in New York on its Web site, in which one unnamed audience member allegedly wrote, "I wasn't sure what to expect when I went to see the musical, *Seussical,* last night. I had heard of the not-so-glowing reviews of the Broadway production, and I went last night slightly skeptical. I left singing the songs, buying the soundtrack, and wanting to see it again."[12] It is doubtful that Clear Channel would have included this encomium in the show's advertising copy in the pre-Internet era, when it was much less likely that an audience member in a touring city would be aware of the press flap surrounding the show in New York.

Clear Channel presents a case study in corporate partnership with independent producers. Disney offers a different approach to creating theatre for Broadway and beyond. According to Disney's Alan Levey,

> *The Lion King* would have remained an animated film released in 1994, to be re-released ten years later in video, and in the interim, it would have remained dormant. Along comes a Broadway musical that opens in 1997, three years after the film opened, and suddenly, there is a reiteration and reinvigoration of *The Lion King*. While a successful stage production's profitability may not meet that of a successful film over the course of the film's theatrical, video, and DVD releases on a dollar-for-dollar basis—although all productions of *The Lion King* internationally are certainly profitable—it does extend the life of, and add equity to, a property significantly. And it generates additional opportunities for merchandising and positive press that otherwise wouldn't exist.

Michael Eisner had no avowed intention of forging a presence on Broadway when he took over the company in the 1980s. But Eisner is known as a visionary executive with catholic tastes. When Peter Schneider, who had years of experience in theatre, took over Disney's feature animation division in the mideighties, Eisner endorsed Schneider's approach to developing animated musical films in a fashion similar to producing for theatre, employing theatre composers and writers like Alan Menken, Howard Ashman, and Tim Rice. The success of movies like *The Little Mermaid* and *Beauty and the Beast* spawned short, live, theme park renditions and demonstrated to Eisner that there was a potential for additional live performances.

Robert Jesse Roth, the director who had engineered *Beauty*'s success in its theme park incarnation, asked Eisner whether he might attempt a production of the show on Broadway. Eisner agreed to finance the preparation of a treatment of the work. After reviewing it favorably, Eisner agreed that Roth should hire a production team, drawn from his theme park colleagues, to mount a Broadway version without the involvement of the feature animation division. After a tryout at Houston's Theatre under the Stars, the show opened on Broadway in 1994 to general critical derision. However, the show broke box office records for day-after-opening sales for a musical, and the production is still running ten years later. It generated a number of international productions and national tours, but despite its success, the show was not intended to be a precursor of future productions. According to Peter Schneider,

Disney back-doored themselves into the Broadway business, took a very arrogant approach to it, overpaid for everything, and announced, when the musical opened, how much it cost—it was made public record. They had no clue they were announcing the highest cost of a Broadway show then. . . . From my perspective, everyone hated how Disney came to Broadway. So they took Disney for every dime they could, the deals were bad, Disney overpaid, they had the wrong kind of people involved. . . . I think that had something to do with Rob and Tom and myself rethinking the whole process.

In 1993, a year before *Beauty*'s Broadway debut, Eisner toured the dilapidated and derelict New Amsterdam Theatre. Despite its state of decrepitude, Eisner discerned the faded beauty and glorious potential of the space. He committed Disney to the renovation and long-term lease of the theatre, envisioning the possibility that *Beauty and the Beast* could play there, which would save Disney the 5 or 6 percent of the gross in rent to a theatre owner. As Peter Schneider pointed out, the ability to control distribution, especially in the claustrophobic and rigidly demarcated confines of Broadway, was essential. "You have to have some place to put your shows. Given that the theatres were all booked, you couldn't plan your lives, you had to wait for a theatre. . . . It was very important for the company to have a flagship space in New York." Eisner was aware that the Broadway of his childhood, in which shows would rarely run for more than a few years, had been radically transformed by the long-running British megamusicals. That kind of longevity and branding potential interested Eisner. The investment of more than $34 million and the obligation to pay off the New York State bonds floated for the renovation garnered Disney a forty-nine-year lease on the space, with an option for another. The move to the New Amsterdam provided an extraordinary boost for the renovation of the street. (Disney's involvement in the saga of Forty-second Street will be explored in greater detail in chapter 7.) The superbly executed remaking of the once spectacular theatre, overseen by architect Hugh Hardy of Hardy Holtzman Pfeiffer Associates, convinced the doubters that Disney was serious about producing on Broadway. Traditionalists were all but keening and rending garments on Times Square, such was the fear that an international conglomerate—one that represented, to many, cartoon and theme park entertainment coupled with a voracious appetite for total control of the entertainment industry—was nesting on Broadway. As Schneider observed, "It was a disaster, initially, opening [the New Amsterdam]. 'Mickey Mousing Broadway!' The articles were ugly. They were terrible for the corporate brand." The ill will was at times profound. Articles about the Disneyfication of Broadway abounded, and the entire industry endured endless speculation about the implications of a Hollywood behemoth in the theatre district. But, Schneider asked, "Is Disney hurting the business? No. . . . There are more jobs, more creativity." Alan Levey added,

> There's this misconception that Disney is on a world-domination tour and our charge at Disney Theatrical is to own every Broadway house and dominate the street. Nothing could be further from the truth. There is a great deal of resentment, you know, about the "Disneyfication of Broadway." But look at the three musicals that we have currently running on Broadway. Have they changed the street in any fundamental way? Compared to what was playing ten or twenty years ago? The standards are just as high. Thematically, have they exerted a profound influence over other work that's being done? Yes, it's a different business model, but the nature of musicals tends to change every decade or so, and that trend predates Disney's presence on Broadway. It's just part of the evolution of the art form.

The British imports of the eighties had already wrought considerable change in the work produced on Broadway.

Eisner then brought Schneider and Schumacher into the process. They had worked for years in theatre, and their enormous successes in feature animation for Disney had amply demonstrated their potential to enhance the company's presence on Broadway. In turn, Stuart Oken and Alan Levey, with considerable experience as leaders in both the commercial and not-for-profit theatre, joined the newly formed Buena Vista Theatrical Group. The New Amsterdam opened in spring 1997, with a limited run of a week of performances of the Alan Menken and Tim Rice oratorio *King David,* produced at considerable cost to the company but viewed as recompense and tribute to the writing team that had been responsible for so many of its feature animation hits.

It was clear to Schneider and Schumacher that for Disney to be truly successful, they would have to create new works for the New Amsterdam. Schumacher noted, "Clearly, you have to focus on what the property requires, what makes it unique, which artists would best bring it to life on stage. We have a very different process than most companies. Most producing companies go shopping for things already created. That doesn't really happen with us." He remarked that *King David* was brought to them by Menken and Rice, but everything else was developed in house, whether an adaptation from a Disney property or material in the public domain, such as *Aida*. "We go about looking for teams of artists for specific properties. We go to people we think have the right sensibility for something and provide them the wherewithal to make it happen."

Initially, it seemed as if *Aida* would be the first new Disney show since *Beauty and the Beast*. Elton John, whose success with the film of *The Lion King* gave him great latitude to suggest his next Disney project, was inclined to compose a stage musical rather than another full-length feature animation piece. John was intrigued by the prospect of reimagining the Verdi opera *Aida* and began preliminary work on the piece. At roughly the same time, Eisner proposed converting the recent animation blockbuster *The Lion King* into a stage musical. At first, his theatrical group believed that it would be exceedingly difficult to maintain on stage the film's sense of narrative, song, and spectacle. How to turn these anthropomorphized animals into musical theatre characters? How to stage a wildebeest stampede without resorting to film projections? Schumacher decided to approach Julie Taymor and gauge her interest in the piece. The director, designer, writer, and puppet maker was known for her experimental, noncommercial works, like *The Green Bird,* in which painstakingly created fantastical puppets inhabited the same world as actors, some in masks. She seemed an unlikely candidate to direct a family-oriented Broadway musical. Schumacher had initially pursued her for a theatre festival he produced in Los Angeles in the eighties, but she was unavailable at the time. "Who gets myth and lore and legend?" he asked. "Who understands ritual? Who has worked on a big scale, like opera, and at the same time can make things handcrafted? I had this notion of getting outside the box on *The Lion King* and not doing the movie but doing some wholly theatrical ritualized version of it, and Julie's name came up, and I called her and said, 'What about it?'"

The results were often stunning. Taymor's ability to translate the cartoon world of the African veldt into a muscular and dynamic theatrical idiom mesmerized critics and audiences alike. Despite some flaws in the libretto, the show, bolstered by rich contributions to the score by composer and musician Lebo M, offered some of the most exuberantly imaginative theatrical moments seen on Broadway in years. The opening sequence featured a parade of actors dressed in a remarkably ingenious array of masks, costumes, and puppet accoutrements wending its way through the audience to chanting and drumming, as a cloth sun rose upstage. It was one of the most enchanting opening numbers in the history of the musical. The show's use of ritualistic, Afro-Asian theatrical conventions to tell what is essentially a crowd-pleasing melodrama with comic interludes seemed occasionally discordant, but Taymor's design and staging delighted and astonished throughout.

The theatre community was surprised that Disney was able to engineer a brilliant coup de théâtre, totally unlike the conventional if pleasingly designed *Beauty and the Beast*. *The Lion King* effectively silenced the pundits who had predicted that the production would be another stage cartoon wrought in childish fashion, and clearly announced that Disney was capable of theatrical magic. Ben Brantley, in his mostly enthusiastic review in the *New York Times,* observed, "There has been much jokey speculation about the artistic marriage of the corporate giant and the bohemian iconoclast, which has been discussed as though Donald Trump and Karen Finley had decided to set up housekeeping. But that rich first number, in which those life-size animal figures assume a transcendent, pulsing existence, seems to suggest that these strange bedfellows might indeed live in blissful harmony."[13] The success of the show was in no small measure the result of initially low expectations, given the critical and community response to *Beauty and the Beast*.

The show tried out at the Orpheum Theatre, a subscription-based road house in Minneapolis, before it made its way to New York. The next Disney musical, *Aida,* began its journey to New York as *Elaborate Lives,* in the fall of 1998 at the Alliance Theatre, a regional company in Atlanta. This marked Disney's first partnership with a not-for-profit theatre, under the banner of Hyperion Theatricals, which was created to produce the shows that were not originally Disney properties. It was Disney's first attempt at creating an original musical for the stage.

After a series of technical and artistic disasters in Atlanta—the enormous mechanized pyramid that was the scenic centerpiece failed to work as designed, and the book was deemed turgid—Disney executives fired the director, the same Robert Jesse Roth who had directed *Beauty and the Beast;* the book writer, Linda Woolverton (who would still retain coauthorship credit on Broadway); and the three primary designers (although lighting designer Natasha Katz was rehired for Broadway more than a year later). Some questioned whether *Aida* would proceed beyond the Alliance, so poor was the word of mouth. But one of the hallmarks of Disney Theatrical is its commitment of time and money to shepherd a production through its developmental stages. By the time the show reached New York in the winter of 2000, under the direction of Robert Falls, with new sets and costumes by Bob Crowley, the show had solved many of its most pressing problems. It was greeted with mixed reviews by New York critics for its attempts to make the Aida story all things to all teenagers. The show featured a preponderance of pop-rock music, a bit of perfunctory comedy, a heavy dose of melodrama, and a cavalcade of stunning but ultimately overwhelming visual effects. The performances, aside from Heather Headley's riveting star turn in the title role, were mostly flat and merely serviceable. Despite these flaws, the show has been a solid hit since it opened and, even in the difficult days that followed September 11, managed to earn a respectable weekly profit.

What surprised people was Disney's commitment to the musical after a disastrous showing in Atlanta. Many independent producers offered that they would have scrapped the show at that point, but Disney persevered. Their financial and production resources allowed them the luxury to completely overhaul the show before Broadway. Attorney Seth Gelblum gave his perspective.

> I thought [*Aida*] would be the real test [for Disney], because it was something they started from scratch, just like everybody on the street trying to create a new property. And frankly, I was impressed, because they had a disaster on their hands in Atlanta when they first opened. They threw out the set. They threw out the director. They added new book writers, and reopened in Chicago with new elements. It got better. And by the time they were on Broadway, they were a hit. They worked at it and they worked at it. And they clearly had the coffers of a multibillion dollar corporation to continue to work on it. Maybe more people would have more successes if they had those kinds of resources to stay at it. But the fact is that there have been people who have spent a huge amount on musicals and never got them right.

Disney Theatrical in many ways now resembles MGM in its heyday, when a number of films were simultaneously in development by contract writers and directors. While Disney does not engage artists for multiyear, exclusive contracts, it has aggressively commissioned new works from some of the most successful and accomplished artists in American theatre. In 2003 Julie Taymor was developing a new version of *Pinocchio,* Pulitzer prize–winning playwright Suzan-Lori Parks was working on the book for *Hoopz!,* a musical version of the story of the Harlem Globetrotters, designer Bob Crowley and rock composer Phil Collins were collaborating on a version of the studio's *Tarzan,* and director Robert Longbottom was preparing a touring production of a musical revue of songs from the vast Disney collection. The Disney approach to producing was expanded on by Thomas Schumacher. "It's a new model, managing a portfolio of projects that you fund through their development, deciding at that point which ones to move forward with. The reason you're managing a portfolio is so you can select which ones have the best chance of success at a given time. Journalists don't understand this because no one else does it." Unlike David Richenthal's proposal to utilize a mutual fund approach to producing, the need to raise money by Disney is obviated by corporate financing. The portfolio largely comprises source material already owned by Disney—*Hoopz!* is one exception—thus saving the company money and time in the pursuit of securing underlying rights. The ability to exploit these holdings has not gone unnoticed by other movie studios, several of which are examining the prospects of Broadway productions.

Disney's approach capitalizes on the company's resources to offer artists the precious commodities of time and money to nurture works in relatively unpressured fashion. Disney can pay them handsomely, in advance, rather than employ conventional theatre deals in which a relatively modest fee secures months or years of work by the creative team, with the promise of better remuneration in the form of royalties should the show succeed. The company can also fund more workshops to hone a piece before it attempts a fully staged pre-Broadway tryout. Alan Levey spent ten years as managing director of the Tony Award–winning regional theatre La Jolla Playhouse, where he oversaw the development of a handful of musicals headed for Broadway, most notably *Big River.* He commented that "a property really suffers, ultimately, because you try and squeeze too much show into a vessel too small to support it. With our development model, we provide the creative team two or three years to do the important work, with the first objective being a reading. Then there's a workshop, the feedback from the workshop, the return to work, another workshop, more feedback. And if the decision is made to continue, only then will there be a production." He conceded that a traditional, less time-consuming process can also generate successful productions, and noted that it is conceivable that not every Disney show may undergo this approach.

Unlike Clear Channel, Disney does not, as a rule, seek investors or coproducers, with the prominent exception of its current partnership with Cameron Mackintosh to produce a musical of *Mary Poppins*. Mackintosh owns the rights to the Travers books, but Disney owns the rights to the film and the songs in it. Normally Disney prefers to produce alone. The company does not own theatrical shops in which to construct the physical production, however, and takes the traditional route of hiring outside contractors to do so. (It does, however, take advantage of the expertise of Disney Imagineering.) As Alan Levey explained,

> The company, because it's a publicly held company, makes the entire investment and takes the entire risk, but as a result, benefits from the success, if the work is good and the stars are in alignment. The company is far more interested in taking maximum advantage of the potential success, and plans for success by making the total investment. Once the property is developed, there are licensed productions in international markets, but in fact we retain total control of the artistic content and production standards by sending the specific production team originally responsible for that content and those standards to those markets.

Disney's independent entrepreneurship makes the company impervious to the clashing demands of coproducers with conflicting agendas and visions, but it also shoulders the full responsibility for success or failure. The impresario of days past has transformed into a corporate entity.

Disney's preference for working alone also means it has resisted joining the League. This move initially displeased many members, who believe that their interests are best served when all producers and owners display a unified front both publicly and in union negotiations. They hoped for the sizable membership fees Disney would have provided and believed that they might better monitor Disney's activities if they were signatories to the League's contracts. According to Barbara Hauptman of the Society of Stage Directors and Choreographers, "Any indie producer's concern at this point with Disney, with [Clear Channel, is that] there's a lot of money being thrown around these days. It's very difficult for them to compete, and so it's painful. I think that's why the League, made up primarily of small, indie producers, is greatly concerned about trying to get some rollbacks, because they're just afraid that the corporations are going to replace everybody." Disney, which has forged separate agreements with the unions that are quite similar to the League contracts, participates in negotiations in coordinated bargaining sessions at League negotiations. Alan Levey said, "There was a feeling, on the corporate level, that we can control our own destiny to a much greater extent by remaining an independent entity, and not being a member of a unit that represents the interests of many theatre owners, limited partnerships, and individual producers." Peter Schneider concurred. "We felt that for various reasons, in terms of labor negotiations, it was the right choice not to [join]. . . . We are very supportive of them . . . but the actual joining of them was not necessary to do business. I think people understood completely; they respected us. I don't think it was negative for us. There was some disappointment, and we thought it might cost us some votes in the Tony races, but it didn't, at the end of the day."

Some independent producers believe that Disney's presence has generated healthy competition. Barry Brown said, "I think success can only breed success on Broadway." But at the outset, Disney was subjected to considerable disdain from a number of fronts, in large part the result of its initial arrogance. While the thought of corporations supplanting independents is disconcerting for most of Broadway's producing community, Barry Grove, executive director of the not-for-profit Manhattan Theatre Club, noted, "I don't see seventy-five other companies lining up to jump in. As long as it stays a mix of free spirits, independently minded producers, iconoclasts, corporate entities, not-for-profits, Broadway is a little bit of everything to everyone. Then, I think you've a very healthy place. If it's dominated by any one kind of producing mechanism and all we saw was Disney and nothing but that, the way you do much more in the world of TV, then that perhaps would be a different concern." Todd Haimes concurred. "I think Disney's involvement is great. Just because the kind of product Disney does is not . . . what I would do, doesn't mean that I don't think there's a huge audience for it. And I also believe passionately that the more theatre, the better."

With control of one theatre and three shows running on Broadway, Disney is not a dominating force relative to either the theatre owners or independent producers. But the apprehension of many independent producers is that Disney's future productions will fill other theatres and displace their own shows. Disney executives, though, long accustomed to thinking globally, acknowledged that the physical parameters of the Broadway theatre district and the relatively small number of available houses do not have to limit the company. As Thomas Schumacher explained,

There are four or five major titles that we're about to do; we will have *too* much product for Manhattan's theatre district. Thus, we may do

Tarzan in a nonconventional theatre space to create a theatrical event, and not do it in a Broadway theatre. We want to do a different thing with it, which requires different thinking. Our mission is to produce commercial theatre, not just to fill Broadway theatres. And anyway, Broadway per se has become an artificial definition of commercial work. That's why we'll start things in London, like *Mary Poppins*. We have to create productions around the world, because there are not enough venues here, there is not enough audience for all the projects we're currently developing.

The company had the chance to establish a broader base on Broadway when it committed to the New Amsterdam, as other theatres were also available on Forty-second Street, but Michael Eisner chose instead to adopt a conservative approach and focus on the one property. As Peter Schneider observed, "I think that Michael felt that we were not in the real estate business, that we were in the theatre business and the entertainment content business. . . . There has been some talk of trying to renovate the Roof [theatre at the New Amsterdam, a separate playing space]. I think the minor mistake was that we didn't spend the X million dollars at the time and do it."

When available theatres are scarce, producers can lose projects because the artists attached to them cannot wait until an appropriate house is open. The charge has been leveled that Disney's financial resources allow the company to run a show longer than their independent competitors, and can endure more losing weeks, because the corporate visibility is worth the loss of revenue. Levey replied that "the bottom line for Disney is no different than any other producer. If a show is losing money and has no chance of returning to profitability, the show will close. Disney will not keep a show running with ongoing losses, no matter what ancillary value there may be to the brand. What I think you are hearing is that Disney shows can withstand losing weeks longer than other shows. That may be the case, but the show has to earn back all losses by year's end or it will close."

Disney's mandate is such that it will likely never produce cutting-edge fare, an approach that is acknowledged by its executives. While the artistry behind the staging of *The Lion King* was impressive, the material itself did not turn Broadway in a new and vibrant direction. That was never the intent. It will fall to the independent producers and the not-for-profits to maintain that commitment to more challenging productions.

Production supervisor Peter Lawrence said, "The upside is that corporations can afford to risk more money than individuals. And when they make that money they'll produce more things. The success of *The Lion King* led to *Aida*. We're employing a lot of people. . . . We've run out of Broadway theatres? Great. Then there will be more shows done off Broadway, and probably more interesting things." Advertising agency owner Nancy Coyne added, "Try to count the number of people Disney has employed . . . especially the number of African Americans. . . . It's phenomenal. And anybody who wants to point their finger and look down their noses at Disney is not taking those things into consideration." Disney's budgets produce shows of impressive size and spectacle, which generate considerable income for the Broadway theatre industry. But great spectacle generates an expectation of and a demand for greater spectacle. A trend that was amplified by the British imports of the eighties has been remagnified by Disney's commitment to dazzle the audiences, sometimes at the expense of content.

Writers and directors, who often encounter fallow periods, are pleased to work for a producer that can pay so handsomely up front. Frank Rich likened it to

> the days when Faulkner and Fitzgerald went out to work and wrote screenplays in Hollywood. That's the price you pay. [Directing *Aida*] may support Robert Falls doing two new Ayckbourn plays at the Goodman [in Chicago, where Falls is artistic director], just as it may have supported Faulkner writing *Light in August*. There's nothing immoral about it, but the problem is the theatre is such a small part of American culture as it is, in terms of how much new work is generated in any given year, and how much support there is for it, that the effect of the corporate culture can be much more profound on it than it can be on other cultural forms that are just so much larger.

And Disney can offer its artists opportunities to work in venues beyond Broadway. Disney's theme park and cruise ship productions are now overseen by Anne Hamburger, once a well-known producer in New York's avant-garde theatre scene. Disney's California Adventure park recently opened a forty-minute redacted stage version of the hit feature animation film *Aladdin,* and its creative team comprised internationally known artists from the opera and theatre worlds. Hamburger has also commissioned additional works, and her theatre contacts confer a growing sense of legitimacy on the work presented at Disney parks around the world.

As Hamburger acknowledged in the *New York Times,* "In 1975 a person like me would never have ended up at Disney. Economics have caused a lot more cross-pollination.... It's healthy for the arts and healthy for the world."[14] This last comment is arguable, but it is apparently healthy for artists' pocketbooks. If that allows them greater freedom to work in the legitimate theatre, then it is reflective of the evolution of the subsidy process in the face of dwindling government support.

Playwright and director Arthur Laurents discussed the rising star of corporate producers. "I think it's reflecting the whole country. We're being killed by entertainment—which goes back to TV, and ratings, and celebrity, and every standard except 'Is it good?' If the theatre isn't going to try to be an art, then it's not worth going on, I don't think. Art, not incidentally, can be entertaining. But it doesn't have a laugh track." The corporate necessity to produce for the widest spectrum of audiences is in no way inimical to the financial health of Broadway; large numbers are essential to keep the industry solvent. Many theatre executives predict, with some trepidation, that corporate producers, and thus independents who will have to keep pace, will create works that cater to audiences' growing appetite for sensational effects and easy, accessible fare. As more film studios seek to exploit their movie holdings and explore producing on the legitimate stage, this movement may gain momentum. If producers give audiences only what they think they want, the chance for theatre to touch not only the eye and the ear, but the heart and the mind, shrivels.

4 When Worlds Collide

● ●

What is commercial producing these days but being the first to take something from a not-for-profit to a commercial venue?
   —Roy Gabay, producer and general manager

You cannot afford the luxury any longer of thinking of two distinct, isolated worlds of theater. Economics have been the driving force between profit and nonprofit, or taxpaying and nontaxpaying, as I call it.
   —Gerald Schoenfeld, chairman of the Shubert Organization, in the *New York Times*, June 15, 2000

If you happen to do a project that's hopefully true to your artistic mission, and it's a big success, then I'm all for exploiting it to the absolute maximum and getting every possible benefit for your company, because the environment for not-for-profit theatre companies is so difficult. You need to do everything you can to survive and prosper.
   —Terrence Dwyer, managing director, La Jolla Playhouse

In 1974, in Princeton, New Jersey, a gathering of theatre makers from the not-for-profit and commercial worlds met for four days to discuss the state of the art—or arts, as quickly grew apparent. The fortunes and aesthetics of these two theatrical spheres of interest seemed polar opposites. Convened by Broadway producer Alexander H. Cohen, the First American Congress of Theater brought together disparate artists, managers, and producers to bridge the wide chasm that separated them. According to writer Jeremy Gerard,

> Cohen . . . like most of his colleagues, had seen his fortunes suffer considerably in the sixties and seventies, when Broadway came to be regarded as just another outmoded Establishment institution worthy of disdain. . . . What little adventurous work was making it to Broadway, even back then, was coming from the Public, as well as theaters like Washington's Arena Stage and Los Angeles' Mark Taper Forum. . . . Alex Cohen knew the [Broadway] business was in trouble—and he knew where salvation lay. . . . The goals were lofty and the expecta-

tions were high; Cohen wanted to accomplish nothing less than to forge ongoing ties where none existed.[1]

No one was certain that the establishment and its adversary would be able to tolerate a few days brokering a rapprochement that would allow for a constructive dialogue.

In a now legendary address to the Congress, Julian Beck, the anarchist-pacifist cofounder of the germinal experimental collective the Living Theatre, railed against the Broadway establishment in a portentously blood-curdling fashion reminiscent of Nikita Khruschev's "We will bury you!" speech at the UN. "The capitalist pig theater must go! It must die! We rejoice in its death!" thundered Beck. A visionary artist, Beck was evidently less successful in predicting the demise of the commercial theatre.

It would be twenty-six years later, in 2000, when a group similarly constituted but with a very different perspective on professional theatre would meet at Harvard for the Second American Congress of Theater (ACT II), sponsored jointly by the League and Theatre Communications Group (TCG), the umbrella organization for not-for-profit theatres in America. After a few decades of increased interdependence, the diatribes were less politically charged and the tone more effusively conciliatory, but the issues brought to the table were of equal weight to the makers of theatre in America. The first conference, according to Barry Grove, the executive director of Manhattan Theatre Club, was less an instance of the not-for-profit world meets the commercial world than of the avant-garde world meets the establishment. In 2000, many worried that the not-for-profit theatres had become establishment themselves, a handmaiden to Broadway, in thrall to commercial producers who had replaced government and private subsidy as a critical source of institutional funding. They questioned whether commercial producers could discover a means to once again produce artistically supple works on Broadway. Could both arenas flourish and cooperate for the greater good of American theatre? Had costs grown so outrageous in both sectors that true experimentation would continue to wither and new voices would be heard only in readings, workshops, and smaller not-for-profit theatres? Would common ground be discovered, or would misapprehensions and suspicions continue to drive a wedge between the two groups?

The ACT II conference unearthed some intriguing perspectives on the ever-changing nature of this critical relationship. Jed Bernstein, the president of the League, said a few months after the conference,

Many people expected there to be pitched battles and bickering at the conference. Others, I think, were more practical, perhaps a little cynical, believing that every nonprofit theatre is, in fact, in the business of making profits—except they call it surplus—whereas every commercial producer is jealous of the nonprofits' ability to write off expenses on their taxes. As always, the truth probably lies somewhere in the middle. So what came out of the conference? I think that at the end of the weekend all participants agreed that we are more alike than different. The next step, yet to be realized, is to identify a collaborative project or issue that we can all get behind.

For all the gnashing of teeth in both camps, and for all the critical distinctions that separate them, times have changed. While in 1974 the connection between the two worlds was tortured and tenuous at best, today necessity has occasioned a new relationship. The absence of pyrotechnical outbursts at ACT II was disappointing to some participants, who relished the prospect of a theatrical brawl, but as the president of the Society of Stage Directors and Choreographers, Barbara Hauptman, put it, "It couldn't have been duller. There were no issues. It is all the same in many ways. And that's not so bad. . . . But I think there are some good things going on. And it's interesting to see, as people mature, where is the next generation?" The bald fact, acknowledged by most practitioners today, is that commercial and not-for-profit producers and managers, and their missions, have become inexorably intertwined. The occasional hostile statement by one side, deriding the other for some egregious injury to American theatre, must be seen more as performance art than as an intentionally venomous attack. And while compromises and miscues have caused disaffection, jealousy, and occasional anger, the American theatre could no longer continue down two separate paths. Despite a degree of mutual wariness and a critical need to safeguard the integrity of both arenas, the task at hand was to determine the most effective ways to coexist. Today, members of both sectors frequently lament that the lines have been blurred and the important distinctions have been undermined. Some of the more vocal keepers of the flame on both sides, who have gazed at the not uncommon sight of producers and general managers "taking meetings" to discuss coproductions, observe that the two are beginning to look more and more alike in certain essential ways. It is reminiscent of the startling discovery made by old Clover the horse at the end of Orwell's *Animal Farm*, who looked in on the card game of pigs and farmers and could no longer distinguish one from the other.

At the heart of the matter is the long-held belief that American theatre thrives on the differences. The disappearance of the old divide, some fear, is not only about erosion of identity but also about the loss of artistic and moral values, and the evanescent nature of culture today. Central to this fear are the questions that continue to plague theatre makers in America. A few decades ago, not-for-profit theatres were the heart and soul of serious artistic expression in American theatre. Now, in a vastly different economic, political, and cultural environment, do they run the risk of being marginalized? Will commercial producers take unfair advantage of struggling regional not-for-profit theatres? Are New York–based not-for-profits adopting the methodologies and appearance of commercial entities? Equity director Alan Eisenberg believed that an overlooked footnote to these questions raised at ACT II was another important issue. "It's mind-boggling that this industry does not have a unified voice, in terms of a position about theatre in this country." Eisenberg pointed out that there is no concerted effort at legislative lobbying or audience development carried on by a group of representatives from both camps.

The progenitors of the not-for-profit theatre movement were disparate groups that blossomed in the middle of the twentieth century, which, despite artistically varied wellsprings, shared one common vision—the need to produce theatre that was not bound by commercial constraints. The Cleveland Play House, the Goodman Theatre in Chicago, and the Barter Theatre in Abingdon, Virginia, were early examples of the pre–World War II regional theatre phenomenon taking root outside New York City. In the thirties, the Federal Theatre Project, under Hallie Flanagan's stalwart leadership, provided opportunities around the nation for thousands of theatre artists to continue to work during the Depression. And despite the fact that the Group Theatre performed mostly in the commercial venue of Broadway, it functioned essentially as a not-for-profit collective, plowing profits back into the organization. After World War II, a handful of forward-thinking artists realized that new resident professional companies could offer artistic sustenance outside the commercial pressures of Broadway. In New York, too, emerging companies sought to provide an anodyne to the increasingly banal work on Broadway that was meant to compete with television. The Off-Broadway movement, by the late fifties, had become a force with which to be reckoned and became the primary source of some of the period's most provocative theatrical offerings. Even though Off-Broadway had already become bifurcated, with some theatres housing commercial productions, the heart of Off-Broadway—and later Off-Off-Broadway—resolutely resided in the not-for-profit arena.

It was not until the late fifties and early sixties that the alternative movements in the rest of the country would be recognized not as satellites revolving around the New York sun but as creatively generative institutions in their own right. Led by dynamic artistic directors like Zelda Fichandler at Arena Stage in Washington DC, Tyrone Guthrie at the theatre that now bears his name in Minneapolis, and Nina Vance at Houston's Alley Theatre, resident theatres began to enjoy a reputation for producing a broad spectrum of daring and honest work, both classic and new. They attracted a new generation of artists who embraced the chance to challenge and flex their artistic muscles. Additionally, civic leaders outside New York discovered the advantages of sponsoring first-class theatres that brought prestige and increased revenues to the community. The integration of permanent resident theatres into host cities signaled a new chapter in the way theatre would be produced outside New York. No longer did communities have to rely solely on amateur theatre guilds and touring productions from Broadway. The movement also signaled an important shift from the perception of professional theatre as moneymaking entertainment. As theatre's regional reputation as a serious art grew, so did government and corporate subsidy. Not-for-profit managing directors began to tinker with the equations of earned income (through subscriptions and single-ticket sales), government grants, and private giving that would keep their theatres solvent.

As Tyrone Guthrie observed in his 1964 book *A New Theatre,* this movement would need to be evaluated with criteria different from those applied to commercial efforts on Broadway. "An experiment of this kind simply cannot be judged in short term. It is essentially an attempt to apply longer-term policies and a more serious, though not I hope on that account pompous, approach to the theatre than is implicit in the pursuit of the Smash Hit."[2] Guthrie's noble vision of theatre artists plying their craft in an attempt, as he put it, "to entertain, to delight" without commercial constraints was a clarion call to theatre artists. In the sixties, the not-for-profit movement was vibrant and innovative, and a moribund Broadway was shocked by the startling ascendance of this new movement. Julius Novick, a distinguished critic and scholar of the contemporary American theatre scene for many years, wrote in 1968 in his book *Beyond Broadway,*

> The American theatre is currently in the midst of a profound redeployment. Broadway is not dying, and it is not going to die, but it can no longer perform all its old functions. It used to be that Broadway *was* the professional theatre in America. . . . Today Broadway has virtually abandoned its old function of reviving the classics, and year by year it comes closer and closer to the abandonment of serious new plays as well. Broadway is becoming an institution devoted more and more to the purveying of light entertainment. (So what else is new?)[3]

The forces that compelled the trailblazers to establish artistic homes in which the work would be the primary focus were the need for permanence and the rejection of the for-profit motive. Commercial Broadway, for all its glamour and prestige, could offer neither with any degree of certainty. A sign of current times is the erosion of the company ethos that dominated the first years of the regional theatre movement. For Guthrie and others, the collective vision and energy of an ensemble of artists, administrators, and technicians would salvage the artistic integrity of the American theatre. Over the years, marketplace factors have made it increasingly difficult for actors to commit to a full year in an ensemble environment, and many of these theatres, including the New York-based Broadway not-for-profits, now typically cast productions on a show-by-show basis, undermining one of the basic precepts that guided the movement in its salad days.

The formation in 1966 of the League of Resident Theatres (LORT) offered the larger, more established not-for-profit theatres a collective bargaining voice that would lead to the creation of the flagship contract between the theatres and most of the leading theatrical unions and guilds, the LORT contract. LORT theatres, numbering about sixty-five today, include the New York–based Vivian Beaumont Theater at Lincoln Center, the Roundabout, and Manhattan Theatre Club, all three of which enjoy Tony-eligible status due to their control or ownership of theatres on Broadway, or within the Tony Award catchment area.[4] Bernard Gersten, with decades of experience at the managerial helm of both the New York Shakespeare Festival–Public Theatre and the Lincoln Center Theaters, noted that the not-for-profit and commercial sectors today are

> occasionally bumping in the night and meeting in funny places. But the not-for-profit theatre is here to stay, which is something that was

not fully acknowledged many years ago. The not-for-profit theatre was just a little kid, a little puppy dog nibbling at the "real" theatre's ankles. It is no longer true. And the manifestations of that are legion, whether it's productions from regional theatres that come to New York, or those that originate in New York not-for-profits and go on to extended runs on or off Broadway, either under their own auspices or taken over by commercial producers.

Gersten's avowal is, if anything, an understatement. The not-for-profits, despite their current financial woes, are entrenched as an essential component of the American theatre scene. The recent blurring of the lines between the commercial and not-for-profit theatres is a function of the inevitable evolution of professional theatre.

Some argue that the intersection of the commercial and not-for-profit worlds has corrupted the mission of the not-for-profit theatres, co-opting their artistic imperatives and encouraging them to produce middlebrow entertainment in exchange for enhancement money, national visibility, and a chance to earn royalties from a successful Broadway transfer. But relatively few not-for-profit theatres have had any interaction with commercial producers. Only a handful of theatres in New York and around the nation have produced work that has moved to Broadway, but like the bleating sheep in *Animal Farm* who chant, "Four legs good! Two legs bad!" some not-for-profit theatre makers sounded a similarly strident note for years when they insisted on the artistic superiority of their patch of theatrical turf. Barbara Hauptman studied theatre administration at Yale under one of the revolutionary champions of the not-for-profit movement, Robert Brustein. She characterized the typical not-for-profit condescension. "I was brought up to abhor commercial theatre. I don't. I often think that the LORT theatre has become a little sanctimonious. I do not think they are the be-all and end-all purveyors of the art of theatre." There is a wide spectrum of theatrical activity mounted on the stages of the nation's not-for-profit theatres, and while the charge of every institution is to do vital and honest work, that may take a variety of incarnations, including unvarnished attempts at crowd-pleasing. Some theatre pundits counter that the not-for-profit movement was only marginally countercultural, and only in the sixties, when the civil rights movement and the Vietnam war created a fringe revolutionary theatre that burned bright but quickly. Jack Viertel of the Jujamcyn Organization observed,

What [resident theatres] produced was by and large, leaving aside a very small number of either highly political or highly experimental theatres, stuff that was on Broadway. So the notion that there was this thriving, revolutionary animal that was corrupted seems very hard to swallow in the face of the evidence. . . . As is true of any time, the art form reflects the world. And it's very hard to find revolutionary theatre these days, which I don't think is a positive thing, but I don't think you can lay that at the feet of the commercial theatre. Is the fact that *The Full Monty* was developed at the Old Globe a negative in any measurable way to the Old Globe? I don't know why it would be, unless you feel that musical theatre is in and of itself inferior . . . which I don't feel at all.

Straight play and musical, the not-for-profit theatre has grown like Topsy in its role as a spawning ground for new work, and a glance at the offerings on Broadway serves as a reminder that the intersection of the two paths is more vital than ever before.

The not-for-profit world is now acknowledged as the point of origin for most new dramatic works seen on stages around the nation, including Broadway. As TCG president Ben Cameron pointed out in an article in the *New York Times,* published just weeks before ACT II, with the exception of Neil Simon's 1991 *Lost in Yonkers,* every Pulitzer prize for best play has gone to a work that originated in a not-for-profit theatre.[5] As Cameron noted, for years most new work at these theatres was supported by sizable grants from the Ford Foundation, the National Endowment for the Arts (NEA), and state arts councils. But today, when the NEA and state arts councils have been eviscerated or eliminated by conservative legislatures or failed economies, and previous levels of private support have deteriorated, many not-for-profit theatres find themselves on the brink of extinction; in the eighties and later, several were forced to permanently close. A theatre that produced daring and highly respected work could afford to run in the red for a season or two, if its board recognized the cyclical nature of these things and supported the mission of the artistic director. That is rarely the case now. Seattle's A Contemporary Theatre came within days of shutting its doors in spring 2003, and only a bailout by its own board members and other concerned groups was able to ensure its presence for another season. Resident theatres are discovering a few hard truths these days. It is increasingly difficult to mount new work that is not immediately accessible. Large-cast plays, except for perhaps one a season by Shakespeare, are unaffordable. As subscription rates decline due to a poor economy, it is mainstream work and revivals that are attracting the increasingly valuable single-ticket buyers.

As subsidies have dried up, not-for-profit theatres have had to look elsewhere for sustenance. The commercial theatre has become a valuable source of funding for the LORT and not-for-profit Off-Broadway theatres that produce shows with commercial appeal. For several years, Broadway producers, including Disney, have turned to the less-expensive arena of resident theatres to try out their new works. Lower salaries, fees, and per diem payments; less costly advertising; affordable housing; and a number of other economic factors all render the regional theatres as attractive alternatives for commercial producers. But it is not as wildly cost-effective as it was a decade ago; commercial producers can now spend from five hundred thousand to more than one million dollars for their share of a new musical at a not-for-profit theatre. Rocco Landesman commented, "We've tended to work with resident theatres because you can get a view of your show in front of an audience at much less cost [than when you go to an out-of-town venue]; *The Producers* in Chicago is going to add more than two million dollars to the capitalization. If you can do it in a resident theatre for half a million or less, you're a lot better off." As Marty Bell pointed out, enhancement money for a not-for-profit production is "total risk money . . . you don't get any piece of the box office, so you can end up with nothing." A producer can come away from a not-for-profit production with valuable knowledge, however, about the show's artistic viability and commercial prospects.

Some critics of this increased cohabitation express apprehension that mainstream Broadway fare dilutes the artistic mission of these institutions. But the most successful not-for-profits today are engaged in the balancing act of finding a middle ground on which to flourish both economically and artistically, and look where they must for support. Now, the condescension with which many not-for-profits regarded Broadway has been replaced by a needful longing for such partnerships. Two complicating factors are the demands and burdens placed on the institutional theatres when they open their doors to high-stakes commercial productions, and the discomfort about commingling commercial and not-for-profit funds. A distinction must be drawn to separate commercial collaborations in not-for-profit theatres, not-for-profit productions that are subsequently produced on Broadway by commercial producers, and Broadway shows staged by the not-for-profit Roundabout Theatre, Manhattan Theatre Club, and Lincoln Center Theater.

In the not-for-profits' salad days, commercial involvement was essentially nonexistent. The two worlds coexisted with minimal interaction, although many artists worked frequently in both arenas. In 1968 Howard Sackler's dazzling new work, *The Great White Hope,* was mounted at the Arena Stage in Washington DC under the supervision of artistic director Zelda Fichandler and managing director Ed Sherin. It was transferred by the intrepid producer Herman Levin to Broadway, and the door was left ajar for future maneuvers by commercial producers. For some time after, transfers to Broadway were typically undertaken by commercial producers who secured the commercial rights during or after the institutional run. As scenic designer Robin Wagner, who designed *The Great White Hope,* remembered, "When shows like that transferred to Broadway, it was because there was a buzz about it. Levin came down, saw it, and brought it to Broadway." A degree of commercial naïveté and an intrinsic distrust of Broadway held sway in the not-for-profit world, so these theatres made relatively little money from transfers in the early days. Now, however, experience and necessity have engendered a much greater sophistication in the not-for-profits.

The New York–based not-for-profits, especially, have developed strong ties with certain Broadway producers. Enhancement money may not be a factor, but these producers will often have the inside track to transfer a success to an open-ended commercial run. Daryl Roth remembered her initial involvement with Charles Busch's hit comedy *The Tale of the Allergist's Wife* on Broadway.

> [Manhattan Theatre Club's artistic director and the show's director] Lynne Meadow passed me the script and said, "We're going to do it at Manhattan Theatre Club; I just want you to know about it because I think you're going to love it, and I want you to be there when we do it." I read the script and I thought, "Oh, my God, this is the funniest thing I've ever read. I really need to do this." ... At an early preview at Manhattan Theatre Club ... I ran up to Lynne and Charles, sitting in the back, and I said, "This is the funniest thing I have ever seen. I don't care what the critics say, we have to move this play." ... When it was well reviewed, and Manhattan Theatre Club decided, yes, they would like to move it, there were a number of producers that wanted to become involved. They put together a group they wanted to work with, and happily, I was in that group.

In some rare instances, an institutional theatre found itself with an artistically and commercially successful show and chose to transfer it to a for-profit venue without the assistance of a commercial producer. In 1971 the New York Shakespeare Festival's production of the musical version of *Two Gentlemen of Verona* was the first transfer of a property to a commercial run due solely to the generosity of a private donor's gift to the theatre, and the theatre was able to reap 100 percent of the profits. The institution benefited similarly—albeit for many more years—from its commercial transfer of *A Chorus Line,* a production that became, in the words of Roy Somlyo, "a cash cow" for the Public Theatre. As Bernard Gersten, then the managing director, put it, "Not one dollar of profit from that show ever went to private investors. And that income is still keeping the New York Shakespeare Festival afloat."

Over time, however, a shift in commercial producing methodologies caused a ripple in the not-for-profit world. As pre-Broadway road tryouts grew prohibitively expensive, producers began to look elsewhere for developmental opportunities. While workshop productions in New York grew in popularity in the seventies and eighties because they offered the chance to explore material without heading out of town, many writers, directors, and producers acknowledged that the response they received in workshops was often suspect, as the audience usually comprised sycophants, family, friends, and competitors. The not-for-profit sector, with its historical commitment to new works, seemed the most promising arena, where shows could expect serious attention and respectable, if not Broadway-caliber, production values. Audiences were not stacked decks, as they often were at workshops, but represented a cross section of that community's theatre-going public.

Producers would not only transfer successful works from not-for-profits; they would actively partner with them and move shows to commercial venues. By means of enhancement money, a producer could handsomely subsidize the not-for-profit's budget. Roy Somlyo remarked that the turning point for many not-for-profit theatres was the desire to discover their own *A Chorus Line*–like gold mine. The landmark musical was transferred to a Broadway run without the involvement of commercial producers in either the Off-Broadway or Broadway incarnations, but the point that Somlyo made speaks more to the evolving weltanschauung in the not-for-profit arena than it does to the specifics of that process.

As a result [of *A Chorus Line*], everybody who was in the position to develop properties started saying, "Hey, that's a wonderful thing, to get a show on Broadway!" So all these regional theatres that were so good at developing properties began to [do so] with one eye turned towards Broadway. And when they started moving one eye and two eyes towards Broadway, they lost sight of what their real value was, which was to work in the creative area. . . . It became [their] goal . . . looking to survive with their cash cow. And you can't blame them. But they misfired. What they were good at was not Broadway, they were good at doing their own material. But they got seduced.

While revenue from a commercial coproduction will rarely save a theatre on the financial brink, it can provide some necessary cash and enhance the theatre's reputation in the community. These assets, in turn, may attract other funding sources or writers who want a nationally recognized platform for their works.

Although enhancement may cost one million dollars or more, it is still considerably less expensive than a road tryout for a large musical. Cameron Mackintosh took his production of the musical *Martin Guerre* to the Guthrie Theatre in 1999 to tune it up for a Broadway run (still unproduced there as of 2004). According to the *New York Times,* that production cost $2.1 million, an extravagant amount of money relative to most LORT budgets (about two and a half times as much as other large Guthrie shows). Mackintosh put up half the cost.[6] This approach allows the producer more time to raise the balance of funds needed for a subsequent commercial production, while observing the development of the work in a less pressured environment where, at least for the sponsoring theatre, box office viability is not the sole guiding precept. Jujamcyn head Rocco Landesman, who solidified his reputation as the producer who shepherded *Big River* through two LORT theatres before its successful Broadway run, pointed out that a LORT production is never followed hard on the heels by a Broadway production, which is usually the case after a commercial out-of-town tryout. "You have, in that kind of situation, the luxury of time between the productions. You're not in Chicago and coming in to New York in two weeks. You're in La Jolla and you have two or three months to really sit down and work with a show." When a show is tried out in a commercial road house, it is usually with the intention to move directly to Broadway when the tryout is concluded, as the expenses incurred to warehouse a production as well as the interruption to the show's momentum would be untenable. By contrast, productions mounted in resident theatres are most often attempted well in advance of a potential Broadway run. The production—usually built in the not-for-profit's shops—is frequently presented on a stage that may not resemble a Broadway theatre's typical proscenium dimensions. Such was the case with the recent Broadway revival of *A Flower Drum Song*, originally seen on the thrust stage of the Mark Taper Forum in Los Angeles. Robin Wagner, who had to redesign the show when it moved to Broadway's Virginia Theatre, created the original sets with the Taper's particular configuration as his only consideration. "I could not have done it any other way. It's more of a production to change the forms from one to another than it is to work with whatever form is there. And the Taper is a specific theatre, a thrust with a kind of Roman seating. And you wouldn't want to do the same production. There's always a hope that the show will be a success, that it could go on to somewhere else. But there was never any intention to design it for its ultimate goal." The Taper's support staff and artistic director Gordon Davidson's enthusiasm for the show, coupled with a large Chinese American presence in Los Angeles, were sufficiently persuasive that the producers could accept the costs of redesign.

When, however, a producer has booked a New York production immediately to follow the residence at the not-for-profit, the design team must tailor the physical elements with consideration for the Broadway house. Martin Markinson, who owns Broadway's Helen Hayes Theatre, provided enhancement money to the Old Globe for a production of *Getting and Spending*. "We knew we were going to get sets and costumes because we gave them the money with the understanding that they were going to be built to travel, built to New York specifications. If you wind up with a fully rehearsed show you can save four weeks of rehearsal costs. You can save on costumes. You can save on sets. And you have a lot of the technical elements worked out. If you intend to move the show, you could be saving the money that you gave for enhancement towards your final capitalization." This approach works only when the production moves immediately, without radical reconceiving.

Even though immediate pre-Broadway pressures are often diminished in a regional production, the team must examine the evolving production with a sharp eye toward its ultimate goal. In many instances, it will determine that the work's flaws are significant, and plans for a Broadway production are postponed or canceled. La Jolla Playhouse, for example, known for the Broadway productions of *Big River, Tommy, How to Succeed . . . , Jane Eyre,* and *Thoroughly Modern Millie,* produced other musicals, including *80 Days, Shout Up a Morning!, Faust, Harmony,* and

Elmer Gantry, that never made it to Broadway. As attorney Seth Gelblum pointed out, a not-for-profit engagement can be attractive for a producer, but there are financial ramifications.

> The not-for-profit producers will be getting a share of net profits, and a share of royalties. You don't have that additional burden on a show [in its subsequent commercial run] if you don't start there. [But] if you really want to save money, and want to see it up on its feet first, and you've never seen it before [in a physical production], then you might be more inclined to go to a regional theatre, because it is less expensive, and it's easier, after the regional theatre production, to sit back and start from scratch and retool. You haven't spent as much money. It's understood that it's more of a developmental process. If you're not sure what you have, you'll often start at one of the regional theatres.

Barry Weissler indicated that "each production takes its own form. If I have something esoteric, I take it to a regional theatre. If I have something bright and easy, an audience-pleasing show with a major star, I try it out of town in major cities, Washington, Boston, L.A." Peter Schneider and Thomas Schumacher chose to originate *The Lion King* in a commercial theatre in Minneapolis, "because of the knowledge of the material, and maybe a little out of ignorance. It was probably too big a show to do anyplace else," as Schneider put it. But *Aida* was first staged as *Elaborate Lives: The Legend of Aida* at the Alliance, a LORT theatre in Atlanta, because, according to Schneider, "it was not a very big show; it fit more into the not-for-profit structure—it needed more time. Clearly we made the right choices with it, in terms of going to Atlanta and realizing nothing worked and making the various changes to it that we made. I think those were all very positive steps. Ultimately the Alliance benefited both financially and creatively, and so did we."

Richard Frankel, a producer of *The Producers,* commented that a number of factors can determine whether a producer seeks a not-for-profit or traditional, commercial road tryout for a Broadway-bound work.

> It's a combination of the particular needs of a particular show. There's no magic to it. And to some degree it's what you can afford. With *The Producers,* we had to go out of town. . . . It's comedy, it has to be tried out in front of audiences that have paid for their tickets, and the audience has to be as close as we can come to a New York audience, simply in order to test the jokes. If we previewed [cold] in New York, we

would be subject to unbearable scrutiny, derision perhaps, when things aren't working, and gleeful trashing of our problems.

The 2003 revival of *Gypsy* did open cold in New York (after previews) and was subject to wild speculation as to whether Bernadette Peters had the ability to pull off the role of Mama Rose. But the show, widely regarded as a pinnacle of accomplishment in the crafting of libretto and score, had succeeded in its previous incarnations on Broadway, and the foundations of the piece did not require the tinkering of a pre-Broadway tryout in either arena.

Frank Rich questioned whether a not-for-profit's mission is compromised when it collaborates with commercial producers, for whom the institution's long-term health may not be a primary consideration during the production process.

> As long as the artistic director and creative personnel keep their artistic prerogatives and have the artistic rights, I don't think it's so bad. However, once that breaks down, once the sweetening money gets mucking around with artistic decisions of an institutional theatre, that's a recipe for disaster. Furthermore, in the—I hope—unlikely event that nonprofit theatres are making their choices on the basis of what they can get money for from outside sources, that to me totally violates the ideal and point of nonprofit theatre. They might as well then become commercial theatres and drop the pretense.

Some commercial producers perceive that not-for-profits—especially the New York–based theatres with whom they compete for audiences—enjoy unfair advantages, such as a favorable tax status and strong subscription bases. Some in the not-for-profit camp worry about the erosion of the once-vital distinction that separated them from the commercial theatre, yet they acknowledge the economic imperative that makes it necessary for theatres to seek out commercial coproductions. Josh Ellis, for many years a leading Broadway press agent before spending a decade as the director of communications at La Jolla Playhouse, said,

> The ideal thing [for a regional theatre] would be if you could do a show and say, "Screw Broadway!" But of course, that doesn't exist. But that would be the ideal. "We're going to be so outrageous and do what we want to do and let's see where it goes!" My guess is that that kind of energy ultimately produces the kind of [show] like *Rent*, which was one of those out-of-left-field shows that became a hit. I don't think

[Jonathan Larson] originally wrote it to be a Broadway hit. I have to believe *The Full Monty* was written to be a Broadway hit.

The income stream from a Broadway transfer can be tantalizing to the not-for-profit, but as Todd Haimes pointed out, "There's not a lot of money in this; if there is real money to be made in any production, it's in being a true producer. Being a small participant in a royalty pool, unless the show is a money machine, [yields] a relatively small amount of money." The Roundabout's revival of *Cabaret* is the stuff of not-for-profit dreams, in which they were the sole producer, without a commercial partner to siphon off the cream of the profits. The musical, which opened in 1998, made more than ten million dollars for the theatre, allowing it to address several financial concerns, complete the building of the American Airlines Theatre, and amass a healthy reserve. But many in the commercial world accuse the Broadway-based not-for-profits of abandoning their mission by charging near-Broadway prices, thus rendering their theatres inaccessible to most members of the community, who are supporting the theatres through their taxes. Additionally, these institutions have access to real estate on Broadway at a subsidized price, while the commercial producer does not, and they do not pay income tax on their operating income.

One possible solution was offered by Manhattan Theatre Club in its production of *A Small Family Business,* a play that started its life in New York directly on Broadway. Executive director Barry Grove explained that

if you are using funds from a commercial entity that insists on joint control, we don't believe it is wise to do that through the not-for-profit. In that circumstance, we formed a wholly owned for-profit subsidiary to the joint venture with the producers who put up all of the capital. We put up the expertise and the rights to the play, with [artistic director] Lynne Meadow directing it, and our producing talents. And they put up the operating capital. And appropriately, in their case, they wanted joint control.

Had the production shown a profit, the subsidiary would have paid tax on it and the remainder would have been reinvested into the institution as a dividend. This move, producers say, would give these theatres the right to charge full ticket prices and relieve them of their not-for-profit responsibility. If not-for-profits produced on Broadway through for-profit subsidiaries, the risk to the company's endowment would decrease, as it often is used to subsidize the commercial production.

Peter Schneider, a vocal participant at ACT II, who earlier in his career ran the not-for-profit St. Nicholas Theatre in Chicago, offered his perspective on the evolution of the relationship of the not-for-profit and commercial sectors, which he sees as the inevitable result of their need to maintain solvency in a changing economic landscape.

> You were seeing the not-for-profits saying to the commercial producers, "We don't like you. . . . We'll do it our own darn way, we like art." And then slowly . . . one or two of those art pieces became commercial . . . [and] the shows leave the not-for-profits with them owning nothing. And someone exploits them [commercially], and makes a lot of money. And the not-for-profit says, "We didn't want to be involved, but gosh, they made a lot of money." So the next step is, "We want to own a piece of it. . . . Why aren't we producing it, as a name producer, so that we could make more money?" . . . So the third step is, "Why aren't we investing our own money in this?" and the board says, "Great . . ." So you have not-for-profits saying "We are now the commercial producers of our work, and all its various territories." So they make money, and the not-for-profits are now in the mode of saying, "We *love* the commercial theatre!"
>
> Another process is that the Peter Schneiders of the world go to them and say, "Can you do this for me?" and they say, "Great!" Because they are now actively looking for things that fit their subscribers and fit their mandate for things that will make more money. So, therefore, you have a complete blending of the two, and the original purpose of the 501(c)(3) not-for-profit was really locally based. Everyone's incorporations were about bringing good theatre and educational processes to the local communities. And with the changing economic situation, changing demographics . . . a few of [these theatres] have become the real drivers of what goes on Broadway these days.

Schneider also responded to the charge that not-for-profits are providing a relatively cheap tryout for commercial producers. "Most shows need a space, an opportunity to have additional artistic work done, and these places offer great environments, great time, great resources to develop the artistic work. Is that a tryout? Yes, in some ways it is; in other ways, it's just doing work." To generate the enthusiasm needed to raise capital for Broadway, producers are inclined to stage these shows as opulently as possible within budgetary constraints. The commercial producer, who realizes that the show's future hinges on its success in the not-for-profit run, can exert undue pressure on the theatre. Large-scale, pre-Broadway musicals can severely tax a theatre's production infrastructure, which is usually not geared to mount works of such scope. Thus theatres are sometimes left to recover from the strain for a season or two while they sort out the problems wrought by overwork and overruns. In some instances, producers fail to fully reimburse the not-for-profit theatre for their share of the costs, and host theatres have suffered weakened financial stability, strained relations with vendors, and the inability to adequately serve the needs of other shows in the season. Terrence Dwyer, the managing director of La Jolla Playhouse, was responsible for brokering the contracts of several productions that made it to Broadway. "It could go wrong more often than it goes right," cautioned Dwyer,

> because the not-for-profit theatre has to have the institutional experience and the institutional capacity to pull off these projects and to control them in a reasonable way, and to have negotiated a reasonable balance with the commercial entity, and I think most not-for-profits don't have that. So there is the danger of the mission or the internal culture of the company being negatively impacted. That problem will be further exacerbated if the commercial producer is not sensitive to the world of the not-for-profit and uses them solely as an out-of-town tryout.

This was amplified by Dwyer's predecessor at La Jolla, Disney's Alan Levey.

> When a not-for-profit theatre mounts a production that has commercial aspirations, the scale of that production tends to be larger than what they would typically undertake. It puts a strain on the institution, it challenges the institution. In some ways, there are probably pluses: the production provides the organization and staff with more varied experience, and presents specific hurdles to be overcome. In some ways, if the resources are not stable, there could be damage to individuals within the organization or even to the organization's reputation and ability to continue. The decision to embark on an enhanced musical is a balancing act. The organization has to be ready for such an undertaking, and capable of handling it. Are there long-term benefits for the organization? If the musical is a success, absolutely.

The best relationships occur when both parties reach an accord, prior to the heat of battle, on how to approach the production. Zelda Fichandler, one of the pioneers of the not-for-profit movement, wrote in the December 2000 issue of *American Theatre,*

> The theatre may be assured that artistic control will remain with them, but it can be difficult for this control to be exercised in an empirical, day-by-day manner, since the project is clearly not being grown for home but with the artistic/economic eyes on some other target. And under the pressure of time, hasty changes in text or personnel, the impending visit of New York critics and the natural power of the piper with regard to the tune, the theatre can easily feel taken over by outside forces rather than creating something it could call its own to share with its community.
>
> I'm sure there are occasions when this kind of relationship has proved to be harmonious and synergistic, and co-partnership has continued on the hoped-for commercial and artistic success. But sometimes the theatre has been left in disarray, its powers depleted, its morale diminished, wondering what the gain really was in the end. Perhaps, if the truth were told, this wasn't even what they would have chosen to produce in the first place—but the incentives proved irresistible.[7]

Josh Ellis cautioned that not-for-profits should not necessarily hitch their fortunes, and their self-images, to the success of a commercial transfer.

> Regional theatres use Broadway success as a benchmark for the success of their theatres, and God knows the media pick up on that first, but I don't think the theatres themselves should use it as a benchmark. If you do a wonderful play that reaches your community and your community loves it, independent of what happens to the show if and when it goes to New York, it doesn't matter. It just means you've done a really great job for your audience and your people who loved it. I think it provides an artificial way of measuring success.

But there are some benefits from a successful transfer; aside from access to coveted house seats, the theatre participates in the royalty pool for anywhere from one-half to one and a half points before recoupment, and one to two points after. Typically, a weekly guarantee is built into the agreement, so that in weaker periods, in which the royalty pool does not receive its full percentage, the theatre will still make anywhere from five hundred to one thousand dollars a week. Once the show recoups, the theatre may also derive a share of net profits, and subsidiary rights can provide another source of income.

Production supervisor Peter Lawrence has overseen several Broadway productions that started at regional theatres.

I don't see anything wrong with the not-for-profits using the commercial theatre and the commercial theatre using the not-for-profits to benefit each other. The Neil Simon plays [at the Old Globe Theatre in San Diego] are the perfect arguing point. Those plays would have happened with or without the Globe. But the profits helped the theatre. I think anything that gets theatre on is a good idea. And what we have to hope is that the not-for-profit theatres . . . are picking the most interesting of the crop that's available to them.

Alan Eisenberg, the executive director of Equity, who attended ACT II, explained that even in the best of circumstances, each constituency needs to view itself as the powerful partner. "It's very much, to use a cliché, a Rashomon situation. All the Broadway people tell me that one way or another, they're controlling the production. They say that directly, they say it indirectly. They do all the hiring, they're there at the LORT theatre all the time. They're pulling the strings in terms of the artistic conceit, most of the time, anyway. And the LORT people tell me, 'We're controlling the product.'" The tension that derives from this power play can cause terrific strain on the artists who become the servants of two masters. Terrence Dwyer made the point that a not-for-profit theatre that actively seeks out partnerships with commercial producers with the primary intent of hitting it big on Broadway is an egregious example of "the system gone wrong." At the same time, Dwyer noted, La Jolla Playhouse, especially under the direction of its current artistic director Des McAnuff, "loves to do big, ambitious projects; we love to do musicals. We think the development and innovative production of new American musicals particularly, and revivals are [also] an important part of our mission. . . . The only way we can afford to do these productions is through these collaborations."

One Broadway producer with experience in both the not-for-profit and commercial worlds said that some LORT theatres produce large new musicals to satisfy the demands of their artistic directors, who direct these shows themselves. Regardless of who initiates the project, the wise not-for-profit administrator will hew firmly to a predetermined budget for the joint venture and place the onus of raising the rest of the money on the commercial producers. Should a budget variance arise, it is in the best interest of the not-for-profit to stand firm, even if the project falls through. As Dwyer observed, "We never contribute to any such product more than we have allocated to any one show in our annual operating budget. . . . We are not about squeezing money from all over the place just to pull off a project."

Just as the commercial producer needs the not-for-profit for the greater affordability and institutional savvy it offers, not-for-profit theatres need the infusion of commercial funds to mount productions of the size and scope of those seen on Broadway. Thirty or forty years ago, many not-for-profits were able to stage several large-scale productions each season (mostly straight plays), as costs were significantly lower. Now, however, most produce only one or two large shows, inevitably musicals or classics. Most contemporary playwrights avoid writing large-cast straight plays because they know that they are not cost-effective for either not-for-profits or commercial producers. Musicals, however, can be marketed more aggressively to a wider audience, but there are risks attached to them. When a not-for-profit engineers a successful Broadway transfer, the theatre may later experience a falloff in contributed income because of a community perception that the organization is solvent. The board, eager for the extra income and enhanced reputation, may demand the production of more musicals. As Dwyer remarked, "You should not do these projects unless you are absolutely sure you have the institutional capacity to pull them off successfully and without financial risk to your company." Key planning strategies to safeguard the health of the theatre include budgeting for unexpected financial blows, planning the rest of the season to avoid a continuous onslaught of production work, and frequently consulting with the board and the staff to contextualize the production in the theatre's mission statement.

La Jolla Playhouse never budgets for projected royalty income from a commercial transfer. To protect the integrity of the organization, theatres like La Jolla Playhouse attempt to exercise caution and wisdom when considering which works to produce. "We don't pick projects because they are being pitched as 'guaranteed' to make it in New York," said Dwyer. "If we did, we would probably be doing musicals every season, and probably at a lower quality on the average. There are a lot of projects that people at least *say* have money attached to them that do not fit within our artistic mission." The Roundabout's Todd Haimes concurred. "As disingenuous as this sounds, with the single exception of *Cabaret* or *Follies,* a commercial run is the farthest thing from our minds when we produce shows. There goes death, if you start worrying about what is going to happen after the Roundabout."

But not every institution has developed appropriate strategies for negotiating with commercial producers. Attorney John Breglio was a panelist at an ACT II symposium that debated how not-for-profit and commercial interests might approach a joint production of a hypothetical new musical. During the course of the discussion, Breglio, playing the role of a board member of the imaginary not-for-profit theatre, offered this observation:

> I am tired of seeing all these not-for-profit organizations spending their hard-earned money at the very beginning, nurturing the material, getting it up; we have a success and then eventually we lose it entirely and we don't get the benefits—the money we need to pour back into the organization. We control the product. We will set the rules. They [the commercial producers] will be there. They will give us their money. *Take* their money. We will protect [the playwright and director] and then we will get as much perhaps out of the commercial success of it as the commercial producer, as opposed to letting it go and watch[ing] somebody else make millions.[8]

While Breglio might have been stretching the point, his argument has a kernel of truth for many theatres. Despite a public show of bravado by not-for-profit theatres engaged in developing commercial properties, theatre managers often rail in private against the overweening control and bullying tactics of commercial producers.

Some not-for-profit theatre administrators resist entirely the advances of commercial producers. Lincoln Center's Bernard Gersten was emphatic when he stated, "Commercial theatre money appears in the sheep's clothing of being a contribution, when it is frequently a self-seeking, inappropriate, and unfortunate influence on the activity of a not-for-profit theatre. That's what it is at its worst. Maybe there is benign enhancement money, but I tend to doubt it. It's the attempt to buy the services of a not-for-profit theatre. That is disquieting." Gersten did, however, admit that Lincoln Center has participated in ventures with commercial producers, but he drew a line of clarification that echoed Breglio's exhortation when he noted, "These collaborations have been primarily initiated by us. And certainly, the productions were always controlled by us. Such financing, usually nonrecourse loans, never paraded under the guise of enhancement money." He pointed to the 1994 production of *Carousel*, produced by Lincoln Center in association with Cameron Mackintosh and the Royal National Theatre. The musical revival, produced first at the Olivier

Theatre at the National in London, required a theatre with dimensions similar to those of the Olivier's thrust stage. When Mackintosh decided to produce it in New York, he approached Lincoln Center with the idea to stage it at the Beaumont, which also has a thrust. Coincidentally, Lincoln Center had tried to obtain the American rights just before it was announced that the play would be part of the National's season. Lincoln Center executives agreed to Mackintosh's proposal, as the cost to produce it themselves would have been prohibitive. Mackintosh put up half the money, said Gersten, "but we were in charge of the production. We managed it in every respect, and this was totally acceptable to our tax attorneys." It would have been difficult for Mackintosh to mount a commercial production of *Carousel* in a traditional Broadway theatre with only one thousand seats—the size of the Beaumont—as the revenue would be too small. But the Beaumont's desirable thrust stage, not-for-profit status, and lower costs rendered the show affordable.

Ben Cameron noted in his *New York Times* piece that despite the potential for compromising a not-for-profit's mission, the two worlds must come together to discuss issues of common interest. "Because the world has changed. Financial disagreements aside, we are now being drawn together in numerous ways as a result of the need to: increase public appreciation and understanding of the theatre; develop and sustain young audiences; find a more efficient and economical means of working; cope with a frequently indifferent or hostile government sector; recognize changing generational patterns in leadership; explore a shifting sense of aesthetics in an increasingly virtual age."[9] Cameron extolled the virtues of the not-for-profit world but acknowledged just how difficult it is to survive in an era in which the not-for-profit impulse is generally held in low regard. Not-for-profits have learned their lessons from a few decades earlier, when they saw their own critical contributions to the success of commercial transfers grossly undercompensated and are now aggressively crafting deals with producers.

In a companion piece to Cameron's, Jujamcyn head Rocco Landesman—who cut his teeth in the not-for-profit world—wrote a blistering diatribe in which he accused the not-for-profit movement of selling out to commercial producers. Landesman observed that in the radically different world of 1974, at the first conference, Broadway was a mere shadow of its former self, and the regional theatre world was humming with excitement and energy. Landesman, who fervently believes that the not-for-profits play a critical part in the landscape of American theatre, was dismayed at their newfound eagerness to attract commercial partners, noting that when he spoke in 1999 at a TCG conference, "the first question came from the managing director of a highly regarded minority theater. 'What can we do to get you to notice our work so it might reach a much larger audience on Broadway?' To me, what is much more disturbing than a nonprofit theater tailoring shows specifically for Broadway is the fact that the big distinctions, so important in 1974, seem so nominal now." He added that "Gerald Schoenfeld, chairman of the Shubert Organization, has observed that the profit/nonprofit dichotomy is obsolete, that the proper terms should be taxable/nontaxable or subsidized/nonsubsidized."[10]

All theatres seek to make a profit, Landesman noted. The artistic divide has been flattened. He wrote, "We on Broadway look like the nonprofit theaters, and they look like us."[11] That is chilling to many artists and managers working in both spheres of professional theatre in America, who viewed the former sizzling tension between the poles as an essential ingredient in the health and prosperity of the American theatre. But Landesman's observation is not surprising. Unlike the previous generation of producers who worked their way up the ladder of Broadway employment, many of the new breed were schooled first in the not-for-profit world and brought that aesthetic and sensibility to the commercial arena. Landesman was tutored at Yale by Robert Brustein. Richard Frankel worked at the Hartman and Circle in the Square. Disney's Peter Schneider ran Chicago's Wisdom Bridge, and Thomas Schumacher, as well as Jujamcyn's Jack Viertel, learned from Gordon Davidson at the Mark Taper Forum. Gerald Schoenfeld of the Shubert Organization was quoted in another *Times* article as saying, "The larger nonprofit institutions are really replications of Broadway. Some are just booking houses for Broadway shows."[12] Although this is hotly debated and seems to refer specifically to the New York not-for-profits, evidence to back up Landesman's assertion can be found by examining the work produced by the mainstream not-for-profit theatres around the nation. Fewer new plays— and even fewer daring new plays—are mounted on main stages, and a pall of complacency seems to have settled over the landscape. The evaporation of funding and the need to cater to a more fiscally wary audience has caused many not-for-profits to shift their programming from the adventurous to the safe.

The countercultural vitality that was a hallmark of the movement, Landesman argued, has transformed into one enormous marketing campaign, whose sole aim is commercial success. While he did name some theatres that continue to produce important work, he excoriated Todd Haimes and the Roundabout for selling out to a corporate sponsor, American Airlines, producing bland works, and devising a user-friendly subscription-based system that has diluted the mission of the theatre in exchange for a large audience base. Haimes, who has defended his alliance with American Airlines in print in the *Times,* was adamant that the mission of the theatre has in no way been compromised. He sought a corporate sponsor because "unlike philanthropic donors, corporate donors basically rent the name for a period of time. So if it's a successful situation, you could have an income stream in perpetuity, whereas obviously a philanthropic donor gives the money once, and that's it." Others have come to the defense of the Roundabout, asserting that the company's enhanced audience amenities do not detract from the theatre's mission. Haimes, who for several years was the theatre's executive director before assuming artistic leadership, oversaw the institution's financial revival and emergence from Chapter 11, in which the company floundered in the 1980s. He engineered the company's move uptown from Union Square to Broadway, where the Roundabout occupied the Criterion Center for several years before moving to its current location on Forty-second Street.[13] He also put the company on the national map with the Roundabout's stunning production of O'Neill's *Anna Christie,* starring Liam Neeson and Natasha Richardson. Haimes has endured public derision for his development of theme nights to attract subscribers, which drew fire from Landesman, but his decisions have boosted the subscription base to a 2001 level of forty thousand. Landesman, a sophisticated and economically astute producer, seemed to discount the financial imperative to which all theatres, regardless of their tax status, must respond. His assertion that "increasingly, the template of success comes from the commercial arena, which is, in the end, not dedicated to the art so much as to the audience" is seen by some as an exercise in splitting hairs.[14] The absence of generous government subsidies and private giving has forced theatres to reinvent the notion of creative funding, and if that need has occasioned a shift to a more centrist artistic position, it does not perforce indicate a wholesale abdication of commitment to a set of vital guiding precepts. Many artistic leaders at not-for-profit theatres complain about the difficulties in balancing the institutional mission with the box office, and express hope that future economic conditions might shift the focus back on greater experimentation. The less optimistic argue that current economic conditions and political winds do not bode well for a return to the days when theatres could ignore the blandishments of commercial producers. As Jack Viertel said, many not-for-profit theatres were never quite as daring and experimental as nostalgia might render them. Most mainstream not-for-profits, including the Broadway-based companies, are foursquare in their catering to a solidly middle-class audience with a mix of new plays, musicals, classics, and revivals.

But Landesman did underscore an essential point when he wrote that the resident not-for-profit theatres in New York City are "often better at commercial producing than some of us veteran Broadway producers."[15] They have been more successful in recent years in producing new straight plays on Broadway than their commercial counterparts, who are less likely to take a chance on works that have not previously displayed the potential for a commercial run. Manhattan Theatre Club's Grove said that when his theatre produced Terrence McNally's *Love! Valor! Compassion!* on Broadway in 1995, there was not another new straight American play running there.

That show was produced under the old Broadway Alliance, the much-heralded but ultimately unsuccessful attempt to define a place on Broadway for the development of new straight plays and to fill those less desirable theatres that often remained dark. After years of negotiations, the League and the unions devised a scheme in which each of the major theatre chains would identify one "endangered" theatre as an Alliance house and would charge not rent but expenses and a royalty for that production. All involved were to work for lower than normal fees and salaries, shows would be less opulently produced, marketing budgets had to adhere to a cap, and ticket prices would be lower as well. The plan was developed in the late eighties and early nineties, at a time when owners were much more inclined to make concessions to see their theatres lit. According to League president Jed Bernstein,

> Part of the problem, specifically in a marketing sense, was that the Broadway Alliance never had a clear objective. Some people believed that it was about producing shows that would otherwise go un-produced. Others believed it was about presenting dramas, as opposed to musicals, to economically challenged audiences, i.e., lower the ticket price and presumably tickets are more accessible. However, when you lower the ticket price, thereby lowering the grosses, you put more cost pressure on the producers. The whole process becomes self-defeating, because in the end, the plays can't get produced.

The unions greeted the concessions demanded by the producers with little to moderate enthusiasm. But as Bernstein also pointed out, the consumer associated lower ticket costs with lower quality, instead of the chance to see "daring theatre at low prices." Edward Strong, a partner in the Dodgers, observed that the Broadway Alliance died from a lack of willingness on both sides to create viable concessions. "It sort of hand-cuffed the producer. There was a cap on what he could spend to market the shows. You built in the seeds of your own failure at the start." While a few shows were successful, the consensus among the industry was that the Alliance was the wrong approach to the longstanding problem of high costs. The production cap rendered shows too sparse, according to Shubert president Philip Smith. He indicated that audiences did not want to pay even these lower prices for a bare-stage production. The circum-stances that existed when the Alliance was developed have shifted to some degree, as producers like Daryl Roth, Roger Berlind, Carol Shorenstein Hays, and others have championed a number of straight plays on Broad-way, albeit usually in collaboration with a not-for-profit theatre.

Productions from the Public Theatre, Lincoln Center, Manhattan The-atre Club, and the Roundabout have moved to Broadway. For many years these theatres, other than Lincoln Center, whose shows at the Vivian Beaumont have been Tony-eligible for some time, would pursue one of two strategies. They could transfer a show after its limited run in the not-for-profit Off-Broadway or LORT home theatre to a commercial Off-Broadway contract in a rental house or to the higher-paying Production contract on Broadway, either as sole producer or, more common, with commercial partners. Another approach would be to collaborate, from a project's inception, with a commercial producer. The show, like Man-hattan Theatre Club's 1992 production of Alan Ayckbourn's comedy *A Small Family Business,* would be staged in a Broadway house from the start. Manhattan Theatre Club maintains a budget line that accommo-dates commercial Off-Broadway transfers but requires outside commer-cial enhancement money when it transfers a production to an indepen-dently owned Broadway theatre. When a not-for-profit theatre receives a gift or endowment to fund a commercial transfer, the theatre eventu-ally reaps the benefits of the full profit, if any, as the Public did with *A Chorus Line* and the Roundabout with *Cabaret.* When the theatre seeks a commercial producing partner—or when a commercial producer pro-poses a transfer—a contract is drawn to provide income streams to both the investment partnership and the institution, which usually receives a percentage from the royalty pool.

But the Tony-eligible not-for-profit theatre with a permanent presence on Broadway is a recent phenomenon. Barry Grove, who has been the executive director of Manhattan Theatre Club since 1975, described the evolution, which underscores the high degree of change over just a few decades. In the late seventies and early eighties, several Manhattan Theatre Club shows were picked up by commercial producers.

> You basically were passive and you waited for someone to come. My job was to make sure that we got the best possible deal we could for the institution. But I didn't have to think beyond that. In the mid-eighties, something changed. [The company produced a string of hit straight plays] with rave reviews, and they were popular with audiences, and when they were over, they closed and nothing happened. The commercial producers had simply stopped knocking at the door. This was a period of time when the big megamusicals had taken over and it seemed as if the play was dead on Broadway. . . . Manhattan Theatre Club came to realize, after that string of shows, that we had to become our own commercial producers. By then, we had seen the effects of *A Chorus Line,* not so much in terms of how much money it made, but just in the notion of doing it yourself.

When a New York not-for-profit, with no commercial funding at the outset, produces a show that quickly becomes a critical and economic success, commercial producers will usually queue up to offer deals to the institution. In other cases, the commercial viability may be less immediately apparent, but the work's artistic potential is deemed worthy of future exploitation. Michael Bush, a former associate artistic director of Manhattan Theatre Club, indicated that such was the case with that group's production of *Proof.* "[Commercial producers] came forward because of what they felt was artistically the strength of the play. I don't think any of those producers signed on because they thought they were going to make money off of *Proof.* They signed on because they loved it and thought it deserved a future life, and wanted to be part of that." The show did excellent business on Broadway, repaid its investors, and provided Manhattan Theatre Club with additional income.

An open-ended run, in which the not-for-profit institution enjoys the full benefit of the profits, allows the theatre to exploit successful productions while maintaining the theatre's regular season offerings in their other spaces. Some not-for-profit productions presented on Broadway are initially conceived as coproductions with commercial producers and are staged at Broadway theatres to exploit anticipated high ticket sales. This scheme, utilized by Manhattan Theatre Club for such shows as *The Weir*, *The Piano Lesson*, and *King Hedley II* both allowed their subscribers the opportunity to buy reduced-rate tickets for the Broadway productions and generated income for the institution. According to Michael Bush, commercial producers embrace this approach because the theatre's subscriber base offers strong and steady ticket sales in what can be a low-income preview period. Richard Frankel, who coproduced *The Weir*, agreed that it was a valuable partnership. "We made a deal with them whereby they sent their subscribers. It was a huge group sale, a twenty-thousand-person group sale. We sold them tickets for all of their subscribers at a reduced rate, but what it meant was that we got through previews and two months running guaranteed that we wouldn't lose money."

Barry Grove tried to frame the merits of not-for-profit and commercial partnerships within a numerical perspective. "In the end, the number of not-for-profit-originated shows that actually become commercial transfers, let alone commercial hits, are still a tiny percentage of the overall output of work that the nonprofit theatre creates. I don't think it's going to be the tail wagging the dog." Manhattan Theatre Club recently acquired its own Broadway theatre, the Biltmore, which minimizes the company's need to rent a Broadway house for transfers or coproductions. It also allows them to enjoy parity with Lincoln Center and the Roundabout, whose spaces are Tony-eligible.

When the Vivian Beaumont Theater is occupied by a hit show whose run Lincoln Center decides to extend, the organization does periodically mount its season's next production in a Broadway theatre but under its not-for-profit status. *Contact*'s run at the Beaumont required Lincoln Center to produce off-site on Broadway, a trend that started in 1989 when the Beaumont was long occupied by *Anything Goes*. Bernard Gersten explained that a determining factor was the unique thrust stage of the Beaumont; some plays work well in that environment and do not adapt easily to the traditional proscenium stage of most Broadway houses.[16] There are rare instances in which Lincoln Center will partner with commercial producers, as it did with *Carousel* and the *Contact* national tour. An earlier, self-produced tour of *Anything Goes* lost a substantial amount of money, so the board decided to minimize their risk exposure on subsequent tours and entered into a partnership with SFX and Scott Nederlander.

The Broadway presence of the not-for-profits may antagonize some commercial producers, but artists are attracted by the chance to develop their work in a less pressurized environment. John Weidman, a playwright whose credits include several collaborations with Stephen Sondheim, wrote the book for the hit dance-theatre musical *Contact*. The show was originally workshopped at Lincoln Center before successive productions in its Off-Broadway Mitzi E. Newhouse Theater and the Vivian Beaumont. The creation of *Contact* in such a manner would have been impossible in the commercial world

> because what this show became was what it evolved into while we made it up and worked on it in a rehearsal room, having been told by [Lincoln Center artistic director] André Bishop and Bernie Gersten that there was no audience of any kind that we needed to satisfy . . . and I don't just mean the people in their seats. I mean producers, or investors, or anybody else. We were doing what we wanted, and we made discoveries about what we were doing as we went along, *because* we were doing what we wanted. . . . If we had developed the show differently it still might have been good, but it never would have been what *Contact* became.

While the not-for-profit's ability to nurture new works is attractive to writers and directors, inequities exist for members of other unions. Equity's Alan Eisenberg identified an area of great concern to his union's membership. Salaries at LORT theatres, except for LORT-Broadway shows, are much lower than those of commercial productions on Broadway. A typical actor salary at a midrange LORT theatre (a determination made by Equity based on box office grosses over several years) is about $650 a week, whereas on Broadway the current actor's minimum is double that—a sensible formula, as LORT ticket prices outside New York are at least half the cost of Broadway tickets. Although most LORT shows run only four or five weeks, after a new play or musical opens, the cast can spend ten hours a week for four weeks honing and refining the material for no extra salary. This rehearsal time affords the creators the chance to further craft the show, which is part of the not-for-profit's original mission. In cases in which commercial enhancement money is involved, however, this period allows producers a much-needed, inexpensive source of professional developmental talent. But if the production eventually moves to Broadway, the actors usually have no contractual guarantee that they will go with the show. Eisenberg said,

> They're using all of that time to rewrite the plays, so you're in rehearsal all the time, earning . . . six hundred . . . dollars a week, and you're really preparing for the next production, which is a commercial production. And there seems to be no acknowledgment of that for the actor in terms of compensation, besides the fact that they're being paid too little anyway. And the position of the industry is "What are you talking about? What are you complaining about? The actor has a job." So they've got a job at a LORT theatre, where they're working a lot of hours to enhance a commercial production, and if they're good and they're lucky and they're talented, they get the job on the Production contract. Everybody has to look at this from their own point of view, but that seems like a very disheartening approach.

Actors, he said, are in a real sense investors in the production, uprooting themselves and relocating to another city for ten or more weeks, working for scale, and servicing the vision of the creators and commercial producers. When he articulated that notion at a Production contract negotiation in the late nineties, he was met with firm resistance from League negotiators. Equity was able to write a clause that allows actors who participate in a LORT production to receive a small bonus of about one thousand dollars should a Broadway transfer recoup 125 percent of its costs—a very small amount that is statistically likely to be generated in fewer than one in seven transfers. Equity members resent the fact that while they receive standard LORT compensation for these pre-Broadway tryouts, which includes housing but no meal expenses, New York–based stagehands who have been brought to the theatre to oversee the technical elements are paid two to three times as much, plus per diem. It is unlikely, in light of the historical power balance among Equity, LORT, and the League, for a substantial change to be effected. In an acknowledgment of market realities, however, actors at the three Tony-eligible LORT theaters in New York City are paid a salary approaching that in the commercial production contract.

Broadway offers artists not only more money than an out-of-town LORT theatre but also greater visibility for the work. As veteran lyricist Sheldon Harnick put it, "At best, it's hard to make a living. The importance of Broadway to a playwright or composer or lyricist is not just a platform where his work will be done with great technical skills and the best performers, orchestra, and so forth. If you have even a modest hit on Broadway, then you are financially set so that you can continue to be a writer, and not have to do other things to support yourself." Theatre artists support the ideals of not-for-profit theatre, but the recognition and remuneration from a Broadway production is unparalleled. A success in a not-for-profit theatre may be gratifying, but it can take a string of productions around the country to equal the visibility and financial rewards available on Broadway. For many artists, an ideal scenario occurs when their work is produced by not-for-profit Broadway institutions. They can focus on the show's development rather than respond to the tension between the institution and a commercial producer with differing agendas and intentions. John Weidman described his very fruitful collaboration with Susan Stroman as they developed *Contact* for Lincoln Center. The show took an ideal path from conception to realization.

[André] Bishop was a fan of Susan Stroman's. . . . He called her and said, "I would like you to develop a piece. I would like to give you my building to work on something. It can be anything you want." She called me, and we talked and then we . . . had a meeting with André, and he gave us the basement rehearsal room for eight weeks. At the end of the eight-week period, Stro showed him what we had, which became the second act of the piece. And at that point, André and Bernie [Gersten] could have done anything with it, or nothing. What they said was, "We'll [produce] this." Stro and I were not aiming for a production—not at the Beaumont, the Newhouse, or anyplace else. It was like we had been given permission to play around in the building. And when André and Bernie saw that piece, they said . . . , "We could do it at the Newhouse, as is." But Stro and I had already started to think of a first act for it, and so we then workshopped that, and it was scheduled to run for two months in the Newhouse. It got fabulous reviews. . . . Stro and I were thrilled that that had happened, that we'd gotten a production. The Newhouse is just a great Off-Broadway house, and we'd gotten a production at the Newhouse, [and] everybody thought that was that.

That's a theatre fulfilling its mission. Here was an artist that André Bishop liked, and he thought that it would be useful, instead of having her simply continue to do numbers for Broadway musicals, to see what she would come up with if she was turned loose on her own. The fact that *Contact* became a big Broadway musical was a pure accident and still seems amazing to me. Not even in the kind of what-if discussions that you have over a drink after rehearsals did Stro and I ever imagine that the show would wind up having the kind of life that it had. . . . And it all happened really fast. That was the other thing that was nice about it. We did the first workshop in January 1999, and we workshopped the first act in June of '99, and then it opened at the Newhouse in the fall of '99, so we did the whole thing quickly. It closed in January of 2000 and reopened two months later at the Beaumont.

Contact's genesis is not unheard of in the annals of not-for-profit development of new work—Michael Bennett enjoyed similar support from Joseph Papp when he began his workshop investigations into the lives of dancers that would become *A Chorus Line.* The absence of a commercial producer's timetable allowed the institution to proceed at a pace that served its needs and those of the artists. *Contact* played at the Beaumont for the remainder of its run of almost two and a half years, because it was in the production's best interests to perform in the thrust theatre for which it was staged. The Beaumont's eligibility for the Tony Award assured that the show would compete with commercial Broadway musicals. Other shows in the Lincoln Center season were produced off-site, in rented Broadway theatres, but remained solely Lincoln Center properties. "We have had plays that have run open-ended at the Beaumont over the years. The most notable were *Anything Goes,* as well as *Six Degrees of Separation* and *Contact,* . . . and *Carousel* and *Arcadia.* When that has happened, we have done the Beaumont season in other theatres, usually on Broadway, and we've referred to [it] as the Beaumont Season on Broadway," said Bernard Gersten. He emphasized that the productions mounted on Broadway by Lincoln Center, such as *Speed-the-Plow, Mule Bone, A Delicate Balance, Chronicle of a Death Foretold,* and *Thou Shalt Not,* were totally financed by Lincoln Center, without partnership. The benefits are obvious—Lincoln Center receives all the profits and maintains complete control over the show's artistic content.

Both not-for-profit and commercial sectors exist in a cultural and economic climate radically different from that of forty years ago. Time and the ever-changing zeitgeist have occasioned the evolution of the noble experiment of the regional and alternative theatre movements. No longer can these institutions rely on the good graces of government support, as the current political climate has bred a palpable and disturbing distrust of anything that smacks of intellectual elitism. The NEA, never a well-funded organization in its glory days, has had its budget reduced repeatedly. State arts councils are similarly challenged, and many have shut down completely for lack of funding. Beyond the bleak financial landscape, however, lies the question of artistic soul and spirit. As not-for-profit theatres have partnered with commercial producers, the iconoclasm and idealism of the not-for-profit movement have eroded. The pervading attitude may have been sanctimonious at times, but the movement birthed a unique way of looking at professional theatre as an organic and constant ingredient in the lives of Americans around the country. Jack Viertel's argument about the middle-of-the-road sensibility of many regional theatres is valid, but these theatres also produced important work that would have been fiscally or aesthetically untenable in a commercial run. Now, while not-for-profits continue to produce good work without the aid of commercial producers, the air of artistic insouciance and indomitability that defined the previous generation has been replaced by one of guarded caution and deflated expectations, as theatre leaders wonder what might lead to a future commercial success. Rocco Landesman may be stretching the point an inch or two when he noted in his *Times* article that "far too many nonprofit theatres chase a decreasing pool of dollars, and theatre companies everywhere are choosing plays and musicals with an eye towards a Broadway transfer,"[17] but he was nonetheless accurate in portraying the current atmosphere of quiet desperation that swirls around the not-for-profit movement. With diminished financial support, theatre boards can tolerate much less experimentation if it does not translate into box office revenue. This raising of the financial bar has resulted in the firing of more than a few artistic directors and the disillusionment of many artists.

What bears scrutiny is that a large segment of the commercial producing world today comprises émigrés from the not-for-profit world, but the tide has not flowed noticeably in the opposite direction. The reason is less, perhaps, the siren song of Broadway than the frustration of toiling in an environment in which the work is increasingly eclipsed by cap-in-hand importuning of every possible funding source. By comparison, Disney is able to subsidize the long-range development of new works. If the work can be done more effectively in an arena in which funding is available, artists will gravitate there.

The effect of the growing interdependence between the two worlds is less pernicious for Broadway than for the not-for-profit sector. The costs of producing tryouts on the road forced producers to discover alterna-tive means of developing works. What better way than to turn to theatres not only where it is less expensive but also where new works are accepted and expected? Broadway producers argue that a stronger relationship will breed greater health and vitality for both movements. Elizabeth McCann, a veteran Broadway producer, warned at the ACT II conference, "We are going to need to work together because in the end the stronger Broad-way is, the more it will help [the not-for-profit theatres]."[18] That remains to be seen. The influx of commercial money will keep a few not-for-profit theatres solvent, but other methodologies need to be identified if the not-for-profit movement as a whole is to be invigorated by its relationship with Broadway. The ACT II conference was perhaps a first step in the discussion of how to cross the philosophical divide for the greater good of theatre in America—a discussion that must continue with vigor and commitment on both sides.

5 The Money Song

It gets hard to make your money back. . . . Money is harder and harder to raise.
  —Rocco Landesman, CEO, Jujamcyn Theatres

The obvious initial decisions that a producer faces are what to produce and where to produce it. Who generates the idea for a production, and where do producers discover material? As Helen Hayes Theatre owner and producer Martin Markinson noted, "I believe there are three ways to produce a show. One is to run around the country or to London when you hear about something that's really good, lift it, and decide to produce it and bring it in to New York. The second way to produce a show is to find a script and take it from the page onto the stage. Quite frankly, that's the most exciting way for me. . . . The third way is to dig deep into your past plays. . . . That's why you have so many revivals." A producer may commission a work, choose one that has been submitted by writers or their agents, or transfer or develop a show from another venue. Producers attend theatre at every level, from fringe festivals to the cream of regional theatres and Off-Broadway, and reading new scripts is essential. According to Jane Harmon, "The main thing is coverage. We cover everything. We read, if we're not there in person. We're reading constantly." Her colleague Nina Keneally added, "It's networking, too, because even things we may not necessarily read, with the other not-for-profits and producers we have contact with, we share information, if they are reading things."

Producers try to work on pieces that excite them, to which they can commit over the long and arduous process, but commercial viability is a sizable determinant as well. As many producers have noted, they are sometimes attracted to plays that they would not attempt on Broadway. For years producers have tried to read the tea leaves to discern what material was likely to succeed. No one could have predicted that an evening based on Ovid's tales could make for attractive Broadway fare, but *Metamorphoses* did quite well; there was general consensus that *Seussical* would be a surefire hit, yet it failed to find a Broadway audience. As Edward

Strong has pointed out, the Broadway audience today is much less elite than it was a few decades ago, and the shift in demographics from New York–centric to tourist has occasioned a sea change in the nature of work produced. "If you look at the [chain] stores on Forty-second Street, I think that Broadway theatre in some way resembles those stores, rather than a literary pinnacle that it may have represented before." Strong pointed to the evolution of audiences and noted that those for straight plays are shrinking. "In a purist, capitalist sense, the people making the product had to find some way to make a product that there was an audience for." He referred to the family fare that abounds on Broadway today and added, "There may be too much of this stuff, and we'll start to cancel out the other. I do really think it bears considering whether we're close to some sort of saturation point in the market, that there's only so much our industry can see. And all these shows doing big grosses, which they need to do in order to get their money back—how much can the market really bear?"

As Marty Bell remarked, many of the great musicals of the twentieth century were originally conceived by producers. He reminisced about the heyday of the producer-as-creator. "Merrick, Prince, Cy Feuer, Robert Whitehead, Kermit Bloomgarden—that whole gang had originated shows." But as teams of producers became necessary to raise money, individual taste was superseded by that of the committee. Bell's goal was "to get that back. My process is to come up with an idea for a show. Doing *Ragtime* was something I wanted to do from the day I read the book. *Seussical* was an idea I got because my kids were sitting on my lap and I was reading Seuss books and I thought, 'You could put all the stories together into one musical.' So my process was to come up with an idea for a show, and then carefully assemble the best team to do it."

An idea for a show is only one—albeit significant—step in the process; having the producing fortitude and wisdom to oversee the work is another. David Merrick, for all his fabled rage and storied imbroglios with his employees and artists, conceived shows like *Gypsy* and *Hello, Dolly!* In both instances, Merrick had to secure the rights to the underlying work (to Gypsy Rose Lee's memoirs and Thornton Wilder's *The Matchmaker*) and hire the creative teams. Rocco Landesman, while driving home from a concert by one of his favorite artists, Roger Miller, had the epiphany that a marriage between Miller and the great American novel *Huckleberry Finn* might produce a lasting work of musical theatre. *Big River* was the result of his years of labor, which included the arduous task of persuading Miller to compose it (along with librettist Bill Hauptman) and overseeing the evolution of the work through two regional productions before bringing it to Broadway, where it won seven Tony Awards in 1985.

None of this work overshadows the contributions of the writers themselves. The writer might be commissioned by a theatre or a producer, but typically the creative spark is the author's. In every instance a producer must provide the means to realize in concrete form what is on the page. The writer must cede some control to a producer, whose artistic vision may vary from his or her own. Rodgers and Hammerstein realized that the best way to maintain control over their shows' destinies and earn even greater income from their productions was to produce themselves, but this decision was made later in their careers when they were established as Broadway's preeminent writing team. Forging a relationship between writer and producer is essential but not always easy. For Gregory A. Kotis, the librettist and co-lyricist of *Urinetown,* which was initially produced as part of the New York Fringe Festival,

> the process . . . was an adventure. It began when the Araca Group approached us with the prospect of putting together a backers audition for the show, and it's still going on. Our background was mostly in way-downtown theatre, or the world of fringe theatre in Chicago. When we started working with the Araca Group, and then Dodger Theatricals, much of the thrill was about not having to do everything ourselves, and also that things that were being done so effectively and professionally.

The three lead producers of the Araca Group, which took up the producing reins after the Fringe Festival,

> were involved creatively . . . giving us plenty of feedback on the material as well as being present to collect the creative team and hire the actors. The Dodgers joined us after the backers audition; they were equally involved. I think *Urinetown* was an exciting challenge for both groups, and I think they enjoyed participating in making creative decisions as much as we did. Since this show was a real discovery, it was also an opportunity to shape it in ways they probably couldn't with known pieces, or known talent.

Kotis offered a crucial authorial observation about producers as they nurture new works. "I think the extent to which a producer is or isn't creative has to do with what's on their plate, whom they're working with, what they're working on, and at what point in their career they are. What-ever discussions they had with each other, they always presented a common front to us. Generally, they challenged us to make the show leaner, faster, funnier, and better." This example represents a fortuitous relation-ship on all fronts; other productions have suffered because creative art-ists and producers find little commonalty. In the case of *Seussical,* though, that commonalty was undermined by a lack of cohesion among the pro-ducers themselves.

In some instances a show will take an even more circuitous route from conception to execution. Frank Wildhorn, the composer of several Broad-way musicals, has a simultaneous career as an extraordinarily successful composer, producer, and arranger of popular music. When he was a stu-dent at the University of Southern California in the late seventies, he visited New York and saw productions of *Sweeney Todd* and *Dracula,* which inspired him "at four o'clock in the morning on a rainy night, to come up with the idea to write *Jekyll and Hyde.*" After he enjoyed suc-cess writing for and producing an album by Whitney Houston, he was introduced to the veteran producer Hilly Elkins, who brought lyricist Leslie Bricusse into the project. About the same time, Wildhorn met singer Linda Eder, now his wife, and realized that "this talent needs a record deal," so she cut a demo disc of songs from *Jekyll and Hyde.* RCA was sufficiently impressed with the material that it signed Eder and re-corded an album of music from the as-yet unproduced show. Subse-quently, the not-for-profit Alley Theatre produced the musical in its first incarnation, and Texas-based PACE then entered the picture as the pri-mary commercial producer. The album sold well, singers such as Sammy Davis Jr. and Liza Minnelli recorded material from the show, and songs were featured at the Super Bowl and the World Cup. "The songs were everywhere," said Wildhorn, "which of course started a whole philoso-phy for me about how to do this for future productions, how to try to make that bridge between the music industry, which can get a song out around the world in a day, and the theatre industry, which thinks so dif-ferently, one theatre at a time." PACE produced a high-profile national tour, which led to the Broadway production.

In other instances a writer will approach a producer to gauge interest in a piece. In the early seventies, playwright John Weidman (whose fa-ther Jerome had written the books for the musicals *Fiorello!, Tenderloin,* and *I Can Get It for You Wholesale*), while still a law student at Harvard, wrote to the legendary producer and director Harold Prince, whom he had met once as a child, asking for a job. Weidman included a postscript in his letter, informing Prince that he had an idea for a show about the opening of Japan in the 1850s. Prince responded that he was interested. At the time, said Weidman, Prince and Sondheim were "riding high; they had done *Company* and *Follies* and *Night Music*. . . . The notion of doing a major musical that used Japanese theatrical techniques with a cast of Asian actors that nobody ever heard of before . . . I've often said that this was a combination of courage and arrogance on Hal's part that you would have not found in anyone else. . . . He believed in what he believed in and then believed in putting it on stage." The result was *Pacific Overtures*. Prince's sharp sense for what makes an exciting musical was honed by work on both sides of the footlights, as producer and then producer-director, and is unique in modern Broadway history.

Sometimes the idea for a work springs from a director or choreographer. *West Side Story* was in large part the creation of Jerome Robbins; Bob Fosse was the driving force behind the development of *Chicago,* and Michael Bennett's initial impulse to investigate the lives of dancers evolved into *A Chorus Line.* In each case, a supportive producer was involved. The director and choreographer Robert Longbottom conceived of a musical based on the life of conjoined twins, the Hilton sisters, after seeing a B movie about their lives. He enlisted playwright Bill Russell and, subsequently, composer Henry Krieger as collaborators. After several years of work, they held a reading. Producer Emanuel Azenberg responded with enthusiasm, according to Longbottom. "He became infected with it, like the rest of us; he loved the concept of my production and the large metaphor as well. He got it. The support he gave that show and me, making my Broadway directorial-choreographic debut, was incredibly generous. Everything we needed, we had. And you listened to Manny because he knew what he was talking about in terms of the book and the process. I learned a lot from him." In some cases, a producer's artistic input is essential; in others, his greatest contribution may be the wisdom to let the artists craft the piece alone.

In the event that a play or musical is to be adapted from other sources—and the large number of musicals, and some plays, are adaptations—the rights to the underlying work must be secured. Works in the public domain rarely present an obstacle, but much source material is protected by copyright, and identification of the owner can take considerable investigation. Disney has been able to capitalize on its vast film holdings, although at times the corporation will produce material whose rights are held by others. Disney's desire to control the rights to its works is essentially a given in Hollywood, and the studio brings that sensibility to the theatrical arena. Once Disney owns the material, it retains control of all self-produced and licensed opportunities of the property as a musical.

When institutional theatres select a show, there is an additional concern about how the work relates to the rest of the season. While a board of directors is usually consulted for final approval, as the Roundabout's Todd Haimes put it, "it's ultimately a very personal decision. You live or die on the taste of whoever is making the decision, and it probably shouldn't be made by committee, which is not to say that I don't welcome input . . . [but] somebody has to make the decision, and go with it, and that's me. I feel comfortable with that role." Haimes's involvement in selecting material has had a dramatic effect on the mission of the Roundabout, a theatre that once was dedicated to revivals. Although revivals still fill an important role in the theatre's mission and make up a sizable portion of each season, since 1996 the company has commissioned new plays. This blend of straight and musical, old and new, has served the Roundabout well, as it has expanded onto Broadway in the last few years.

A producer must decide whether Broadway is the appropriate venue for the work. Off-Broadway presents a viable and sometimes attractive alternative, especially for straight plays that may have a better chance to succeed in the smaller houses found there. The most persuasive arguments are the costs and the audience-performer dynamic. Roy Gabay, whose production of *Wit* enjoyed a lucrative and critically heralded Off-Broadway run, indicated that deciding the appropriate venue can be difficult. "There have been shows in the past that I brought to Broadway that I would have brought to Off-Broadway, and vice versa. I think [*Wit*] would have been successful on Broadway but would not have had the financial success that it ultimately had Off-Broadway. The only thing more we could have gotten if we were on Broadway was a Tony Award. On Broadway it wouldn't have run as long." Daryl Roth, whose Off-Broadway work includes *Wit* and Edward Albee's *Three Tall Women,* considered that it was time, in the late nineties, to return the straight play to its rightful place on Broadway. She believed that the good fortunes of shows like David Hare's *The Blue Room* opened the door to transfers of *Proof* and *The Tale of the Allergist's Wife.* Roth identified the slow equalization of financial factors as another determinant. The expenses of producing Off-Broadway have escalated in recent years; it can cost only an additional three or four hundred dollars to produce a small-cast straight play on Broadway.

But the pendulum swings swiftly in New York theatre, and in the recent season of 2002–3, only a small handful of straight plays opened on Broadway; most commercial straight works were produced Off-Broadway. Musicals have flourished Off-Broadway, although they are invariably of smaller scale and often more stylistically daring than their Broadway counterparts; Alan Menken and Howard Ashman's *Little Shop of Horrors* was an impressive hit for David Geffen and the Shuberts in an Off-Broadway venue when it first opened. While they had ample opportunity to transfer it, they believed that its simple production values, small cast, and downtown sensibility worked more effectively in its intimate Off-Broadway house. Had they made the move to Broadway, they would have had to expand the visual scope, and the show's charms would have been compromised. The Broadway revival in fall 2003 received poor reviews in large part due to the expansion of the physical production that sapped the intimate pleasures from the work.

Producers not infrequently have chosen Broadway as the appropriate venue and have been mistaken in their assumption that shows could work in larger theatres. The Ed Kleban musical *A Class Act,* staged first at Musical Theatre Works and later at Manhattan Theatre Club, moved to Broadway's Ambassador Theatre in 2001. The show was favorably received in its first two incarnations, and the producers were optimistic about its chances on Broadway. Despite a strong score by the late lyricist of *A Chorus Line* and a talented cast and inventive production, the intimate show about Kleban's artistic dreams and personal demons failed to find a Broadway audience. Several of those involved with the show were impressed by the producers' keen desire to make the show work but confessed that it probably would have done so more effectively in a commercial Off-Broadway run. There was much dismay when the show failed, as many Broadway practitioners watched it carefully to see whether success might mark a reversal in the trend toward more expensive and lavish productions.

Once the work is secured and the venue determined, financing becomes the crucial issue for producers. Corporate producers working alone will usually have the money in place at the start, but independents almost always need to raise the capitalization. In simpler financial times, the standard for producing was the limited partnership, in which one or more producers would act as the general partner or partners and seek funding from investors, or limited partners (the term *angel* being common parlance for decades). An investor's liability was limited to the amount of the investment, and the general partner bore all financial and legal responsibility. Additionally, the investors were liable for taxes only once if profits were paid; corporate profits are liable twice, on initial earnings and on dividends to stockholders. In a pure scenario—which occurred rather infrequently—the producer would receive a modest weekly fee, usually a small percentage of operating profits, but would not make any significant money until after recoupment. During the first phase of a show's life—sometimes its only phase, if it does not recoup—when its weekly operating profits are largely applied to paying back investors and the royalty pool, producers would not earn anything else unless they had invested themselves. After recoupment the producers would begin to earn more sizable income, as they and the investors would share in a fifty-fifty split of all weekly net profits remaining after the royalty pool was reimbursed. In some instances during the preproduction or rehearsal phase, the producers would discover that the show was underbudgeted. While there was a mechanism in some contracts that could be exercised to require an extra investment from the limited partners, most producers lately have opted not to utilize this "overcall." Producers who needed more money could not legally sell extra percentage points of the initial capitalization, as that would dilute the original investors' guaranteed returns. Instead, they would have to sell off portions of their own 50 percent of the eventual profits to lure more capital.

Producers are not required by law to invest in their own shows, and for many years several astute producers followed that rule. Today, though, some find that they need to invest to demonstrate good faith and their belief in the economic viability of the show. The partnership is formed around the core calculation of each producer's ability to fund a specified percentage of the capitalization. Some producers will commit to raise a portion of that money from investors and make up the remainder with their own. One veteran Broadway producer observed that "there are a lot of producers who never put up one penny of their own money. I get a little resentful about these guys," because they participate in the general partners' profits without risking their own capital.

In the late seventies, the LLC, or limited liability company, replaced the limited partnership as the producing method of choice. According to attorney Seth Gelblum, "The LLCs are pass-through tax entities. The managing members have no personal liability and effectively as much control as the general partners of a limited partnership. [LLCs are] the final culmination of a movement toward eliminating double taxation, providing a shield from liability, and giving complete control to the managers."

The financial challenge developed as more producers found it necessary to band together to raise money, thinning out their individual shares of their 50 percent of net operating profits. Three producers who split 50 percent would each receive 16⅔ percent of a show's profits; the more producers, the lower that percentage. Now producers have to create more inventive means of making enough money, money that in turn reflects their efforts on behalf of the show. The lead, or "torchbearer," producer—who identified the property, acquired the rights, and assembled the creative team—will sometimes take 5 percent off the top of the 50 percent, with all sorts of formulas applied to divide up the remaining profits. Before recoupment, however, when all net profits are used to pay back the investors, the only way for producers to make money is through participation in the royalty pool, but the water is getting shallower as the pool gets wider. Today not only do the creative artists participate but so do some major investors. The more producers, the smaller their individual portion of the producers' royalty from the pool, usually about 2 percent total to start. So producers have raised the amount they deduct from weekly operating expenses for office costs. Seth Gelblum believes that "it is one of the unfair anomalous things about the theatre. We have producers who will put in an enormous amount of time working on a show, and they're the ones who don't get a fee solely for producing." To compensate for this inequity, Gelblum said, producers must develop more creative ways to protect their dwindling percentage of the profits.

This is one reason that we have so few professional producers who can afford to pay their bills from theatre revenue, rather than wealthy people who made their money elsewhere. As a result, we see the invention of additional producer fees. I've seen "executive producer" fees and "marketing fees," which are kept by the lead producers alone to make up for sharing the royalty with so many other producers. Sophisticated authors will require that the operating expenses, for the purpose of calculating the profit pool, not include these fees, so they end up being borne by the investors. And certain producers have developed divisions to perform functions that the producer would otherwise have to hire an outside party to do, such as general management, tour booking, and merchandising, generating significant additional fees. All of these fees are fully disclosed to the investors, who accept them as necessary to induce producers to take on the job of mounting a production.

Some producers, however, preferring to keep their investors content in order to work with them on future productions, siphon off as little as possible before recoupment. A producer's approach in this matter is a function of both personal credo and personal finances.

Finding the money is the great test. Under current law, an unlimited number of accredited investors (corporations, trusts, or wealthy people) and up to thirty-five other individuals can all join in one production's investment pool under most producing structures. In the not-so-distant past, an individual of modest means who wanted to experience the peculiar thrill of participating in a Broadway show could invest a small amount, perhaps five thousand dollars. Aside from one or two producers today who raise money from a large pool of small investors, most have found that raising ten or twelve million dollars in small increments can be exhausting and untenable, and prefer to work with wealthy individuals who can afford to take a total loss on their investment. The most potent lure for an investor is a producer's track record. Barry Weissler said, "I have a core of investors. I pick up the phone and, for the last two years, I've been able to raise money with telephone calls. . . . There is a relationship to the success that I've delivered. [The investors] have made a lot of money with me. It's like a financial manager. You pick the right stocks, the people stay with you; you have a downturn, they run for the hills."

Once the money is in place, the relationship between the producer and the theatre owner takes center stage. The level of income a theatre owner can reap from a show can be formidable, and clauses in the rental contract allow an owner to evict a production should its gross box office receipts fall below a certain point for a specified number of consecutive weeks. Rental cost is frequently cited as one of the primary factors in the skyrocketing expenses of producing on Broadway. Playwright Arthur Laurents chaired a committee to investigate ways to expedite the production of straight plays on Broadway, and that group commissioned a management firm to study the issue. According to Laurents, the one cost that outstripped all others in growth rate was theatre rental. A survey conducted to examine the relative cost of each element involved in producing a show revealed that theatre rental had ballooned more than any other, a 432 percent increase during the previous ten years. In addition, advance ticket sale revenue is placed in the theatre owner's account, and the owner, rather than the producer, draws the interest.

Midtown real estate is such a lucrative investment, and theatres, especially dark ones, are so expensive to maintain, that the owners have at times seen fit to sell or use their theatres for other purposes. The venerable Mark Hellinger Theatre was leased by the Nederlanders to a church at a time in the eighties when theatre owners were searching for occupants. At one point, Gerald Schoenfeld considered leasing or selling the Shuberts' Longacre Theatre to the city for use as a municipal court, despite its landmark status. Currently, with all but a few of the commercial Broadway theatres controlled in part or fully by three theatre chains, much power is wielded by the three men who own or control the fates of the organizations: James Binger, James M. Nederlander, and Gerald Schoenfeld, men who, according to Jack Viertel, "come from the world where you rent your theatre to Hal Prince, and he takes the show out of town and brings it in. And they've lived to a great degree on the English megamusicals, which I think [are] really winding down at this point." Many question how the next generation of theatre owners will respond to the changing nature of Broadway.

Booking the appropriate theatre is both a financial and an artistic decision. The aesthetics and pragmatics of each house are markedly different, due to several factors: architecture; decor; seating configuration; size of stage, orchestra pit, and wings; number of dressing rooms; location; and number of seats. The newer theatres offer a very different ambiance from that of the older houses. Daryl Roth maintained that "the choice of a theatre is always about 'Will the play sit well there?' 'Is this the right match?' It's less about the producer than it is about the collaborative decision between the director, the producers, and the theatre owners, on behalf of the piece. It's really about that match." Producers will consider the input from the director and designers as to the aesthetic considerations, but the number of seats is a significant factor. More seats will likely correspond to higher rent, so a producer needs to be secure in his ability to fill them.

While most owners offer competitive deals to producers with attractive shows seeking a home, Bernard Gersten of Lincoln Center, who has negotiated with all three chains over the years for transfers of his shows, felt that "there is no general rule about the deals that landlords will offer for plays. The negotiation for theatres is always based upon the play itself, who the producers are, and whether it's a buyer's or seller's market."

He added that it usually makes no difference to an owner whether the production is commercial or not-for-profit. The desire of the Shuberts to house *A Chorus Line* was based on their perception that the musical could be a significant production for them. Realizing that the show was likely to be an unusually long-running one, they aggressively pursued the contract and even urged Papp, Gersten, and Bennett to book a larger theatre than they had first intended. An owner is more likely to offer a favorable deal to an established producer with a proven track record than to a newcomer, although an inexperienced producer with a desirable property from Off-Broadway or LORT might broker a reasonable agreement.

In a buyer's, or producer's, market, when theatres are plentiful and the number of new productions sparse, owners are inclined to offer more generous terms. At times owners have joined as coproducers to keep the theatres lit, a ploy that is necessary only when shows are scarce. Nick Scandalios of the Nederlanders said, "The best thing a producer could do is go to a theatre owner and not want any money from them, because everybody wants money. So, in a way, if you have two shows that are equal, and one wants half a million dollars, and the other doesn't want any investment from you at all, and you can rent the theatre, what would you do?"

When Rocco Landesman assumed the presidency of Jujamcyn in 1987, he adopted an aggressive posture as a producing owner, a maneuver necessary to keep his five houses occupied. As the smallest of the chains, Jujamcyn was liable to suffer a greater loss if any of its theatres was dark. Jack Viertel pointed to the time that they were able to lure August Wilson's *The Piano Lesson* to their Walter Kerr Theatre. Viertel was an enthusiastic admirer of the play in its not-for-profit run at the Yale Repertory Theatre; when he arrived at Jujamcyn in the late eighties, "one of the first things I did was to call [Yale Rep's managing director] Ben Mordecai, who I knew was producing it, and say, 'I love this play, and we have a house for you.' He said, 'Well, we've done all our other plays with the Shubert Organization. And they will have first crack at this one because we don't want to break up that relationship.'" But an appropriate Shubert house was not available, and the organization was unable to fund a significant portion of the capitalization costs, an essential ingredient for these producers. Viertel continued, "We were in a situation then, in 1989, when we were putting very substantial investments into shows. So we got a number of shows that other theatre owners were happy to provide theatres for, because we were willing to commit to actually produce them." The

Nederlanders' nine theatres and the Shuberts' sixteen and a half (they own half interest in the Music Box) allow them to weather becalmed booking periods with greater ease. According to Martin Markinson, owner of the independent Helen Hayes Theatre, "If you have an empty theatre, and all you want to do is book it, because it's very expensive to run when you're not booked, you take shows that you ordinarily wouldn't take."[1] The threat of an empty theatre is not, however, the only reason an owner invests in a production. On occasion, an owner participates in the production of an attractive property even if he must do it in someone else's house. Recently, the Shubert Organization was the lead producer of the comedy *Dirty Blonde* in Markinson's Helen Hayes Theatre, housed there because the producers determined that the small-capacity Hayes was the best venue for the intimate piece. At the same time, James M. and Scott Nederlander were among the producing team for *Copenhagen,* which played at the Shubert's Royale Theatre.

In times of theatre scarcity, when an owner must choose among several possible suitors, identifying a potential hit can be a challenge. Each owner seems to have his own divining rod, often in the personae of an in-house team of artistic advisers. Philip J. Smith, the president of the Shubert Organization, described their process.

[It's] based on the people in our play department who read the plays, Gerry Schoenfeld, who reads the plays. Obviously, the creative team that's involved with the play or the musical [is a factor]. Put quite simply, if Andrew Lloyd Webber writes a musical and comes to you, and Tim Rice has done the lyrics, you don't have to go into too much of an executive session to make a decision. Or if somebody who's a respected producer, like Cameron Mackintosh, comes with a project. If he feels strongly about it, you have a similar situation. You book it.

Nick Scandalios expanded on this. "It's a factor of the relationships, the creatives, and the least amount of dark time a theatre can have, because a dark theatre does nothing but cost money and not service the public. Dark theatres have no value; they are useless without shows in them. You weigh those components, but ultimately it has to do with who the producers are, how much you can trust them, what your long-standing relationship is with them."

In the seventies and eighties, Bernard Jacobs and Gerald Schoenfeld of the Shubert Organization were long held to be the true powers at the center of the League, given their control of the lion's share of Broadway houses and their producing and investing record. One League official observed that the union contract negotiations were for years driven by the Shuberts, whose interests did not always coincide with those of the producers. John Weidman, who is currently the president of the Dramatists Guild, agreed. "Conventional wisdom is that Bernie Jacobs essentially drove labor negotiations, and because the Shuberts were theatre owners, they were prepared in the end to give the unions almost whatever they wanted in order to keep their theatres lit, in order to avoid a shutdown." Now, say insiders, with the death of Jacobs and more shows on Broadway and in the production queue, the League's power base has consolidated in a core of producers. Marty Bell recalled that a gradual change occurred in the eighties, when the splinter faction, the Producers Group, formed. "We were all doing our first shows around then, and we felt that the theatre owners controlled the League, and we didn't have a voice. We were kind of the antiestablishment, and had meetings that started out as a secret, and then got into the *New York Times,* and it became a big issue. And I think we had an effect on business. Now, I guess we've become the establishment, and I wish someone else would become the antiestablishment. But we opened up the League more, got a lot of younger people on committees." Bell pointed to the owners' involvement in producing as the crux of the conflict, as this dual control of productions gave them considerable authority that eclipsed the will of the independent producers. Bell believed that at the time, an aura of invincibility surrounded the owners. "I think some of the theatre organizations thought that they could produce everything, and the era of the independent producer was over."

In recent years, when availability of houses is scarce, owners can command very high rents from producers, who usually pay for just about everything that transpires within—and often outside—the walls of the theatre.[2] In the seventies and early eighties, owners were often willing to accept their fee in the form of profit participation, rather than from the first dollar of gross receipts; if the show was marginal, so was their percentage. Now, as one insider put it, "That's gone with the wind." Typically, owners now demand 6 or 7 percent of the gross and an additional percentage of profits. While everyone else might have jumped into the royalty pool, owners can usually sit dry at poolside and earn their weekly percentage. This situation has irked producers, investors, and artists for years, especially as many of them are in thrall to the constraints of the royalty pools. Martin Markinson indicated that owners can make a sizable impact on the fortunes of a producer, especially when the show is running but not commanding exceptional business. In such circumstances, producers will often approach him and request that he take a cut in his percentage. "I'm not bound to, by contract. But I have rarely said no, unless I really don't want the show anymore. Normally, I work with the show to make the show work." Unless another, potentially more lucrative show is queued up, an owner will usually let a marginal show remain, as the owner's expenses are covered entirely by the production; he would have to cover those fixed expenses himself if the house was dark. As Markinson wryly observed,

> It's like the old theatre joke. A woman comes to the box office and asks if there are any tickets to the performance that night, and the box office treasurer says yes. She asks how much, and he says it's sixty-five dollars. She says, "Sixty-five dollars? Oh, my God, I can't afford sixty-five dollars!" So the treasurer shrugs his head and says, "I'm sorry, lady." Meanwhile, the owner is standing right there, and he asks, "Well, how much could you afford?" And she replies, "Fifteen dollars." So the owner turns to the treasurer and says, "Give her one of our fifteen-dollar seats."

James L. Nederlander described his company's policy toward shows that are struggling. "If you see the show is slowly sinking into the quicksand, and you don't see any rescue, we try to give them help, and we say, 'Look, we don't kick people out of our theatres.' But there is a time when you have to say, 'You guys are losing one hundred thousand dollars a week, are you sure you want to do this?' They may say yes, but if it's at a point where we've got another show coming in, it's not really productive for anybody, and most of the time, they get it."

Markinson observed that in periods in which theatres are scarce, the owner has more choices. "You weigh it on the basis of what you think is going to give you the most legs, what's going to sell the most tickets. If it's something that's never been done as opposed to something that's coming from London or from Off-Broadway, then of course you're going to go with the one that already proved itself. However, there are exceptions to the rule." The producers of the Off-Broadway hit *Wit* inquired about booking the Hayes for a Broadway transfer. With 597 seats, it is the most intimate Broadway house and a strong candidate to house a small-cast straight drama. But despite the show's ecstatic reviews, Markinson turned them down.

At the time, there were three or four shows that wanted the theatre. I thought the best show was *Wit*. My decision not to take it astounded a lot of people. I told the producers, "The show may be great where it is. I really believe it should be Off-Broadway. And if I were to produce it I would bring it to Off-Broadway. Because it will cost half the amount of money to run. If you're as good as I believe it is, you'll get the accolades." It is a show that is "iffy" for a multitude of people because of the content. I opted to go with another show that I thought would have had more legs. I was wrong in picking the show that I picked, because it didn't run.

Control of real estate equals control of a show's destiny. Disney and Livent realized that and wisely engineered deals for the New Amsterdam and the Ford Center. With theatres such valuable commodities, it remains to be seen whether any of the three chains will sell off any property. Few independent producers could afford the exorbitant price tag, however, and the producing corporations or other theatre chains would be the likely bidders.

Production expenses, of which theatre rent is only one line item, have a direct effect on ticket prices. The complex nexus of economic factors that has caused Broadway producers to charge up to one hundred dollars is the greatest concern for every sector of the industry, not the least of which is the audience. Thomas Schumacher pointed out, "The first thing people do when they bemoan the cost of producing shows is blame labor. And there are issues regarding labor that I think will ultimately get in the way of producing. But theatre rents are high, marketing costs are very high, and production costs are *really* high. When you think about the ratio of ticket prices to operating expenses, it's dramatically different today than it was for *Oklahoma!*" Budgets have escalated rapidly, outstripping inflation. The primary components of a Broadway production are responsible to varying degrees: salaries and fees, the expense of the physical production, rehearsals, theatre rent, and advertising and marketing. The corporations' apparent ability to address these costs with greater ease than independent producers contributes to the dismay with which many independents survey the landscape.

Each show's budget is markedly different, but the largest line items are typically the physical production and advertising. Together, they may account for as much as 40 percent of a show's initial budget, and while producers rail against rising prices in all areas of production, it is the cost of advertising that producers consistently decry. Production supervisor Peter Lawrence suggested, "Just look at the spreadsheet of a production. Look at what they set aside for advertising now. It's much more than 10 percent of the budget. And it never used to be that. I know producers are always blaming the unions, but union costs have come to something less than 8 percent of the overall budget." Advertising costs can also approach 20 percent of a show's weekly operating costs after opening.

The exorbitant price of spectacle can inflate the budget beyond the actual necessity of the production's design concept. On the fifteen-million-dollar musical *Sunset Boulevard,* written and produced by Andrew Lloyd Webber, Lawrence remembered that "at a production meeting, Lloyd Webber said, 'I had lunch with Billy Wilder today [who cowrote and directed the original film], and Billy Wilder said we have to have a car in the show.' And then we did. It was a $150,000 car." This sort of extravagant gadgetry notwithstanding, designers and directors can and often do demand exceptional attention to the smallest physical details to achieve the particular look they are seeking. But according to the former actor and producer, now a group sales executive, Ronald Lee, "To achieve opulence on a tight budget, that's genius. If you achieve opulence by spending twice what opulence should cost, that's not genius." Peter Lawrence added that a strong producer is sometimes able to countermand artistic whim and excess and maintain fiscal responsibility. But, he added, some producers do not have the expertise to determine how to keep costs down. In cases of overspending, Lawrence said, "I always blame the producer. There is no reason for a designer, given his or her head, to say, 'No, I'd rather spend fifty thousand dollars on a set than five million dollars on a set.' A designer can do more and it's more interesting to spend more money. They can do more gimmicks. It's up to the producers to say 'You can't do that.'"

According to scenic designer Robin Wagner, who has been working on Broadway for more than forty years, it was common years ago for producers to solicit director and designer input regarding their vision of the show's needs, but that generosity of spirit has faded over the years as costs have grown and producers have focused more on the their bottom line from the outset. Wagner noted, too, an evolution in the manner in which producers and general managers approach the bid sessions, at which production shops vie for the opportunity to build a set or costumes, or rent lighting or sound equipment. In years past, managers would genuinely consider all bids, and while price is always a compelling factor, the job might be awarded to a higher bidder because that shop could provide the best service. Today, said Wagner, pure finances drive the decisions much more frequently, and he attributes this change to a belief that many of today's producers and managers did not train in the commercial theatre. The need to keep costs down has, he said, created a scenario in which the bids for one set might be parceled out to six different scene shops, which is, he declared, ridiculous. "Nothing ever goes together until it gets onstage. And this is supposedly saving money. Well, it doesn't save a nickel . . . it doesn't save anything, because it never fits together, and you have to rebuild, and you have to make it fit." One stage manager recalled the load-in for the set of the musical *Big River,* in 1985, at the Eugene O'Neill Theatre.

> There was no room for a lot of the scenery in the small backstage area or in the fly space. Huge set pieces were strewn around the orchestra seats. Didn't anyone look at the theatre and realize that all this scenery would never fit? Some pieces were so large that they didn't fit through the loading doors, had to be cut up into pieces, brought into the theatre, and put back together, adding to labor costs. On every show certain scenery will get eliminated, because it just doesn't look right or the scene itself is cut. But there are too many instances of poor planning, and a lot of money is wasted.

Costs must be analyzed from the perspectives of both the initial capitalization, that is, the funds needed to mount the show and open it, and the weekly operating expenses incurred throughout the life of the show. As noted earlier, a large-cast musical spectacle can cost more than ten million dollars to mount and another five hundred thousand or more in weekly expenses. A smaller-cast straight play can cost two million, and considerably less to run, depending on the size of the cast and the star power (and salary demands) of its leads.[3]

Once a show is capitalized, the producers can begin in earnest the task of making theatre. Bonds are posted with the unions to begin casting and hiring. Designs are completed and bid sessions held. The theatre and rehearsal hall bookings are finalized, and the advertising campaign initiated. As the producer's and general manager's offices fall into the rhythms of putting the pieces of the production puzzle together, money is spent daily. From the date of the first rehearsal to opening night, assuming a show is opening directly in New York, about three months will elapse. Four or five weeks will be spent rehearsing the work. Rehearsals are held six days a week, usually in a rehearsal hall, as vacant Broadway theatres are generally far too expensive to rent for such purposes. The theatre that will house the show will itself be turned into a construction site as the design takes shape onstage. About two weeks are devoted to the painstaking process of technical and dress rehearsals, when the cast rehearses on the set with lights, sound, and costumes, and long days are devoted to focusing the disparate production elements into one coherent theatrical statement. Previews follow for a few weeks, and daytime rehearsals augment the normal eight-show performance schedule. It is then that rewrites, new staging and choreography, different technical maneuvers, and general performance polishing are effected. A few days before opening night, the show is "frozen," after which no significant changes are allowed, to give the production a chance to gel. No longer is opening night the stuff of old movies, in which the critics rush up the aisles after the final curtain in a mad dash to file their reviews in time for their deadline. Now, most critics attend the last few previews, as this allows them more time to craft their reviews.

Some capitalization costs will be used to offset initial expenses incurred by the producer, most notably the money needed to secure an option to produce the writer's work. The Dramatists Guild's Approved Production Contract (APC) is the most frequently used agreement that dictates payments for straight plays and musicals; when writers are not Guild members, producers will often use the contract as a model. The amounts initially paid to the writers are considered advances against royalties earned after the show recoups. If a show runs for years and generates a weekly royalty but never recoups, the writers keep their entire advance as well as all their royalty payments. A writer's option is currently set at eighteen thousand dollars for the first year, nine thousand dollars for the second year, and nine hundred dollars a month for the third year. Once the show is capitalized, he or she receives an additional sixty thousand dollars as an advance, although the initial option payment is applied against that, so the net advance is forty-two thousand dollars. If a show is under option for three years—and many shows today take that long or more to get produced—an author might make an average of just twenty-six thousand dollars a year before the show opens. Disney, like many movie studios, tends to offer a higher fee at the start of the project to compensate the author, or director, for developmental work. Disney, which will not reveal its fee structures, is reputed to pay lower royalties than some independent producers once the show is running. As the Dramatists Guild is not a union, it cannot mandate that writers employed on Broadway join it or that producers work as signatories to the contract. (Most of the major unions working on Broadway, however, can require union membership within thirty days of the start of employment.) This policy creates a reinvention of the wheel each time a producer negotiates with a writer, because there are no ironclad rules for advances and royalties as there are with the unions.

Recent legislation, however, would mandate changes in the way that the Guild and the League do business. A bill introduced in the U.S. House of Representatives by Barney Frank (Democrat of Massachusetts) and Henry Hyde (Republican of Illinois) and in the Senate by Orrin Hatch (Republican of Utah) and Charles Schumer (Democrat of New York) would modify existing antitrust legislation relative to the Guild. While it would not create a union, it would allow the Guild to enter into collective bargaining with the League. According to Guild president John Weidman, there is much need to revise the APC. Writers and producers, perhaps influenced by Hollywood studio control of scripts, have historically had contentious relationships. Weidman said,

> It's what distinguishes writing for the theatre from writing for television or movies, and although it's not fundamentally an economic issue, it's fundamentally an artistic issue. . . . I think we all believe that it is important to protect the unique, idiosyncratic voices of people who write for the stage; that regardless of what the dollars involved are, that copyright remains with the playwright, so that the theatre remains a place where Arthur Miller decides what happens to Willie Loman at the end of his play, as opposed to seven producers who feel that the show would run longer if it had a happy ending.

Producers were initially reluctant to negotiate with the Guild, citing those very antitrust laws as impediments. According to Weidman, "The only way to bring the producers back to the table was to do something that we had never done before, which was to go to Washington and get help. What this legislation would do is create a formal exemption to the antitrust law, which would authorize collective bargaining between playwrights as a group and producers as a group. The antitrust objection, which has been raised by the producers themselves, would be cleared away by this legislation." But several writers said they do not expect producers to support the bill, and cited the League's preference to avoid collective bargaining and revisiting the days when writer royalty models made it more difficult to recoup.

Weidman pointed out that because there has been no substantive change in the APC in almost two decades, the true inflationary labor factors are to be found in contracts with the unions, with whom the League is compelled to negotiate each time a contract expires. (Actors' Equity contracts, for example, expire every three years.) "The one group involved in a theatrical production who have remained outside the collective bargaining process are the playwrights. . . . When the producers come up for air, the only people they can turn to to try to make up their losses are the playwrights, and that's essentially what is happening," said Weidman. Producers, in turn, claim that writers can earn significant income from lucrative productions. Barry Weissler suggested that "successful writers on Broadway make far more than writers in Hollywood. Just look at the royalty section of any offering and think of a successful show, and multiply that by six hundred or seven hundred thousand a week, and look at fifty-two weeks against a million dollars that a writer gets in Hollywood. You'll find that the pay on Broadway is dramatic." The three writers of a musical (composer, lyricist, librettist) share equally in 15.56 percent of the profits before recoupment, slightly more after, against a guarantee of six thousand dollars a week. If a blockbuster generates five hundred thousand dollars over operating expenses, they each make about twenty-five thousand dollars a week, or $1.3 million a year. This might taper off slightly after the first couple of years, but over five years, a writer might earn five or six million dollars from a Broadway production alone; the national tour, international productions, and subsidiary rights will bring in even more. The chance to earn this level of income in royalties is one way in which theatre can be differentiated from the movie business, said Seth Gelblum.

The theatre is a back-end business, the opposite of the movie business. In the movie business, it's all up-front money. If the movie is a success or a failure, it doesn't make a difference, everyone got paid their fees. The back end is wholly illusory, unless you're a big star or big director. It doesn't matter how collegial they are, or how good their work is, they're paid the same amount of money. In the theatre, the front end is minimal. The back end can be very substantial, but only if the show works. The result of that is that it can be a lot more fun to work in the theatre. It's a lot more collegial business and everyone has to work together to make it work. The movie business tends to be more about the deal; the theatre business tends to be more about the show.

While theatre has always been known as the most collaborative of arts by virtue of its form, it is intriguing to think that this collaboration is in part fostered by the prospect of greater financial returns in the future.

The Society of Stage Directors and Choreographers' Broadway contract similarly demands a fee and an advance against royalties that together reach about fifty thousand dollars for a director on a musical; for a straight play that amount is slightly lower. A choreographer will receive about forty thousand, and a director-choreographer will receive an amount that is just under the total of the two individual fees. Royalty payments are mandated by the contract, but the amounts are minimums, and directors and choreographers with a proven Broadway track record receive considerably more than those. Producers can opt to pay directors and choreographers a lower percentage based on the gross or a higher percentage based on operating profits. Producers of musicals pay royalties based on operating profits, as those will likely never reach the level of pay based on the gross receipts, whereas producers of straight plays will usually opt to pay a royalty on the gross, as the weekly expenses will often be minimal and a profit payment could outstrip the gross payment. Some star directors of musicals may receive 5 percent or more of profits (twenty-five thousand dollars on a musical with a weekly net operating profit of five hundred thousand dollars), and those who collaborate with the writers to shape and nurture the show over months or years will often receive an additional royalty to reflect that work, as much as an additional 2.6 percent of profits.

Thirteen theatrical unions maintain contracts with the League, but aside from the writers, director, and choreographer, only the designers and the orchestrator, arranger, and musical director receive a weekly royalty (often a flat fee rather than a percentage).[4] Members of the other unions receive weekly salaries or hourly wages. There are exceptions; star actors may receive, in addition to their salaries, a royalty as a percentage of the gross. On one current musical, the star receives 7 percent of the adjusted gross if it reaches anywhere from six hundred to eight hundred thousand dollars, and eight percent if it exceeds that. A show with a gross potential of $1.2 million playing at 100 percent capacity at full price could generate twenty-six thousand dollars a week for the actor.

For producers the sticking points in labor negotiations are the number of union employees required and what producers view as excessively restrictive labor rules. The brouhaha over the minimum number of musicians, which resulted in a short strike in 2003, exemplified the strong antipathy between the producers and the unions. The rank-and-file membership of Broadway's unions frequently repeat the conventional wisdom that the corporate approach to producing is an attempt to eviscerate the unions and turn Broadway into an East Coast version of Las Vegas, offering bland but spectacular fare at ever-higher prices. The friction between labor and management has existed for many decades. The formation of Equity in 1913 was the result of powerful antiunion efforts by a coalition of producers, key among whom was George M. Cohan. Today both corporate and independent producers publicly aver that the unions are beneficiaries of too many antiquated employment perks and that costly featherbedding is endemic. The musicians' contract was the first to endure this latest salvo, but Equity and IATSE, the stagehands' union, have been similarly accused of contentious labor practices.

While the new house minimums for musicians, arrived at in 2003, were the result of a negotiated settlement, their reduction was viewed as a victory for the producers. The decision frustrated many on the artistic side. Robert Billig, a longtime musical supervisor and conductor for shows like *The Best Little Whorehouse in Texas, Les Misérables, Miss Saigon,* the revival of *Man of La Mancha,* and *Never Gonna Dance,* believed that the producers were too aggressive in the negotiations. A show like *Les Misérables,* Billig believes, would suffer greatly if it were produced today with the minimum number of musicians now required in a large Broadway house. The thinking that drove the establishment of minimums was not an arbitrary process but reflected a determination of the musical needs of the shows that would play those theatres. Before the advent of synthesizers, large-cast Broadway musicals required a large orchestra to provide the musical heft and texture envisioned by the composer and orchestrator. Today, *Les Misérables* would need to employ several synthesizers to make up for the loss of nine or more musicians, but the synthesizers would not compensate for the loss of texture and aural specificity. According to Billig, "The reason that doesn't work is number one, that's not really music. It's not a real instrument. A synthesizer can't really duplicate the sound of a bow hitting a string, the attack. You can do something like it; you can sample a sound and get something close to a sustained sound, but you're never going to get the attack of the bow on the string or a really good pizzicato. You can't replace real instruments." The League's Web site is entitled "Live Broadway," but the producers' willingness to employ virtual orchestras and more synthesizers makes a profound statement about "liveness."

It is to the producers' advantage to keep pressure on the unions in contract negotiations, but it will be difficult for the League to demand similar concessions from the actors or stagehands, as there is no obvious analogue to the use of virtual orchestras. Equity president Eisenberg observed that in the last Production (Broadway) contract negotiation with the League, while concessions were made on both sides on a number of issues, there was a change in the temperature of the proceedings. Management struck a more aggressive posture than that in past sessions, a change that might be attributable to the shift in power from the owners to the producers. League president Jed Bernstein attempted to put the issue of League-union negotiations into perspective. "They want more money, and we want more flexibility in getting the work done." He acknowledged that the specific issues may have changed, but the larger picture is much the same. Some union leaders fear that the producers are intent on weakening the power of the unions by adopting increasingly more intransigent approaches in negotiations and threatening nonunion productions. But one longtime producer argued that "there's a sense that we're always trying to beat them, that in fact producers somehow are hiding that they're making tons of money, and that we don't really care. And the really byzantine interpretations of the work rules by the IA [International Alliance of Theatrical Stage Employees] and the musicians' union, and the lack of willingness to come into the twenty-first century and have productive work situations, are very galling."

The stagehands' union has enjoyed perhaps the greatest success in maintaining the viability of its contract on Broadway. Many shows utilize a complicated two-pronged system of stagehand employment, in which a core group is hired by the producer as salaried employees (from any of more than six hundred locals of IATSE) who oversee the production's construction and ongoing physical and artistic welfare. Another, often larger group from Manhattan's Local One is hired by the theatre owner for hourly wages, although the money flows from the producer's accounts through the theatre owner's to the stagehands (and musicians and other theatre employees). This double hiring can cause a labor overlap that the producers sometimes characterize as featherbedding. Bizarre examples abound: an automated winch that controls a moving piece of scenery requires an operator to hit a "go" button but must be simultaneously operated by two stagehands, one each from the producer and theatre sides, to preserve the sanctity of both contracts. While producers have succeeded to some extent at pruning the more obvious examples of staffing excess, they hope to gain more concessions in future negotiations with IATSE. The union, however, has typically adopted a resistant stance in League negotiations.

When the costs of production are totaled, a producer must calculate the most effective strategy in determining ticket prices that will enhance a quick recoupment. Top tickets hover around one hundred dollars for musicals and seventy-five dollars for straight plays; producers never thought a few years ago that they would ever be able to—or need to—charge that much. Industry insiders question who will be the first to break through the psychological ceiling of the century mark and actually price tickets higher (a ticket to the 2000 revival of *The Iceman Cometh,* with Kevin Spacey, cost $120 due to the show's limited engagement and long nightly running time, which occasioned overtime payments).

Edward Strong sounded a worrisome note. He remembered that the Dodgers' first sizable Broadway venture, the 1985 musical *Big River,* was capitalized at $2.5 million, while their 2000 revival of *The Music Man* cost more than eight million. Neither show relied on lavish spectacle or employed big-name stars, and both were of similar size in cast and orchestra. In 1985 the top ticket price was forty-five dollars; in 2000 it was ninety. The production costs more than tripled while the ticket prices only doubled in that fifteen-year period. Strong noted that the discrepancy between production costs and ticket prices over a longer time span was even more striking; the 1992 Dodger revival of *Guys and Dolls* was about twenty times more expensive than the original 1950 production, whereas top tickets had multiplied by only a factor of nine. "An extrapolation would mean that you should charge about $130 just to keep pace. And obviously, nobody is going to do that. No one could. But it means that our task is ever more difficult, to have these huge capitalization costs and large running costs, to have to run for however many years just to get your money back." He assailed ticket brokers for making money, sometimes excessive amounts, on the face value of a ticket, easily charging three or four times the price for hard-to-get tickets for hit shows. The producer, he noted, sees only the face value of the ticket price and nothing more.

Shubert Organization president Philip J. Smith, whose long view in theatre finances goes back several decades, agreed with Strong. "If you don't raise the price, you're not going to recoup." Smith pointed to the direct and pernicious correlation between higher ticket prices and more lavish production values. If a producer charges high prices, he must deliver "much more scenic effects, much greater costumes, which is all driving up the costs. So it's a vicious cycle." The Broadway Alliance's failure emphatically underscored that audiences will not happily pay top price for a modestly designed show, especially one without stars. Unless a production features some marketable lure, like a major revival featuring a stellar cast, or an "issue" play or a "snob" hit, which do not require extravagant design values, producers continue to spend lavishly. Smith added that "we have created an atmosphere where everyone has to be in an Armani suit. If he's not in an Armani suit, he can't go onstage." Technological advances, such as innovations in mechanized scenery and computerized lighting, which offer designers a much more sophisticated, and expensive, palette, have contributed to the growing spectacle and attendant costs.

Smith indicated that each ticket price rise is followed by a public outcry, and when prices escalate, the general audience pool is reduced, "either in overall number, or in the number of times an individual goes over the course of a year. . . . So nobody consciously raises prices, because you know what you're doing—you're cutting down your own potential. You're going to run for a lesser period of time or you're going to play to fewer people." He added, however, that in the case of "that one hit show, price is absolutely irrelevant," and audiences will clamor to see it regardless of cost. In this instance, theatregoing takes on an air of conspicuous consumption; one sees the show to be able to boast that one has seen the show.

But not all tickets sell at top prices. Even the most successful musicals typically sell a handful of tickets at much lower prices directly at the box office. Shows that are not runaway hits will usually send a portion of that day's remaining tickets to the TKTS booth at Duffy Square, run by Theatre Development Fund, for sale at a quarter or half off the face value. Disney sells a few tickets for its shows for about twenty dollars, but any seat priced at that level will invariably be in the top row or two of the last balcony. Experienced theatregoers know where to find less costly tickets, whether it is at the TKTS booth or on a Web site. Disney's Thomas Schumacher attempted to explode the idea that Broadway is not affordable.

> Theatre has variable pricing, not to mention that at certain times of the year—September, January, or February, for example—people can buy tickets on sale. The TKTS booth is open every day, selling discounted tickets to some shows. But, for whatever reason, people look at the top ticket price and say, 'Tickets are too expensive.' If we played that game with clothing, we could say, 'Clothes are too expensive, be-

cause I saw a cashmere sweater for three hundred dollars.' The fact is, you and I can walk into the Gap and buy a nice wool sweater for thirty-two dollars. Some people want cashmere and pay for it, and some people wear wool. Some people want fifth row center orchestra, and some people sit in the balcony. That's the reality of life.

Schumacher also commented on the perception that Broadway is more expensive than other similar luxury expenditures. "It is true that the best seat in the house is too expensive. But so is the best food in the best restaurant, so is the best watch, so is the best necklace . . . and no one ever thinks of it that way. The theatre is held to an altogether different standard, and I'm not sure why." Aside from movie theatres, in which all general admission tickets cost the same, other forms of live entertainment, from sporting events to classical music concerts, typically employ a wider variety of tiered prices, but producers seem reluctant to return to the days of a broader spectrum of ticket pricing from orchestra to balcony. There was a brief period in the midnineties, when relatively inexpensive musicals like *Rent, Bring in Da Noise, Bring in Da Funk,* and *Chicago* convinced the public that producers were embracing the return to producing dramatically exciting and lucrative shows for reasonable sums and at reasonable ticket prices. Seth Gelblum pointed out that a less expensive hit show with lower running costs presents the producer with the opportunity to make significant income without needing a huge gross. In addition, if the show fails, much less money is lost. "You hope that something small can still work," he said. But producers evidently did not hew to this approach and reverted to staging lavish, expensive productions. The 2003 revival of *Gypsy,* with Bernadette Peters, endured criticism that its less opulent production values looked pale by comparison with many of its competitor musicals.

A spreadsheet quickly informs a producer as to how quickly the show can expect to recoup under different box office scenarios that are based on variances in ticket pricing, discounts, and group sales. In decades past, the old rule of thumb in figuring out royalties was to multiply the total royalty percentage for a show, perhaps around 16 percent of the gross, by the gross receipts, and subtract that, along with weekly operating expenses, from the adjusted gross. If anything remained, it would be used to pay off investors or pay a profit after recoupment, at which point royalties escalated slightly. The problem was that this practice often left relatively little to return to investors. A show could run for years in the black but fail to generate sufficient profit to pay back the investors or turn a profit. This scenario has occurred in countless productions. The royalty pool, now in place for about twenty years, accommodates the producer's need for the quicker recoupment necessary to keep investors returning for successive shows. Disney, though, is said to have experienced difficulty in persuading royalty earners to accept the concept of pool participation at the start of a production, since there are no direct investors who need to be repaid. If a Disney show eventually stumbles financially, and the royalty payments prevent a show from meeting its weekly running costs, Disney would suggest a pool agreement to keep the show running.

There are countless royalty pool calculations. The net operating profits are figured by subtracting weekly operating expenses, or the "nut," as well as the theatre owner's 5 or 6 percent, from the adjusted gross receipts, which themselves are calculated by subtracting items like credit card commissions and theatre ticket taxes from the gross receipts. Typically the weekly net operating profits are split into two segments. One share of the profits, about 65 percent, goes to the investors, and the remaining 35 percent is paid to the royalty pool. These figures usually are adjusted to 60 and 40 percent, respectively, after recoupment; once the investors have recouped, the artists deserve a slightly larger share. But as production costs and weekly expenses continue to rise, shows that fail to sell at or near 100 percent of gross potential find it increasingly difficult to recoup—hence higher ticket prices. For example, on a show with a weekly net operating profit of fifty thousand dollars, the investors will split 65 percent, only $32,500. If the show cost ten million dollars to produce, it will take almost six years to recoup. Big musicals with high weekly operating expenses employ an amortization schedule to increase the rate of recoupment, in which an amortized amount of the total production costs, usually about 1 or 2 percent, is subtracted from the operating profits and paid to the investors. On a ten-million-dollar show, this schedule might translate into an additional one hundred thousand dollars or more in a week. This plan aids in a quicker recoupment but subtracts money from the royalty pool, causing increased friction between artists and producers. Smaller musicals, as well as straight plays, tend to avoid the amortization scheme.

Most producers keep a show running as long as it earns weekly profits, even minimal ones. According to Seth Gelblum, "The longer you stay open, the more you seem like a hit, in terms of concurrent tours and subsequent exploitations." Many shows never recoup on Broadway but do so from national tours and foreign engagements. Edward Strong said that a producer's best intentions and most astute financial predictions can be derailed by any one of several factors in the course of developing and running a show, which will inhibit the ability to pay back in a timely fashion. He noted that "in some respects [success on] Broadway is about making the brand here in order to capitalize in other places." Clear Channel's investment in *Swing,* which lost money on Broadway but recouped on tour, is an example of that not infrequent scenario. The relationship between Broadway and the road, which plays an increasingly vital role in the decision-making process of which shows are produced in New York, will be examined in the next chapter.

Once the show is selected, the money is in place, and the initial deals are cemented, a new set of challenges must be faced as the production heads toward opening night.

6 Page to Stage

The reason to go out of town is to learn from an audience.
—Barry Brown, producer

They say if Hitler ever came back and they wanted to punish him, they'd send him on the road with a musical.
—anonymous producer

A pivotal moment in the life of any Broadway show occurs when its creators and producers draw its road map to Broadway. In years past, a production would travel out of town to address its flaws and polish it in front of audiences before opening in New York. The prohibitive costs now of such an approach dictate that most producers hone their works in other arenas. Readings, in which actors—not necessarily the ones who will ultimately perform on Broadway—work with scripts in hand, often while seated in chairs in a rehearsal room with no production trappings, allow the creators and producers the chance to hear the words (and music) and make initial decisions about the direction of the text. Often, readings will be held before a producer considers approaching investors, as this first phase is crucial in determining the viability of the material.

Workshops present another opportunity to ascertain both the show's potential and its flaws. Workshops today may cost hundreds of thousands of dollars, and these more lavish efforts have both detractors and supporters within the Broadway community. According to Stephen Sondheim, the practice of getting a show on its feet before the actual rehearsal process began more than forty years ago with *A Funny Thing Happened on the Way to the Forum*, produced by Harold Prince and Robert Griffith, and directed and choreographed by George Abbott and Jerome Robbins. Sondheim said that Robbins initially was reluctant to work on the show and suggested that the producers gather a group of actors in a hotel ballroom to read and sing the work in front of the producers and writers Sondheim, Larry Gelbart, and Burt Shevelove. There was no audience in attendance, just the producers and creative artists.

Hal and I thought it was a waste of time. We all did, we all thought it was a waste of time, but it was to indulge Jerry. So, in fact, we did it, and of course, to our astonishment, found that we learned so much more about the script and about the score, and even about the casting. . . . Hal and I thought it was so valuable, that every show we did after that, we went through this process. We would start, usually the first time, in Hal's office, with Hal reading the script aloud, me playing the score, and the author listening, and sometimes, if there were any design staff in tow, have them come in, too.

Subsequently, the writers and directors discussed and tinkered, and often reconvened some weeks later with a group of actors, as they had on *Forum*. The point, said Sondheim, "was that we worked a number of kinks out, before rehearsals began, which had never been thought of before."

Sondheim, a veteran of Broadway since *West Side Story* in 1957, offered a critical observation about the way in which this new step in the production process afforded a vital function. He pointed to the musicals of the forties and fifties, and noted that most of them have strong first acts and weak second acts. The reason, he said, is "there was never any time out of town to correct the second act. By the time you got the first act done with, and all the songs in, you'd be coming to New York, so there was very little time to work on the second act." The new developmental phase "allowed us time to work on both acts, and work some of the kinks out before rehearsal, so that, as I used to be fond of saying, 'You go into rehearsal with a perfect show and then find out what dreadful trouble you were in.'" Sondheim is a strong proponent of this process, and his most recent work, *Bounce*, written with John Weidman, traveled a slow and cautious route. It first had a workshop production with British director Sam Mendes, under its original title, *Wise Guys*, but according to participants, the material was not yet ready for another production. After rewrites, a switch of directors—to Harold Prince—and a name change, to *Gold!*, the musical was given a reading. In the summer of 2003 it was produced in its third incarnation at the Goodman Theatre, a LORT house in Chicago, and then again in the fall at the Kennedy Center.

Today the spartan approach adopted by Prince and Sondheim for readings and workshops has been frequently superseded by a more costly process, in which considerable sums are spent to stage the show with scenery, costumes, lighting, sound, and a small orchestra. While directors and designers often embrace the chance to explore rudimentary staging and design concepts before the Broadway run, there are risks. Sondheim expressed his belief, shared by others in the community, that most of these workshops are essentially glorified backers auditions. In the past, a producer invited a cadre of potential investors, as well as representatives of group sales organizations, to listen to a few actors, or even the writers themselves, read and sing selected bits of the show. Today, many producers find that to win over investors and other essential participants, greater emphasis is placed on the initial dazzle. The original point of workshops and readings, to examine the work on its feet, is rarely the case these days. Roy Somlyo said, "Today a workshop is done to expose it to potential investors." A successful workshop can bring in millions; Marty Bell said that the workshop for *Sweet Smell of Success* generated over twenty million dollars in offers.

Director and choreographer Robert Longbottom created the 1997 musical *Side Show,* based on the lives of conjoined twins, the Hilton Sisters. From a directorial standpoint, he enjoyed a prerogative rarely seen on Broadway—the chance to workshop the musical in a Broadway theatre. In this case it turned out to be the same theatre the show would ultimately play. The Hilton sisters spent much of their lives working in vaudeville and in carnivals, and the theatrical atmosphere was essential in creating an appropriate environment.

> We had the most extraordinary workshop. I don't know one that has been so beautifully handled. We got the Richard Rodgers Theatre empty, and had a very sweet time in there for six weeks. We brought in a set of bleachers, and [scenic designer] Robin [Wagner] hung blacks [velour drapes]. We had maybe twelve lighting instruments— just enough to produce this show in a way that you really didn't need costumes and sets. The actors and your imagination filled in everything.... It was just a stunning workshop. I know years before, Tommy Tune had workshopped *Nine* and *Grand Hotel,* also in Broadway theatres. But it was just happening less and less, because everything was booked.

Broadway theatres are more expensive to rent than rehearsal halls, but the experience of working in a real theatre is always advantageous. Longbottom found the experience a transformative one for the production. "I can't tell you what it does for me as a director to be working in an old theatre like that, stripped down to the bones with all the ghosts listening. It was amazing what we actually pulled from that theatre. It contributed to the work." The pragmatic elements were also valuable. "I could get twelve rows back, where you couldn't do that in a rehearsal studio. It makes a lot of sense to rehearse on a stage if you can. It forces the actors very quickly to navigate what the performance is going to be, and to fill the house." Longbottom agreed that workshops can provide a pivotal step in a show's development. "The problem with a workshop is that so many people come in and judge it prematurely, and don't give you the benefit of the doubt that this is but a step in the process of making a show. And you're going to go further than that."

A producer's perspective on play development was offered by Edward Strong. "Every show is different. It really depends on the personalities of the people involved. I would say, instinctively, when you're just starting, it's nice to have it in your neighborhood—low-cost, nearby—so you can get good people and some idea of it without going through the disorienting process of production." Strong, whose group was a lead producer on the musical *Titanic,* noted that a developmental production of a show of that size and visual scope—the scenery was built on mechanized jacks that allowed the set of the ship's superstructure to tilt as well as "sink" into the stage—would have been impossible in other venues. "*Titanic* was an example of something that we workshopped here extensively. But then, realistically, the next step had to be Broadway, because . . . you couldn't have done it in a regional theatre. It would have been beyond the technical abilities of the not-for-profit, and an out-of-town tryout would have been prohibitive." It would be logistically and financially impossible for a LORT theatre to rip out its stage floor to install the necessary automation.

Sondheim is a proponent of the reading over even the most sparsely designed workshop, because "you're concentrating on the material, which is the whole point, not on presentation." Some producers invite audiences to workshops to better gauge reaction, but this practice can yield mixed results. Richard Frankel argued that he never utilizes a workshop for such purposes. "We're looking to judge, the best we can, whether the show works in a dramaturgical sense, whether the characters have arcs, whether there's a plot that makes any sense, whether there's sufficient motivation, whether the right songs are there, whether you have songs that advance the story and tell you what you need to know about the characters' wishes and dreams. That's what we look for from readings and workshops." To determine an audience's response, he would place the work in a production context, on the road or in a regional theatre.

A bare-bones workshop may suit some marginal shows better than an eventual lavish Broadway production that can either obliterate the work's small charms or highlight its lack of heft. One veteran Broadway stage manager remembered the 1983 Alan Jay Lerner and Charles Strouse musical disaster, *Dance a Little Closer*.

> At the end of the rehearsal period, we gave several workshoplike performances in the basement theatre of Michael Bennett's rehearsal hall complex. These were no-frills run-throughs to give Alan and Charles a sense of what was going on, and to give the actors a chance to play in front of an audience before we went into tech rehearsals and lost the sense of the show. We opened up the bleacher seats down there to audiences culled from Theatre Development Fund lists and showed them what we had, with only the most basic rehearsal costumes and props, on a bare stage with no scenery and a couple of musicians.

The audiences accepted the show's weaknesses in this stark, unadorned presentation and responded positively to its strengths. When the show was finally presented several weeks later on an overdesigned and poorly functioning Broadway set, with the actors cavorting in garish, expensive costumes, all of the show's faults were glaringly evident, and the production closed the day after opening night, losing its entire investment of more than two million dollars.

But a more fully-fleshed workshop would not have helped. As Sondheim noted, the addition of production elements often obscures both the work's flaws and strengths and diffuses the focus of the creators as they shape the work. Sondheim said, "It's only important that we have a chance to hear the work sung and read. It's not important to have an audience. In fact, I think it's probably misleading to have an audience. I do not approve of workshops with audiences, because you get misled. They're usually friends, to begin with, or professionals, so you have a mixture of people who want you to succeed and want you to fail. And that's just not valuable." Robert Longbottom added that

> the workshop isn't necessarily just useful for audience reaction; it's useful for the creative team. The workshop of *Side Show* was highly beneficial to me, because we were dealing with something that nobody had ever done before—singing and dancing Siamese twins onstage, and wanting to do it with four rolling sets of bleachers. I thought, if we're not going to go out of town, and we're not going to do a regional

theatre production, I've got to have my hands on this, and I want to have my hands on this before the six-week rehearsal period starts rolling and I find myself in tech. . . . But if a workshop is a backers audition, which it almost always is, it can be tricky.

The emphasis on spectacle places a burden on those producers who believe that to generate strong word of mouth, a handsome workshop is a necessity. Still, most producers will not invite strangers at this delicate and critical juncture. Rather than risking the potentially disastrous effects from negative word of mouth, they selectively invite potential backers, family, friends, and industry colleagues. This policy, too, can yield mixed results, said Miles Wilkin of Clear Channel. "When one has two hundred closest friends there cheering for you, it is not the same as having a real audience. And it can be deceptive, painfully deceptive at times. I can name quite a few shows that had the classic 'wonderful' workshop and went on thinking it was in the bag and had horrendous experiences after that." Rocco Landesman concurred, noting, "The problem with workshops is you don't really have an audience. . . . It's nice to see a show in front of a paying audience. I think you learn much more from that than you do from a workshop. You save a lot of money with workshops [relative to out-of-town or not-for-profit productions], but I'm not sure you don't lose more." Edward Strong agreed. "I'm a big proponent of the workshop without physical production as an element. I've had experiences recently where the workshop was fantastic, and then, when you got to the theatre, it's not so fantastic. I suspect there is something misleading about the kind of womblike experience of the workshop that ends up costing a lot of money."

Marty Bell, the originating producer of *Ragtime*, remembered the process of bringing the Terrence McNally–Lynn Ahrens–Stephen Flaherty musical of E. L. Doctorow's novel to Broadway for Livent. After the composer and lyricist had been selected, the writing team began work in March 1995. The authors met with Drabinsky and Bell in a hotel room in Toronto and spent a day discussing the structure of the musical. A reading was scheduled for five months later, and Bell hired a cast, in part to secure the best actors and in part to provide a compelling deadline for the writers. A two-week rehearsal and reading process ensued in August, which generated many rewrites. The readings were closed to outsiders, except for some Livent staffers. After four months of additional rewrites, a second reading was held, "where we really knew we had something special." The following May, they staged a full workshop of the show, "a completely staged, choreographed vision of the show, but with no scenery or costumes or lights, and just with a piano." They had planned to produce the show on Broadway the following spring, but the workshop went so smoothly that they started rehearsals that September. Less than two years had elapsed, a relatively short journey these days. Bell believes that most shows do not need a longer time frame, as long as the writers are able to "write on their feet, and get to hear everything as soon as it's written." He endorses Sondheim's consideration of the importance of hearing a show, "because things are very different when actors do it than they are on the page. And I think writers have to continually hear their work."

The microscopic gaze under which so many new works labor is intense in New York City. But the extra layer of protection that many producers believed they gained from an out-of-town tryout has largely evaporated, in part because of the pernicious effects of the Internet. Now legions of theatre gossipmongers can post scabrous messages on bulletin boards, chat rooms, and e-mail list-serves. This barrage seriously crippled *Seussical* in its Boston tryout. The show was hampered by numerous artistic problems, but the point of a tryout is to identify and fix them. The negative Internet gossip from Boston was cited as a significant factor in the weak advance sale in New York. Despite this problem, Nina Keneally believes that there is value in taking a show out of town. "There's something to be gained from taking the company away from their everyday lives . . . and putting them somewhere where they're all in the boat together, and no one has to go home and walk the dog or see their Con Ed bill, and there's a certain unifying process for working and eating together. I think that really allows for work to be done in a more concentrated manner. . . . Just being all together, even above the choppy seas, has great advantage."

An out-of-town tryout in either a commercial or not-for-profit theatre is no guarantee of a subsequent Broadway run. The productions that died outside New York are legion. Some perished because of serious dramatic flaws; others failed to make the journey because the producer lost faith in the show, was unable to raise money, or chose not to invest additional time and money fixing the problems that were revealed. Actor Danny Burstein recalled his participation in a new musical version of Jack Finney's novel *Time and Again,* originally staged at the Old Globe Theatre in San Diego, directed by Tony-winning Jack O'Brien. The producers were so certain that the show was going to enjoy Broadway success that the cast simultaneously executed both Broadway and LORT contracts before rehearsals began in San Diego. "It was not a question of whether or not we were moving in to New York; it was just a matter of how the show would go in San Diego. They thought it would move, given the director and the designers and the cast they had. It would *definitely* move. It just did not." The show received mixed reviews, finished its Old Globe run, and stopped there. The actors received a severance payment of two weeks of Broadway minimum salary, and the producers informed the cast, according to Burstein, "that the show just wasn't ready. The show did not get the reviews that they thought we'd get. And it was going to cost a lot of money; it was a big cast, with a big set." Richard Frankel was involved with the show. "In San Diego, we thought that the book was fine and the characters were fine, and what we needed to know was whether or not we could do the time travel physical effects properly. We were completely wrong. The show wasn't right. The book wasn't in good shape. There were huge problems with the basic dramaturgy of the show, and it was a huge mistake to do that production. So we went back to the drawing board, in a way, and had the show restructured. And now, we no longer believe that giant sets and effects are necessary." The show was eventually produced at Manhattan Theatre Club, but it never saw the lights of Broadway. The producers spent about four million dollars over eight years to develop the production.

Salaries for readings and workshops are low—understandable in the context of a developmental phase with no ticket sales—but that does not deter actors from participating. As Tony Award–winning Randy Graff put it, "This year's reading is next year's gig. If you get called to do a reading of a project that you really like, you do it with the hopes of moving on with it. I've gotten a couple of jobs this way." While there are mechanisms for workshop actors to share in a very small percentage of royalties from a Broadway run, it takes a long-running hit to make a sizable difference to most actors.

Actors have little clout when negotiating with producers. Eager for high-paying Broadway jobs, rank-and-file actors have little bargaining power with so many other performers waiting in the wings. Equity does not allow agents to negotiate contracts for chorus members, who receive standardized salaries, with very few of them earning more than minimum. Most actors on principal contracts employ agents in exchange for 10 percent of their weekly salary. Except for stars, there is not much leeway in salary negotiations, but other factors are often of greater concern to actors than a few extra dollars, like a private dressing room (not usually possible in a large-cast show, except for leading performers), a limousine service to drive home after the show, a private wardrobe assistant, a guaranteed number of weeks off for vacation or the chance to do a film or a workshop of another show, and billing. Randy Graff, who has worked for a number of different producers, identified veteran producer Emanuel Azenberg as one of her favorites, because "he believes that if you take care of your actors, they'll do a good job for you and they won't want to leave. And he's right. He likes and respects actors, and you feel that during the negotiation process. When a producer doesn't like or respect you, you also feel that right away in the negotiation process."

The greatest concern for most actors is continuity of employment. Until the early 1980s, a producer could, with fair ease, fire an actor at any point. If an actor was inadequate to the task or, more frequently, poorly cast in the first place, the producer felt that it was his prerogative to terminate the contract. During the run of the musical *Annie,* the director and producers determined that several cast members were not performing up to par, and terminated their contracts. This galvanized the union membership, and in subsequent League-Equity negotiations, a "just cause" clause was inserted into the contract. Now, while a producer may terminate a contract during the rehearsal period and in the first four weeks after the first paid public performance—including previews—without just cause, it is more difficult to do so afterward, and the decision must be based on either a nonperformance issue like chronic lateness or other unacceptable behavior, or on some concrete observation of the failure to perform as directed. In practice, actors are terminated rather infrequently. Actors working on standard contracts with a two- or four-week termination clause can, in theory, work on the show in perpetuity unless just cause is invoked, in which case the actor can appeal to an arbiter. If the case is determined in favor of the actor, a payment schedule based on the number of weeks the actor had already worked applies. Chorus actors who have signed six-month riders and principal actors on term contracts of several months or a year will receive, in theory, the remainder of their contractual salary should the arbitrator determine that there was insufficient cause for termination.

However, contractual protection is not always sufficient to stave off a producer's desire to clean house. A memorable example occurred in late 1996, when Cameron Mackintosh and John Caird, the producer and the codirector of *Les Misérables,* announced, in anticipation of the production's tenth anniversary in March 1997, that the show looked tired and sluggish and had lost its vibrancy. As a result, the entire cast would be evaluated and overhauled. Twelve actors were fired, others were invited back to audition for the show (not necessarily for their current roles), and a few were asked to remain. Many Equity members ventured, on Internet chat rooms and in the Equity lounge—the working actor's refuge in midtown Manhattan—that the move was a shameless publicity ploy to bolster the show's waning receipts. Even more to the point, actors said, the maneuver smacked of a flagrant disregard for actors' job security in a famously insecure profession. The joke that had made the rounds after the *Annie* debacle was heard again. Producer: "You're fired!" Actor: "Why?!" Producer: "Oh, just 'cause." Mackintosh was willing to forgo the hearings and arbitrations and simply pay the actors in excess of the contractually stipulated amount, but the matter devastated those affected performers. Director Caird responded that he empathized with the concerns of the actors but was quoted in several articles unfavorably comparing the show's recent performances with Madame Tussaud's wax museum. The cast's anger and frustration were exacerbated when they discovered that Equity leadership had been informed earlier by Mackintosh's office of the intended terminations but had not informed the cast in advance of the startling announcement. Much wrangling in the press and behind closed arbitration doors resulted in Mackintosh prevailing. He did not violate the contract and did pay each actor more than was warranted. In March, after the national touring cast stepped in to perform while the new cast rehearsed, the show reopened. According to Peter Marks of the *New York Times,* the radical maneuver provided the necessary magic bullet that restored luster to the musical. "*Les Misérables* unveiled its refurbished Broadway production last night, and, like a faded fresco lovingly restored, many of the original colors have returned. With some intelligent recasting decisions, a sumptuous costume makeover and an infusion of vocal energy, the show has recovered from its near-death experience last fall, when Cameron Mackintosh, the producer, and John Caird, the co-director (with Trevor Nunn), sacked half the 38-member cast and vowed to rehabilitate a production that had gone limp from creative exhaustion and neglect."[1]

While contractual continuity of employment is an essential safeguard against producer or director caprice in the firing of actors, many productions suffer from a creeping and insidious staleness of performance during long runs. Some actors do not know how to keep a show fresh over time. It is all too easy for a cast to slide into a shopworn and mechanical performance. Actor William Parry, whose first Broadway appearance was in the 1971 original production of *Jesus Christ Superstar,* understudied Richard Burton in the 1980 Broadway revival of *Camelot.* He recalled that "Burton said that it takes at least two months to really begin to connect to a role, and after six months, you've probably explored all the nuances of it. If you continue in that same role much longer, you'll only find yourself repeating those same discoveries over and over, which is death. That said, I watched him do *Camelot* for a year with a goodly amount of verve." Parry, who played the role of the boatman for the entire seventeen-month Broadway run of *Sunday in the Park with George,* added that the challenge of performing a part countless times flies in the face of one of the primary precepts of acting.

> The process of discovering and developing and exploring that goes on as you work on a role is obviously crucial to the depth, the intensity, the vitality that come across to the audience. Up to a certain point, there's fresh exploration and exciting discovery taking place. And even after some time, a fresh nuance will present itself, which adds a new shade to the scene. But to expect an actor to recreate—as opposed to create—that over an extended period of time is somehow antithetical to the freshness of the moment.

Actress Rebecca Luker had leading roles in five Broadway musicals over fourteen years, all ranging from one to three years in duration.

> I can safely say that I've had the long run experience. I discovered over time that to survive the sometimes bone-tiredness I felt as a result of the relentlessness of eight shows a week, I devised games for myself. These involved the usual good acting techniques that, when we begin a show, are easy to access, but which don't come easily once you've sung the same song and recited the same lines for two years. So I had to actively make myself listen to my fellow actors and try to be in the moment—every night. Eventually, what I would find was that I actually discovered new moments in a show I'd been doing for years. Those experiences were few but when they occurred, they were wonderful. There's also the old "long run rule" to remember: the audience has never seen the show before. Keeping this in mind is very helpful when you're trying to keep a show spontaneous and fresh. It *is* fresh to the audience. It also helped me immensely when I had the good fortune to be cast

in a show that I loved. For instance, I don't think I ever tired of singing *The Secret Garden* or *The Music Man* scores. When the material is
brilliant it makes doing it night after night so much more rewarding.

It can be argued that actors deserve the chance to enjoy the benefits
of long-term employment, but a counterargument states that job security should not outweigh the preservation of the production's integrity.
The onus of maintaining a production falls squarely on management.
The production's stage manager is responsible for maintaining the show
after opening, along with the musical director and dance captain on a
musical, but may lack the artistic ability or influence to keep the show
fresh. The phenomenon of long runs, in part the result of fewer new
shows, has spawned a new breed of Broadway performer. Chorus members were known for decades as gypsies for their habit of moving from
show to show. Today, many chorus gypsies find themselves inhabiting the
same camp for years. With so few options annually, many actors choose
security of employment in a long run over a new artistic challenge on a
new show that may fail. Danny Burstein explained the balancing act that
is necessary.

I think long runs are great for an actor financially, but artistically
they're an incredible challenge. The best-case scenario is when a show
is running for a long time, the producer is flexible and lets his or her
actors leave the show for other jobs and then brings them back at a
later time. Say an actor wants to play Lear in summer stock but he's
performing every night in *Kiss Me, Kate* on Broadway. If a producer
is smart, he'll allow the actor to take a hiatus from the show, recharge
the batteries, and return fresh to the show after the break. This happens rarely, sadly, but when it does, I've found, it always works.

William Parry said, "The great majority of actors pray for a long run, and
if they're lucky, some of them get it—some of them, for a *long* time. Those
shows have certainly paid off a lot of actors' mortgages and kept a slew
of people solvent who otherwise would have been wrestling for the few
jobs available in the shrinking world of Broadway shows."

Before contracts are issued for a new musical, the producer outlines
for Equity the intended contractual designation —principal or chorus—
for each actor. Equity examines the script, attends rehearsals, and solidi-
fies a ruling when the show is frozen before opening. The category of the
actor's contract affects several areas, from payments to agents to the

length of term contracts. Producers want flexibility to dismiss actors when needed but also want to ensure that reliable actors remain with the show for as long as possible, as replacing them can be time-consuming, costly, and damaging to the fabric of the production. Decades ago, when most musicals were constructed with an obvious delineation between principals and chorus, it was fairly easy to determine the appropriate contractual designation. As the form of musicals evolved, and the traditional dancing and singing chorus gave way to an ensemble of performers taking on many roles, the designation process grew more imprecise. In 1985, when *Big River* was produced on Broadway, the producers, led by Rocco Landesman and the Dodgers, hired a cast of twenty-one actors. They presented a persuasive case to Equity that there was no traditional dancing and singing chorus. Rather the cast included four main parts and an ensemble of actors—not gypsies—who were usually cast in principal roles and who would each take on a number of small parts in the musical. The producers had initially offered all twenty-one principal contracts, but Equity countered that only the four leading roles were principals; the rest were designated as chorus. The producers worried that some of the actors would not sign the chorus contract, because there is something of a class divide within Equity. Although all Equity members enjoy the same standing and there is no distinction in the union among chorus, principals, or stage managers, those members who have made their career primarily as chorus performers view their contributions with pride and wish to preserve their contractual prerogatives. Actors who work most frequently as principals worry that a chorus contract can be viewed as a lower rung on the performance ladder. In *Big River,* although the actors were persuaded to sign the chorus contracts, the producers were hurt by a contractual loophole in the six-month rider they executed, which allows chorus members to give notice if they secure principal work on another production. Several of these actors were soon offered principal roles, and an exodus began. Had they been signed as principals on term contracts, the producers would not have had to recast half a dozen actors within the first six months of the run. While Equity may view some of the contractual issues as sacrosanct, a show's integrity can be damaged by union intransigence.

A production's life cycle does not necessarily end on closing night on Broadway. Touring figures prominently in a producer's expectation of potential profits. Barry Weissler observed that "there's money to be made" on the road. "There's an audience that has grown exponentially. It's huge."

Income from a tour, if produced with funds from the original Broadway production, can propel a show over the hump of recoupment. Before the advent of regional theatres, apart from summer stock companies, Broadway tours offered most theatregoers in America their only opportunity to see competent, professional theatrical talent. In the mid-twentieth century, dozens of tours crisscrossed the nation each year. Today the relationship between Broadway and the national touring circuit is more complex and reveals an evolution in priorities.

In an ideal scenario, a producer would mount more than one tour during the original Broadway run, cashing in on the currency of the commodity. While each tour requires the investment of additional capitalization or the utilization of a substantial part of the original show's income—a large musical tour might cost close to three million dollars—the show's artistic and technical road map has already been drawn and proven viable. This allows for a shorter rehearsal process and sometimes the construction of less complex and expensive sets, as loading a show in and out of a number of theatres requires greater simplicity of design and scope. In rare cases, a show like *The Phantom of the Opera*—the most successful touring production of the modern era—is so attractive to a local presenter that the expense of altering the theatre to accommodate the complex scenery is worth the investment. Jack Viertel said, "If you could bring *Phantom* into your market for eight weeks, where you would normally have a one- or two-week run of a typical show, you could then justify digging up the basement of your theatre and putting in elevators." Some Broadway hits might be produced in an open-ended run in Los Angeles, while a national tour plays primary cities like San Francisco, Boston, Washington DC, and Chicago for at least a month, and often more. When the Los Angeles company finishes its run, perhaps a year after opening if successful, it might be technically retooled to accommodate touring and take to the road as a second national company. Although some shows are enshrined as perennials, like *Cats*, and can run "now and forever," it is wise for a producer to take advantage of the prevailing winds and exploit the riches of the road while the Broadway production, and its attendant hoopla, are still fresh. Touring productions of current Broadway shows, as well as revivals of shows not presently playing in New York, earn more box office revenue than Broadway itself. In 2002 this income came to almost $650 million, down from almost $800 million in the midnineties, when *Phantom* and *Miss Saigon* earned unmatchable revenue. These figures include income from productions that were never intended to play Broadway. Some producers realize that there is money to be made from yet another revival of *South Pacific* or some other favorite that features a bankable personality, usually a television actor, in the leading role.

The paradigm for such a tour was relatively simple in decades past. A producer would raise additional money or utilize some of the profits from Broadway to mount a tour and hire a booking agency to map out a route and negotiate with road presenters. In another option, the original producer would lease the rights to a second producer who specialized in touring, take a sizable percentage of the gross, and let the tour producer do the yeoman's work. A well-produced and carefully booked tour could produce income for years. Although ticket prices on the road are usually lower than on Broadway, they have increased considerably over the years, almost rivaling Broadway prices in some major markets. Because road theatres are typically much larger than Broadway houses, there is the potential for considerable profit.

Today, though, the ground has shifted. Less expensive nonunion tours have gained in popularity with producers who have chosen to curb their rising costs by avoiding Equity rates. Shows that failed on Broadway, like *Seussical*, have spawned successful national tours. Clear Channel's hegemony in the national touring circuit, with control of almost sixty North American markets, has altered not only the ways and means of touring but the nature of the shows themselves. Their decision not to book a show can translate into rough going for that producer who is shut out of so many markets. As Rocco Landesman observed, "Their support of a show can be decisive . . . because they can deliver twenty markets with one phone call."

The evolving relationship between the road and Broadway has created a belief that the tail is now wagging the dog. What is essential for Clear Channel and other large presenters is a sufficient number of productions annually to service the marketplace. Some shows are now produced on Broadway not because it is likely that they will flourish there but because they want the Broadway imprimatur to help them succeed on the road. "Direct from Broadway" has at least as much impact on the road as an advertisement featuring laudatory remarks from the major New York newspapers. James L. Nederlander, however, said he believed that a show can succeed on tour without ever having played Broadway and cited the pre-Broadway *Jekyll and Hyde* that ran for almost a year on the road before it landed on Broadway. Director Des McAnuff expressed his concern that it may be, ultimately, the most destructive thing about the form if we're not careful, the idea that you don't go to Broadway anymore to make money . . . the idea of trying to get as many good reviews as possible and trying to be accepted, if not embraced, by the intelligentsia—all those things were important. If that's not what's important [now], if it's simply getting in and out of there so that you can get a rubber stamp on it, and get it out into other markets to make money, I think that could encourage [people] to do more and more schlock.

The involvement of Clear Channel and Disney in such entertainments as truck rallies, rock concerts, and theme parks has allowed them to tap new audiences. No one in the industry gainsays the import of developing new audiences; the misgivings stem from a belief that unsophisticated audiences are being served increasing portions of unsophisticated fare, with little attempt to expose them to more challenging works.

Broadway is a concept to be applied to marketing shows. Scott Zeiger of Clear Channel was quoted, in a 2001 article in *Variety*, by Chris Jones: "We are trying to brand the experience of coming to a first-class Broadway show all around the country. . . . We think our patrons should feel like they are part of a prestigious and important subscription family. . . . Consumers will be assured of the best customer service in the venue and that they will be seeing the best and the brightest shows coming from New York."[2] Unfortunately, some of what they see never originated in New York in their current incarnations, while other shows are culled from a cross section of mediocre offerings and of shows that failed in New York. If audiences in touring markets were exposed to only the best shows coming from New York, there would currently not be sufficient productions to flesh out a subscription season. Selling rehashed and retrofitted versions of Broadway flops is not an indictable offense. The quality of these shows is often acceptable from a purely technical perspective, but the material often suffers from a variety of maladies. Unfortunately, a powerful message is sent that middling fare can command a hefty ticket price and should be regarded as high quality. The same applies to some productions on Broadway, and success in New York provides no accurate reading of a show's artistic merit. But once a show has taken an egregious belly flop on the boards in New York, it is disingenuous to foist this material as the best of Broadway on less discriminating audiences in order to flesh out a season.

It is perceived family value that sells many shows on tour. New York reviews carry little weight on the road. When the producers of *Saturday*

Night Fever sent out a national tour, despite dreadful reviews in New York, they calculated that the show would succeed because of the extraordinary popularity of the original movie. As producer Jon Platt was quoted in *Variety*, "I'm willing to bet . . . that the people who will be buying tickets to this show did not read the reviews in New York."[3] The theatrical sensibility of an audience in Salt Lake City is probably different from one in midtown Manhattan. For example, not every audience will appreciate the humor of Mel Brooks as those audiences in New York, Chicago, and Los Angeles will. *The Producers* will sell out in smaller markets—it is a "must-see" hit—but it may not play as well there.

Many touring houses operate a Broadway series or a similarly named subscription. For a theatregoer to purchase tickets for the one show he really wants to attend, usually the big hit of the series, he has to buy a full or partial season subscription, which may include filler shows like *Riverdance.* If he chooses to save money and buy individual tickets to only the one show, he will probably have little choice from a pool of the least desirable seats or may be shut out entirely if the subscriptions sell well. As there are, at the most, two bona fide hit musicals on Broadway in any season—straight plays rarely succeed on the road—a subscriber has to spend several hundred dollars to secure tickets for the one show he truly wants to see. It is intelligent marketing, but it provides little incentive for a presenter to offer the best shows possible. If a mediocre show does well because of its inclusion in the same series as *Mamma Mia!,* it makes it easier for the local presenter to fill out the season. Before the proliferation of subscription packages, shows had to succeed on their own merit. When *The Lion King*'s tour was first announced in early 2001, local presenters were overjoyed as they calculated how this enormously popular musical could salvage an otherwise poor slate of touring shows. As Chris Jones wrote in *Variety*, "Not only will tickets fly out the door for a multiweek engagement in any city of size, but this kind of attraction is a hook on which sub-par subscription seasons can be hung with impunity."[4]

On the other hand, shows like *Seussical* do not have the instant name recognition or the mass appeal needed for a long run in one city, but a sold-out week or two in Houston or Detroit can earn the producers a few hundred thousand dollars in net profits. If a show has a star—a television personality rather than an established Broadway performer—it is that much more attractive. Cathy Rigby, for example, is a perennial road favorite, and while her *Peter Pan* sold well on Broadway in four different limited engagements over eight years, she is a much bigger draw on the road. A country-western star like Larry Gatlin can sell a show to the rafters. Name recognition of a star is critical for marketing a show that is not a must-see phenomenon, while audiences have no interest in the particular casting of a blockbuster like *The Lion King*.

While it might seem that only one group of shows travels from city to city, much like the days of the old vaudeville circuits, in truth, some options allow presenters to respond to the variance in local tastes. This availability of choice requires not just the six or eight productions that one subscription house will book but perhaps fifteen or twenty to satisfy markets around the country. No single organization could produce this many shows on its own, so presenters book productions from multiple producers. Some presenters offer nonunion shows but market them as part of a Broadway series. This practice does not quite constitute false advertising, as some of these productions, such as a recent tour of *The Music Man* that followed hard on the heels of the Broadway revival, are either staged by the original Broadway director or mounted in accordance with the director's original concept, and feature well-wrought touring versions of the original designs. As noted in chapter 2, these tours are the bane of Equity and present a notable challenge to the continued health of union tours.

The hot-button issue today is the rising cost of touring. Local presenters usually pay the tour's producers a guaranteed fee plus a negotiated percentage of the profits above a trigger point. Barry Weissler noted that the break-even point on the road may be more than $150,000 greater than on Broadway, due to trucking, loading in and loading out the show at each venue, and individualized marketing and advertising campaigns. Higher, too, is the amount that producers and presenters take. Local presenters often demand a greater percentage of the gross than Broadway theatre owners do, because their financial risk increases during a shorter run. Equity salaries, however, have grown minimally, and they cannot be considered the primary factor in the excessive costs of sending out a production, regardless of how the League crafts its argument. Equity is perceived as a weaker union than the musicians or stagehands, and the specter of nonunion tours has allowed producers to wrest many concessions from the union. With over 80 percent of the union's more than forty thousand members unemployed at any one time, producers realize that Equity is often willing to agree to concessions in order to preserve the primacy of union tours. However, the imbroglio over the reduced salaries and per diems for *42nd Street* generated such hostility from union membership that Equity's leadership adopted a tougher stance in subsequent discussions with touring producers. But more producers are willing, it seems, to call Equity's bluff. Cameron Mackintosh surprised other producers and union leaders alike when he chose to produce nonunion tours of *Oliver* and *Oklahoma!* after Equity balked at his request for salary reductions. Local presenters view full-cost productions as so prohibitively expensive that they believe that ticket prices will inevitably rise to a level equal to those in New York, an increase that would devastate the markets in most cities.

In 1997 Rocco Landesman and Clear Channel's predecessor, PACE, cobbled together a deal in which Jujamcyn and PACE would produce shows for Broadway that would subsequently tour PACE's markets. This agreement matched the needs of both organizations handsomely; for Jujamcyn, a wealthy investment source was tapped, and PACE was able to avail itself of a sure source of new works. "In the past," said Miles Wilkin, "in some years there was too much product or too little product or not the right mix of product. What this allows us to do is to plan together. Now, it's not just hope and prayer. It's a plan."[5] Rocco Landesman did observe a few years later that "it's always scary when there's that sort of monolithic tower in any place. And a lot of independent road presenters and a lot of the producers are nervous, anxious about that and always will be. On the other hand, if they're with you and you can play all those markets, you have a big leg up."

The greater interdependence between Clear Channel and Broadway has salutary effects for both, but it is worrisome to those who view it as another critical link in Broadway's evolution toward increasingly banal entertainments. Clear Channel has little interest in presenting tours of straight plays, except for the occasional star turn. Broadway producers will generally not mount large-cast straight plays owing to the expense-to-profit ratio, except for limited-run revivals, and the small cast plays they do produce are often overwhelmed by the two- and three-thousand seat houses on the touring circuit. Tours of straight plays were able to succeed on the road in decades past, especially before the larger civic theatres were built, but today, television and the movies satiate an audience's need for pure drama or comedy. Now, straight plays that succeed on Broadway will likely see their next incarnations in regional theatres, not in touring houses, so there is even less incentive for producers to send them on the road.

If a star is the prime attraction for a straight play, the producer's problem is compounded, because most top-flight stars will not commit to a lengthy tour, necessary to turn a profit for lower-priced and harder-to-sell straight plays. Jed Bernstein offered a suggestion, while discussing the success of a limited-run tour of *Death of a Salesman* after its Tony Award–winning revival on Broadway.

> The fact that touring companies of dramas are, in general, not an extra income stream is unfortunate, because we need all of the income streams we can get. But it just means we have to be clever and think of something else. . . . Maybe we don't imagine that you could convince Brian Dennehy to do fifty-two weeks of the tour of *Salesman,* but maybe you could get him to do ten, and then get another star to do ten. Yes, there would be extra rehearsal costs, but on the other hand, at the end of the day you'd have a forty-week tour instead of a ten-week tour.

One advantage that derives from producing a straight play on tour is that the presenter typically pays a much lower guarantee to the producer, making it more affordable. Roy Gabay believes that a viable market for straight plays does exist, although he admits that "a whole circuit needs to be developed of nine-hundred- and one-thousand-seat theatres for a play series." Straight plays are also less expensive to mount because they invariably are designed without the lavish trappings audiences have come to expect and demand from musicals. The expense of a technically complex design is counted not just at the outset, when the scenery and other physical elements are constructed, but at each venue, where a smaller production requires fewer stagehands unloading only a handful of trucks. Large musicals utilize a dozen or more full-length trucks for sets, lights, sound equipment, costumes, and props. Occasionally, a show will require as many as twenty or thirty trucks, although this scale of production is associated with blockbuster musicals moving from one long sit-down date to another. Automation has rendered larger and more complex design concepts simpler to execute, so shows have grown exponentially in size, and those costs are passed on to the presenter at each load-in and load-out. But as costs have grown, so have producers' inclinations to cut as many corners as possible to maintain fiscal stability.

Not too many years ago, a musical on a first national tour playing primary markets might be allotted three or four days to load in to a theatre, in anticipation of a run of several weeks. As each house is architecturally idiosyncratic, with different loading and backstage facilities, some adjustments must be made to the physical production in each city. The producer and presenter are required to hire the number of stagehands mandated by IATSE in accord with the producer. Although the cost of thirty or forty stagehands for the load-in period is high, the sooner the show opens, the sooner it begins to earn income. But a few dozen stagehands still need many hours to load in a complete stage deck (used to mask the automation tracks and cables for moving scenery) and the attendant stage mechanics; hang the flying scenery; load in, hang, and focus as many as a thousand lighting instruments; set up the sophisticated sound equipment and run the cables; store the furniture and props; and set up the orchestra pit, dressing rooms, and wardrobe areas. In addition, there must be some minimal time allotted before the first performance for the full orchestra to play in the pit, with the actors singing onstage, for the sound engineers to balance the show's acoustics. Often there is no time left to rehearse any scene changes and instruct the local stagehands, who augment the core touring crew, in how to run the show. The first performance can be fraught with close calls or even unfortunate technical mishaps. First-night audiences in a road house will often see a bumpy performance, as producers cannot afford the extravagance of a dress rehearsal at the risk of losing the income from a performance.

Robin Wagner, who has designed many touring versions of his Broadway shows over the last thirty-five years, noted a change in the way tours are now handled. The tour of *The Producers*, for which he designed the sets, had been allotted sixteen hours for the load-in of the modest seven trucks of equipment. He added that shows now seem put together with a strict eye toward cost as the guiding precept, with the artistic elements a secondary concern to the producers. "What they really care about is scheduling and booking. It's not about how do you make this show work on the road. . . [Producers are worried about] their guarantees, about making those hours [work]: no overtime, and how few trucks they can get it out with. These are issues that never came up before. And I don't remember people going broke because you were doing big shows and taking two days to put in the stuff." That sixteen-hour load-in has more in common with the amount of time allocated to the scaled-down bus-and-truck tours that play split weeks and one-night stands in the smallest markets. Today, many producers are sending out what would have been billed in previous years as bus-and-truck tours but are using the super-sized "Direct from Broadway, National Tour" moniker. "I got a call [about] *Saturday Night Fever* . . . and the managers were saying, 'We want to lose the bridge set, and we want to lose the mirrors and the dressing room sets. We've got to cut a truck,'" said Wagner. A truck may cost up to two thousand dollars weekly, for fuel, insurance, and drivers' salaries, plus the stagehands' wages to load in whatever the truck carries. Cost cutting is understandable, but when decisions are made after a show has been conceived and staged, they compromise the original integrity of the production. But a common sentiment among producers is that once a tour has garnered its first set of strong reviews, which will be used to advertise the show during the rest of the run, they can jettison some of the production values and attendant costs without risking too much damaging fallout. This practice represents either poor production management during the planning phase of the tour or a disregard for the conceptual work of the creative team, or both. The justification offered, that this is the only way to keep marginal productions afloat, has some validity, but in most instances, the decision is made to bolster sagging profit margins. The unfortunate truth is that most audiences will never know the difference. However, from time to time, local theatre critics will have seen the production at an earlier engagement and will note in their review the parsimonious nature of the current version. Most producers accept the criticism in stride, in light of the savings.

The demographics of touring audiences are worth noting. According to the last study commissioned by the League, during the 1999–2000 season, the twelve million tickets sold for tours represented more than half of all tickets sold for productions around the nation and eclipsed the number of tickets sold on Broadway. The single most persuasive selling tool was word of mouth and not reviews, advertising, or marketing. The average theatregoer in these markets attended six shows during the year, two more than the average Broadway theatregoer, a number that results from 45 percent of touring audiences purchasing subscription packages, which do not exist in commercial Broadway houses. One similarity between touring and Broadway audiences is that the composition is primarily female, over fifty years old, affluent, well educated, and Caucasian.[6]

On Broadway, where theatregoers attending commercial productions must buy single tickets, there exists a remarkably enterprising subsector devoted to marketing, advertising, and selling tickets. To lure those middle-aged women and their families and friends, and to broaden the market, producers are no longer content with only posters; flyers; newspaper, subway, and bus ads; and similar ploys that for years were the stock-in-trade of the industry. Today producers find themselves, sometimes reluctantly, in thrall to a host of public relations, advertising, press, marketing, and group sales representatives, who help them craft the best strategy to sell their shows.

The newest buzzword in the Broadway lexicon is *branding,* and it is now employed not just by the corporations but by the rank-and-file membership of the League. At the ACT II conference in Cambridge, the closing session was devoted to an overview of techniques that could be used to brand "theatre." According to one of the speakers at the conference, Alan Adamson, the managing director of Landor Associates, a leading firm in the field of brand identity, branding "is a shortcut for making decisions. It's a way—particularly by Americans but more and more around the world—people make choices. Because making choices any other way has become very complicated."[7] While such egregious corporate newspeak annoys some traditionalists, the point that Adamson underscored was that the industry needed to raise the profile of theatre in the cultural life of America. The concept of selling theatre itself as a brand, rather than targeting individual shows, would have the benefit of increasing business across the board, he maintained. According to the account given by Jeremy Gerard, many ideas were discussed, including rethinking performance times, pricing structures, and a greater openness in sharing information about how shows are selling.[8]

Jed Bernstein offered his view, a few months after the conference, that Broadway does not exploit its full marketing potential. Many producers and artists alike, he said, are reluctant to adopt new approaches to selling their shows, indeed to selling theatre, because the industry is afraid to explore new avenues of marketing, thus impeding the chance to expand the audience base. The germinal, unique experience of sharing a dramatic event can be augmented with merchandising and other ways of reliving the event, but they will never replace the event itself. "In theatre, it's almost as if we've been martyrs for so long, we're so insecure, that we don't have enough self-confidence to believe in the product. In fact, the product is pretty unique, pretty unbelievably great. And we've got to believe in it, and not think that fifty-two ersatz ways of experiencing it can replace it. If managed correctly, they will enhance it." If the makers of theatre in America cannot determine a way to prove its value for the nation in a forceful and emphatic fashion, theatregoing will drop off precipitously. At that point, said Bernstein, "it's going to be a ritual, and eventually, the last person that remembers the ritual is going to die, and that will be it. And that would be terrible."

Producers can spend considerable sums on advertising and marketing, with ten percent of a preproduction budget currently the norm. Theatre is a handcrafted industry, and all of the pressure, work, and money spent to create a play or musical will still result in only one production playing in one space eight times a week—a number that is unlikely to rise due to union resistance.

A not-for-profit theatre with a subscription base will rely heavily on direct mail to tout its wares. Todd Haimes, at the Roundabout, attempted to generate new audiences by marketing subscriptions constructed around themes; there was a singles' subscription series, a wine-tasting subscription, and so forth. Although this move was regarded with some disdain in certain producing quarters as shameless pandering—possibly the result of envy of the Roundabout's innovation rather than sincere criticism—others applauded the company for its attempt to diversify its outreach. Disney, with worldwide name recognition, can market its shows in a variety of venues unavailable to most independent producers.

The choices available to independent producers are somewhat more circumscribed by financial limitations. For producers to counter the power of the corporations, which, as one producer put it, "are marketing machines," they must continue to explore new ways to get the word out about their shows, especially in the event of mixed or poor reviews. Said Rocco Landesman, "It used to be basically just advertising. Now, the marketing element has taken on a bigger and bigger part of it, which is to get a shot at people's consciousness in ways other than sheer advertising: promotions, and PR, and marketing stunts, and so forth. The level of marketing savvy has increased manifold since we started out." Roy Somlyo, though, observed that "marketing has always existed in the theatre. We may not have called it that, but I had a marketing director on my shows, going back to the eighties . . . a person who tied in with various commercial products, whether they were subtle product placement, or whether they were companies buying tickets for their employees." Although, as president of the American Theatre Wing, he was in a position to extol the virtues of "theatre," he questioned the value of marketing Broadway as a commodity, because, as he pointed out, "people don't decide on going to a Broadway show; they decide they're going to *The Lion King* or *Aida* or *The Full Monty*. They pick their product. I guess we don't hurt anything by marketing Broadway, [but] I don't think that awareness of Broadway is something you can market." If Somlyo is right, the League's intention to do just that may generate little more than another unnecessary assault on the American senses.

One reason, perhaps, that Broadway feels so compelled to adopt more aggressive campaigns is that theatre has lost much of its former cachet as a vibrant and attractive source of entertainment. Josh Ellis, formerly one of New York's leading press agents, noted that

> over the time I was a press agent in New York, publications would do a fall preview issue, telling us what was coming up in movies and TV, and theatre was always one of those areas they were talking about. Over time, theatre fell into that "miscellaneous" category, and then it fell off entirely, unless that miscellaneous segment had a star, or was an event like *Seussical.* For the most part, there is no large concern about what happens in the theatre, unless it's one of those megashows that has been so pretested that the national publications feel relatively safe.

The relative inaccessibility and expense of theatre—in relation to movies, television, home videos and games, and Internet entertainment—are difficult to overcome no matter how smartly theatre is marketed. When rising prices and changing demographics occasioned Broadway's transition from a staple of the cultural life of New York to special event status, fewer potential audience members were willing to make the effort and incur the expense.

One valuable tool for marketing Broadway is the annual Tony Awards television broadcast. While viewership continues to decline, the Tonys offer Broadway its best chance at capturing the hearts and minds of millions of potential theatregoers for two hours on a Sunday night in early June. The Tonys have evolved from a traditional awards show that allotted time to every category to one in which star badinage and more production numbers have forced many "lesser" award categories off the air. But the bigger problem with the Tony telecast is that the producers of the show have not figured out a way to present scenes from straight plays. As a result, although awards are given to these shows, audiences see only scenes from musicals, reinforcing the notion that straight plays are marginal or unappetizing. When Alexander Cohen produced the telecast, he tried to include scenes from straight plays, but the network felt that a scene out of context made a strange two- or three-minute sound bite. A musical song-and-dance number is a more complete theatrical moment. In the fifties and sixties, former show business columnist Ed Sullivan was always pleased to present scenes from both plays and musicals on his Sunday night show. But this was the era of televised productions of dramatic, theatrical works, and audiences were better able to contextualize the presentation of those small offerings. Now, no such widely viewed television outlet would incur the expense needed to present these scenes. The marginalization of straight plays and the corporations' avowed interest in pursuing only large-scale, big-ticket musicals have rendered plays an afterthought in the marketing of Broadway.

Marketing schemes have taken on a life of their own, beyond the work itself. Marty Bell had a previous career in journalism and knows what kind of lead-in or catch writers look for. He described a marketing idea for *A Class Act,* about the struggles of composer Ed Kleban to get his songs produced in the theatre: "a national song-writing contest. We'll get a sponsor involved, and on eight Sunday afternoons, after the matinees, the eight finalists will be on a Broadway stage performing their songs for the audience. And then we'll narrow it down to a finalist, and the winner will probably get his songs recorded by the company that is doing the original cast album. And what that does is to make the show a bigger event. It communicates exactly what the show is to the audience; it makes a national idea instead of just a local idea." Daryl Roth worked with a promotional company for the Broadway production of *Tale of the Allergist's Wife,* whose heroine is an inveterate shopper at upscale New York stores. Bloomingdale's created a store window featuring the show, and Saks sent out mailers about the show to their credit card customers. These ploys are an essential selling device, say producers, contemporary versions of Broadway's ongoing efforts to burrow its way into the public's consciousness. The master marketer was David Merrick. The impresario pulled a stunning coup—more notable for the notoriety it gained him than for the box office boost for his show—to publicize the 1961 musical *Subways Are for Sleeping.* Merrick ordered an assistant to comb the pages of the local phone books to find a handful of people with the same names as the major theatre critics for the New York press. They were invited to the show and wined and dined at Sardi's. Each "contributed" a rave quote extolling the show's virtues. When the show received mediocre reviews, Merrick ran an ad blaring the quotes from the critics' namesakes, and carefully included tiny photos of each "critic" in order to deflect any charge of intentional disinformation. The ads ran briefly before the newspapers caught on, and the subsequent brouhaha garnered Merrick extraordinary press.[9]

Absent such shamelessly devious grandstanding, a crucial decision in crafting a campaign is how to spend the money available. Large-scale musicals in bigger houses must be marketed to families, allowing a producer to sell more tickets at one go, and must be pitched to an audience that lives beyond the core metropolitan area. A national campaign, featuring more television advertising, may be best suited to the show's needs. Many straight plays, and musicals in smaller houses that are oriented to an adult market, can rely on print ads, particularly in the *New York Times*. However, that expense is extremely high, with a one-time, full-page ad in the Sunday Arts and Leisure section costing more than eighty thousand dollars. (One Broadway producer wryly noted that "the *New York Times* periodically writes articles decrying the rise in ticket prices, failing to mention that, come hell or high water, every January first their ad rates go up, significantly, like clockwork"). Word of mouth can often generate sufficient additional sales, but after one or two years, a different strategy is needed to tap other markets.

Garth Drabinsky was known to be a strong and enthusiastic advocate of focus groups, and crafted campaigns around the input gleaned from them, but this approach is generally reviled by traditionalists. Josh Ellis concurred. "Gut instinct told us. We didn't do a lot of market surveys." The impetus to use focus groups comes from the corporate film world, where Drabinsky enjoyed his salad days, where sneak previews are employed to gauge an audience's reaction. The preview period for a Broadway show allows the producer and artists that opportunity to rework the show, but audiences are rarely consulted to determine how they would like to see the play adjusted. Most artists believe that therein lies madness.

Josh Ellis identified two points in time as pivotal in the evolution of marketing on Broadway. The first occurred in 1973, when Bob Fosse directed a one-minute television commercial for his musical *Pippin*. The second resulted from the marketing approach that Cameron Mackintosh and Andrew Lloyd Webber brought from England a few years later, unlike anything that Broadway had seen before. "The fact that you had a hit song before the show opened, the idea that you had a music video— we're talking about a new era," said Ellis.

Rick Elice is now an artistic consultant with Disney Theatrical. After his first career, as a Yale Drama School–trained actor in New York, he spent eighteen years as a creative director for the most prestigious and successful of Broadway advertising agencies, Serino Coyne. During that time, he worked on four hundred Broadway shows and thousands of television and radio commercials and print campaigns. Elice recalled that early television ads for Broadway consisted of still photographs with crude graphics. He concurred with Josh Ellis that Fosse's commercial for

Pippin was a turning point in selling shows. Fosse, whose star at the time was at its apogee, determined that the best way to address the sagging fortunes of the show was to create a commercial that featured an extended dance sequence. The kind of dance material that would work best for a commercial, however, did not exist in the show, so Fosse created a new number based on the extant dances, featuring Ben Vereen and Anne Reinking. The voiceover promised the audience richer delights if they went to the Imperial Theatre. Said Elice, "The commercial became so successful that the sequence was interpolated into the show, but it was Fosse's big idea that people would respond to an advertisement that was as entertaining as the show that it was representing, and that was a whole new way of thinking, of how to portray theatrical productions in advertising." He cited Nancy Coyne, who cofounded Serino Coyne in 1977, with creating even more imaginative approaches to selling shows. Coyne, who began her advertising career at the forerunner of many of today's agencies, Blaine Thompson, had the notion to shoot the television ad for the musical *Shenandoah* in the countryside, because, as Elice pointed out, "She understood that what works in a theatrical reality doesn't necessarily translate to the literary reality of TV." It was her work on commercials for *Grease* and *A Chorus Line* that put her in the limelight and allowed her to start her own agency. She believes that television was an almost surefire savior for any foundering show in the midseventies and early eighties. "All you needed to run was a really good TV commercial."

Now television ads are prohibitively expensive, and sixty-second spots, even if affordable, would be hard-pressed to hold the attention of today's audiences. Producers use television campaigns much more sparingly now. They will often wait until after December 26 to run their television ads, when air time costs drop by almost 40 percent. The timing is appropriate, too, as the postholiday season typically presents one of the two big drops in box office attendance (the other, for many new, marginal shows, occurs in June if they fail to capture critical Tony Awards). Most Broadway commercials play only in the New York metropolitan area, as the costs to do so nationally would be exceedingly expensive with little resultant payoff. (National tours do run advance television ads frequently in key markets, often employing some or all of the Broadway ad.)

Nancy Coyne defends the costs of advertising on Broadway. While she admitted that expenses have risen, she observed that many other costs have escalated even more dramatically. Still, as she ruefully acknowledged, even one million dollars in 2000 would probably not buy a producer a significant presence in all of the major media outlets. But her agency rarely utilizes more than 10 percent of a show's gross potential for advertising in any given week, a percentage that she said had never risen. Radio ads may work well for a revival with recognizable songs or for an easily accessible new musical with a pop music score. Television is a more effective tool for shows with a big star or a stunning visual component. As Coyne characterized her approach, "Each show has to be examined under a microscope for its strengths, and then you have to match its strengths to the medium that can best exploit [them]. I like to think that our talent as an ad agency is particularizing a campaign. We have no boilerplates, no 'this is the way we do it.' We don't have any formulas." Even a revival of a show she has previously advertised will warrant an entirely different approach.

Producers have had to explore more cost-effective marketing approaches. Direct mail is an effective way to tout a show's worth, but it is invariably used in conjunction with discounted ticket pricing. Initially the industry believed that it could work only for subscription-based theatres. Now, independent producers have discovered that with the right three ingredients, as Nancy Coyne identified them—"a limited engagement, a star, and a discount"—direct mail can be quite effective. One surprising discovery she made, however, is that the Internet is not an effective tool for selling Broadway shows. "People delete their e-mail. They don't open e-mail, wisely, if they don't know who the sender is. Banner ads are useless, at best. As for sending people to a show Web site, I'd much rather send them to a ticket Web site. Why have them do two-stop shopping when I can send them directly to the source? If they want to know more about [a show], chances are they've already seen [it] and just want to browse. That's fine, but that's not the business I'm in." But even direct advertising cannot accomplish much if the client is the producer of a straight play. Coyne decided in the late nineties to avoid handling them, "because the market isn't there. The market is here for musicals. That's what people, tourists, who undoubtedly are not going to see straight plays in their own home town, want."

Coyne compared the amount of money she spends weekly on a show with the amount of money McDonald's spends on its advertising, and explained that McDonald's offers an inexpensive essential item, food, while she sells a higher-priced luxury commodity. Additionally, theatre is a luxury. "You have to schlep to an inconvenient location to get it, and it's only available eight times a week. In order to convince you to purchase this much more incredibly expensive item, I have a fraction of the dollars McDonald's has to sell its hamburgers." Movie producers can capitalize on a show's success by saturating the market with more showings on more screens, but Broadway producers cannot. "It's a frustrating economic challenge when you have that ceiling at all times." There was some talk that Disney might produce a second company of *The Lion King* to run in another Broadway theatre, but that never proved economically advisable.

Coyne's frustrations are shared by many producers of large-scale, hit musicals who yearn for larger houses. This issue compelled Disney to seek alternative venues in midtown Manhattan for future productions, as they believe that the size and scope of much of their anticipated work will necessitate larger theatres with greater seating capacity. Most independent producers cannot afford the costs of converting an existing space into a Broadway-style theatre. Thus far the theatre chains have evinced more interest in the development of smaller venues, like the Off-Broadway houses on West Forty-second Street, west of Ninth Avenue.

One final transaction must transpire before the theatregoer is seated: the sale of a ticket. It is a truism that the only people who pay full price for a ticket are either first-time tourists or wealthy executives on expense account. Many infrequent theatregoers buy tickets at brokers, who tack on expensive service charges to secure tickets for hits, but tickets for many shows are available for less than face price. The most visible source is the TKTS booth, in Duffy Square, five short blocks north of Forty-second Street, with another site at South Street Seaport. The booth sells about 2.5 million theatre seats annually for both Broadway and Off-Broadway, as well as dance and music performances, at both half price and a 25 percent discount. Box office managers determine daily how many unsold tickets will be "sent" electronically to the booth. (In the early days, after the booth's opening in 1973, hard tickets were delivered by box office representatives.) There are two drawbacks to buying tickets at the booth. A prospective buyer will never know with certainty what shows will be available until she reaches the ticket counter. To do so, she must wait in line, often in miserable weather, for quite some time, depending on individual tenacity and the degree of desire to get the best tickets available. Theatre Development Fund, which oversees the booth, also offers a series of discounted tickets to a mailing list of over seventy-five thousand union members, students, seniors, teachers, clergy, servicemen and women, and members of other special-interest groups. The booth has been of immeasurable assistance to producers, allowing them to shore up sagging grosses, as an unsold ticket has no shelf life after the date of performance.

The advent of computerized ticket sales in the late seventies was a signal event for producers and audience members alike for three crucial reasons. It made tickets more readily available and trackable, it allowed tickets to be sold for a date further in the future, and it effectively put an end to the very costly and illegal practice known as "ice." This box office ticket-scalping scam had plagued producers for decades, and it was a New York state attorney general's investigation in 1964 that first brought it to public attention. *Ice* referred to the illegal sale by box office workers of unsold, unused house seats—those desirable, top-priced seats set aside by the producers for use by themselves and company members—to brokers. The brokers would in turn sell them at an astonishing markup and kick back a sizable commission to the box office treasurer. The producer saw only the profits from the initial face value recorded sale. Although some box office treasurers and theatre owners preferred to keep their business shrouded with a cloak of old-school secrecy, the producers became advocates of computerized systems to better track ticket sales and end the persistent problem of ice.

By the end of the seventies, Telecharge and Ticketron sold tickets on the phone, marking another crucial step in the evolution of the process. Previously, a buyer had a few options, none of which were particularly convenient—to travel to the theatre and perhaps wait in a long line, to mail in a check to the box office, or to patronize a broker. Before the advent of telephone sales, in-person or mail-order sales could be effected only by use of cash or check—box offices did not accept credit cards, as the owners did not want to pay the fees. The new phone services required computerization of the sales system, and while a walk-up customer could still buy a hard ticket sold off the rack rather than generated by computer, there was now the beginning of a modern and streamlined system. Although it took a few years to coordinate the phone system and the burgeoning in-theatre computers, a new means of selling tickets was finally in place by the late eighties. Tickets could now be sold at a variety of venues rather than only at the theatre or through a broker or hotel concierge. When tickets were sold in hard form only, at the theatre, it was feasible to sell them in only thirty-day advance blocks. Once computers proved effective, producers realized that they could sell tickets over a longer time frame and generate bigger advance sales.

The changes in the selling of tickets occurred at the same time that

Nancy Coyne was making her mark by changing the way Broadway sold its shows. Those two factors, ventured Rick Elice, together occasioned the presence of more blockbuster musicals with longer runs. *Cats*, in 1982, said Elice, was the

> the first show with a great big advance sale, the first time a show's advance—and the *Cats* advance was enormous for its time—became news. And because tickets were so unavailable, the ad campaign became not about selling out this week or this month, but about convincing the public that buying tickets *six* months from now and looking forward to going was part of the fun. Emphasizing the pleasures of anticipation was a whole new way to sell the theatre-going experience, which, up to that time, had generally been about instant gratification ... "Let's go to the theatre tonight!" And that strategy, of course, not only helped maintain the advance, it helped the show run longer.

Computers now allowed producers and theatre owners to view buying trends and to craft their marketing campaigns with greater accuracy. The age of the blockbuster English musical had arrived on Broadway. No longer was a run of four or five years considered extraordinary; *Cats*, *Les Misérables*, *A Chorus Line*, *Miss Saigon*, and *The Phantom of the Opera* all ran at least three times as long. They became institutions, redefining the nature of what a musical could accomplish at the box office and spawning enormous successes in international and touring venues. Since movie versions of hit Broadway musicals have not been in vogue for decades— the recent success of the film *Chicago* was an anomaly—producers could no longer count on that significant potential income. Longer runs now fill that income gap.

The age of the computer-generated ticket has been augmented by the age of the Internet discount ticket. A variety of Web sites, maintained by a diverse array of theatre owners, corporate producers, industry groups, and entrepreneurs, all compete for the chance to sell cheaper tickets to all but the biggest hits. In some ways, this discounting was necessitated by the aftermath of September 11, 2001, subsequent international tensions, and war, when producers scrambled to sell their shows after a substantial falloff in tourism. There has not yet been a sufficient resurgence in tourist attendance on Broadway to occasion the elimination of deep discounting, so producers continue to operate under the assumption that a ticket sold for a discounted price is better than a ticket unsold, and plan their recoupment charts around different discounting percentages. Roy

Gabay observed, "We're now pricing things to be discounted . . . [and] I don't know how to break out of that. We've instilled the mentality that you can get theatre tickets for a discount. It's not even how much of a discount, or that people can't afford the full price. It's the concept of 'why should I pay retail?' We may have dug ourselves into that hole too deeply." This discounting is emblematic of the changing economics of selling commodities in America. The Internet, in particular, has made discount purchasing an increasingly common practice that cuts across many income classes. Producers have learned that Broadway shows must keep pace with other entertainment sectors that utilize Internet sales and discounting.

Group sales companies have offered blocks of discounted tickets for several decades. Ronald Lee, owner of the largest of the approximately fifteen companies in the sector, has been involved in group sales for more than forty years. Such companies first worked only with nonprofit, charitable organizations, but today they sell to any affinity group, from schools to social clubs, from travel agencies to theatre tours. They employ telephone solicitation, direct mail, and theatrical presentations to excite sales. Lee, whose company handles roughly a third of current musicals, acts as a middleman for groups and theatre box offices and, because of his strong and enduring relationship with producers and theatre owners, is able to commandeer excellent tickets for hard-to-get shows. While the theatre owners and corporate producers maintain their own group sales divisions, they are, according to Lee, not a major drain on his business "because they are reactive. When the phone rings, they answer. I promote business by actively telemarketing." Lee sells his tickets for a straight 10 percent commission, typically paid by the producer. As Lee pointed out, the virtue of group sales for the producer is the ability to amass a larger advance; "the bigger the advance sale, the better the financial cushion." One unfortunate change in the nature of Broadway, Lee has noted, is the difficulty in selling straight plays. Audiences now tend to view theatre more as pure entertainment and less as thought-provoking fare, "and the serious play has to struggle to find a market. And you can't have too many plays that can attract an audience at the same time."

While discounts are now a more familiar component of the Broadway landscape, a relative newcomer is the premium ticket. Livent sold luxury seats to *Ragtime,* much like a sporting event, offering champagne and other amenities to those willing to pay $125. But an even more astonishing example of ticket markup was introduced in 2001 by some of the producers of *The Producers.* Broadway Inner Circle offered high-flying

consumers the chance to pay $480 for each of fifty tickets for any per-
formance of that show. This scheme was geared to very wealthy or corporate patrons who wanted the best seats at a moment's notice. While
the Circle producers argued that they did so to make tickets available to
those willing to pay the price, their pricing was also intended to cut into
the profits made by scalpers, who can charge two or three times the face
value of a ticket to a hit show. Some critics of the Circle's pricing responded
that it would serve only to make theatre appear even more elitist than it
already seemed, like opera, and was the mark of greedy producers who
wanted to wring every last cent from the audience. While eighty dollars of
the price goes to the coffers of Broadway Inner Circle, the rest—four times
the current top ticket price—goes to the show's accounts. A show that sells
out at full price and utilizes the Circle scheme now has the chance to earn
more than 100 percent of its gross potential in a week. The Circle managers argued that it allowed an extra amount weekly to be paid to the
creators and investors, who ordinarily would see nothing more than the
usual return on a scalped ticket, the price of which cannot be controlled
by the producer.[10] But one Broadway producer observed that the eighty
dollars in fees that went directly to the Circle managers earned them an
extra four thousand dollars weekly. In some fashion, however, the Circle
pricing is in keeping with the producers' conventional wisdom that one
must exploit a hit for its greatest potential.

As the most vested of all interest groups, producers and owners must
cultivate a greater awareness of Broadway and the pleasures and benefits
of attending theatre there. To do so, both the American Theatre Wing and
the League have developed extensive outreach and education programs.
The Wing, in addition to overseeing the annual Tony Awards show, produces televised seminars on working in the theatre and sponsors high
school outings to Broadway shows, where, according to Roy Somlyo, they
pay $2.50 for a ticket and arrive not on a school bus but on their own.
This, he said, inculcates in them a degree of familiarity with the process
of paying to see theatre—albeit at a relatively insignificant cost—and trav-
eling to get there. The Wing also sends panelists and teachers to schools
around the city to conduct workshops and classes in the theatrical process. The League maintains similar outreach programs, like a Kids Night
on Broadway, in which parents can purchase tickets for their children at
half price. This scheme has been modestly successful, although there is
some question as to how frequently producers can afford that decrease
in box office revenue. It is a marketing showpiece rather than a truly

viable tool to encourage theatregoing. The industry's greatest challenge is combating the perception that Broadway theatre is elitist and overpriced. The League has harnessed its energies to create an image for Broadway that is attractive to a middle-class, middle-American audience whose theatre-going habits and tastes are quite different from those of the previous generation of Broadway audiences. The radical renovation of the theatre district and the evolution of the work performed on its stages reflect a new direction for Broadway.

7 The Nature of the Beast

Somehow, everybody seems to think that Broadway used to be really smart, and today, for some reason, they think that Broadway is really stupid. Wait a minute!
 —Thomas Schumacher, Disney Theatrical

There are not a lot of risk takers left. That's the sad part.
 —Scott Zeiger, CEO, Clear Channel Entertainment Theatrical Group, North America

The biggest marquee on Forty-second Street heralds not the delights of *The Lion King* or another blockbuster musical but the more prosaic wares of that ubiquitous outpost of the American culinary landscape, McDonald's. The presence of a fast-food chain on a prime strip of New York real estate is not unusual, but that its supersized theatrical calling card outstrips that of any legitimate theatre on the street speaks volumes about the Broadway district today. The changes to the area, the result of years of internecine struggles within city and state government and local business interest groups, bear scrutiny to discern the current zeitgeist and the possible future of Broadway.

The heart of the theatre district lies roughly between Sixth and Eighth Avenues, and Forty-second and Fifty-second Streets, with Lincoln Center another half-mile uptown in the West Sixties. The very terms *theatre district, Broadway, Times Square,* and *Forty-second Street* are often used to denote the same place, but subtle differences exist. Times Square, for example—originally Longacre Square—is often applied to the entire district but actually refers to the area immediately north of Forty-second Street where Broadway and Seventh Avenue intersect. The entire neighborhood, however, has been associated with entertainment for the better part of the twentieth century and has long enjoyed iconic status as the avatar of popular, live performance, as well as sundry other easily consumable cultural offerings.

Most of the extant theatres date to the first few decades of the twentieth century, with a preponderance of the houses built before the Depression. While many theatres either were razed to give way to more lucrative real estate ventures or have been converted to other uses, the core few dozen of the older houses still form the heart and soul of Broadway, architecturally as well as spiritually. Most artists agree that no matter how comfortable, spacious, and well appointed the newer spaces are—the Gershwin, Minskoff, Circle in the Square, Beaumont–Lincoln Center, and Marquis—they lack the history and atmosphere of the older theatres. Audiences, too, although perhaps unable to quite articulate the distinction, experience amidst the splendor of the Majestic or the New Amsterdam an event very different from that in the relatively sterile confines of the more recently constructed houses.

For decades, the tawdry glitter of Broadway, captured in so many films, photographs, songs, stories, and plays provided a vividly picturesque and quintessentially theatrical backdrop for the artistic endeavors inside the theatres. The opening sequence of the 1950 musical *Guys and Dolls* expresses the metatheatrical commentary on the zest and spirit of the place and time. Broadway signified a curiously compelling and very American notion of entertainment, a locus of every form of performative pleasure, from plays and musicals and opera and movies to nightclub shows and titillating variety acts. For decades Broadway was regarded as a place unlike any other, where "there's a bright light for every broken heart," a street of garish and gaudy delights and intense hucksterism. That the veneer of sophistication and glamour purveyed on Broadway might be tissue-thin added in some way to its mystique and charm. It was a place where the tacky could easily cohabit with the profound. There pulsed, on Broadway, a concatenation of aural and visual signs that screamed that it was the place to be, twenty-four hours a day.

While some keen observers of the urban scene have remarked that the Broadway district has been slowly decaying since the Depression, by the sixties, the spirit of artistic plenty had completely withered. Occasioned by the sad confluence of urban deterioration and economic blight, the area had given way to a tarnished and depressing parade of petty criminals, drug dealers and users, prostitutes of every stripe, and street hustlers (1969's *Midnight Cowboy* captured the dispiriting and menacing ambiance of the neighborhood). While commercial theatres continued to ply their trade, the growing presence of porn movie houses, massage parlors, and intimidating and unsavory characters increasingly sapped the lifeblood of the district. While audiences still attended Broadway shows, there was a severe drop-off in attendance in the seventies and early eighties. The flight of the urban middle class in the sixties from the dangerous city to the safer and more salubrious suburbs was perhaps the most significant factor. As writers fled to Hollywood in search of more lucrative work, the perception grew that Broadway had atrophied artistically, and Broadway's decline was palpably reinforced by the unpleasant experience of attending a show—especially at night and even more so when taking the subway. While some natives displayed a perverse New York pride in their ability to take in stride the grim decline of the district, most, including theatre workers, found it either embarrassing or deplorable, or both. By the sixties, the stretch of Forty-second Street between Seventh and Eighth Avenues had gained a reputation as one of the most sordid urban combat zones in the nation.

Today, of course, the area has received a cosmetic and aesthetic makeover of remarkable proportion. Beginning in the sixties, a series of city and state-funded studies produced a number of different plans to revitalize the area, but economic and bureaucratic obstacles prevented any serious developments until the late eighties. Until then the area languished in a twilight sleep, waiting for a fairy godmother to wave her magic wand and transform the ugly duckling into a beautiful swan. In the late seventies, a minirenovation of sorts was accomplished, just west of the Broadway district, with the construction of Theatre Row, a string of Off- and Off-Off-Broadway theatres, and Manhattan Plaza, two massive apartment towers that were designed as subsidized housing for thousands of working artists. While the eighties did bring some redevelopment to the area, it was perceived by many as the wrong sort. The 1982 demolition of the Helen Hayes, Morosco, and Bijou Theatres that made way for what is now the Marriott Marquis hotel and theatre generated a bitter and well-publicized outcry by the theatre community, which viewed the city's deal with the hotel's developer, the Portman Corporation, as a pact with the devil.[1] The net loss from the construction was two theatres, and it seemed emblematic of the city's attitude of neglect toward the theatre industry, which was the soul of the district in the first place. But to many who took the longer view, the hotel was seen as a necessary, initial step in the development of Times Square, because it demonstrated a midwestern company's belief in and commitment to the restoration of the area.

Aside from the bitter battle over the Portman project, most of the planning for a complete makeover was largely invisible to the public, as one roadmap after another for reinvigorating Times Square as a dynamic business district was discarded. Still, in the eighties, there was a shift in urban planning policy. Old edifices along Seventh Avenue and Broadway

began to fall to the wrecking ball, and new hotel towers and office buildings were erected. The real estate crash of the early nineties occasioned
a downturn in development, however. While parts of Seventh Avenue and
Broadway had been remade, the western edge of the district, at Eighth
Avenue, remained a seedy and disreputable outpost, dotted with pornography arcades and anchored by the architecturally brutish and squalid
Port Authority Terminal on the southwest corner of Eighth and Forty-
second Street. Most notably, the fabled one-block stretch of Forty-second Street itself from Eighth to Seventh Avenue was still a bastion of every
sort of unsavory activity imaginable, both behind closed doors and on
the street. A gap-toothed row of movie houses, some of which had been
legitimate theatres, featured porn and martial arts films. Massage parlors and adult bookstores proliferated. It was an appalling example of
urban decay, and despite the attentions of the police and civic leaders,
nothing could seem to dislodge the dregs from the street.

Plans had been in the works since the early days of the Koch administration in the seventies, but Forty-second Street would not emerge from
its chrysalis until the midnineties, during Rudolph Giuliani's term in City
Hall. By then, a deliberately crafted blueprint to reinvent the area as a new
entertainment center had been the beneficiary of a change in corporate
attitude toward New York, new zoning laws that facilitated the eviction
of almost the entire skin trade, and the construction of several new office towers. Cora Cahan, the dynamic leader of the New Forty-second
Street, Inc. (New 42), whose charge it was to oversee the transformation
of six of the nine theatres on the street, had already spearheaded the
development of a not-for-profit children's theatre in the New Victory, on
the north side of the street. A children's theatre declared in no uncertain
terms that Forty-second Street was going to change. By this time, some
key corporations had already gambled that the area would continue its
upmarket shift and had established offices and outlets in Times Square.
A new skyscraper at 1540 Broadway became the home to the publishing
conglomerate Bertelsman, and other companies followed suit.

The pivotal organization in the renaissance was the 42nd Street Development Project (or 42DP), a state agency born in the late seventies with
the express purpose of coordinating the revitalization of West Forty-second Street between Broadway and Eighth Avenue. The agency's first maneuver was to utilize state powers of condemnation to reclaim most of the
buildings on the street and force the sex shops to relocate to other areas.
The plan went through several phases, and its early stages proceeded in

desultory fashion due to a series of lawsuits by the pornography trade, as well as difficulty in identifying major tenants and developers. Throughout the duration of the project, the three constant bulwarks remained the construction of three office towers; the reclamation of nine theatres, two of which were mandated as not-for-profits; and the building of a hotel on the western end of the street. The bulkier new constructions anchored the corners, and the middle of the block was to remain low-rise.

Because the only theatre designated as a landmark on the street was the New Amsterdam, a plan was needed to develop the other, unprotected spaces. Some were to be converted to other uses, but a core group was to remain as theatres, and they needed considerable upgrades. Unrenovated theatres built during the early part of the twentieth century typically are uncomfortable and lack ample wing space. Many had second balconies, now considered a box office liability. The Lyric and Academy (formerly the Apollo) Theatres were converted into one large space and leased by New 42 to Livent, which dubbed it the Ford Center. The Selwyn was leased to the Roundabout and renamed the American Airlines Theatre. Sorely needed rehearsal spaces were built elsewhere on the street, and several producers relocated to office buildings there. The AMC corporation bought the Empire Theatre and constructed a multiscreen movie complex, preserving much of the glorious facade of the original proscenium arch in its new lobby. Chain stores and chain restaurants joined the fray, and soon the remade street was aglow with neon and chaser lights. Families, groups of tourists, and even some native New Yorkers began to flock to Forty-second Street to enjoy the corporate delights that were offered there, the newcomers largely unaware of the drastic change that had occurred in less than a decade. The signal event, architecturally as well as symbolically, that started the redevelopment chain reaction was the formal announcement in July 1995, after more than a year of negotiations, that the Walt Disney Company was going to establish a theatre on Broadway in the long-derelict New Amsterdam.

Initially, many pundits voiced surprise. How did Disney, synonymous with clean, good-spirited, family fun, assume that it could survive on the most disreputable street in New York City? No matter how much it spent on renovating the theatre, unless Disney took over the entire street—which it had no intention of doing—it would be only one component in a larger commercial and retail framework, quite unlike its amusement and theme parks around the world. The New Amsterdam itself had been in a terrible state of disrepair for years. The home of the original Ziegfeld

Follies was a magnificent structure but had long been unoccupied and was crumbling from age and neglect. Disney, however, was seeking new ways to position itself internationally. The failure of some high-profile ventures both at home and abroad, and the success of its newly revitalized feature animation division, convinced Michael Eisner that a Broadway presence, and its subsequent potential for vertical integration internationally, might be a viable maneuver.[2] Eisner was persuaded by his friend, the architect Robert Stern, a board member of 42DP, to tour the theatre in March 1993 and consider it as a possible home for Disney's first Broadway production, *Beauty and the Beast*. Disney executives were hoping to find their own venue, both to control their destiny and to preserve the 5 or 6 percent of the gross typically paid in rent to a theatre owner. Encouraged by the long runs of shows like *The Phantom of the Opera*, Disney believed that the time was ripe for its own move to Broadway.

Eisner was evidently taken with the art nouveau theatre. He recognized its enormous potential for renewed life and splendor, as well the chance to establish a well-publicized presence in Manhattan for his company. The negotiations commenced, and the corporate world took note of Disney's willingness to gamble its New York fortunes on the renovation of the area. The city and the state agencies worked to meet Disney's demands, which included a detailed list of improvements to the street. One condition, according to an insider, was that two entertainment entities be signed in advance of Disney's commitment. Madame Tussaud's and AMC were convinced of the opportunities for success if Disney agreed. State and city planners were thrilled at the rapid development of good fortune. Although the deal was not cemented until 1995, forcing Disney to seek a traditionally leased home for *Beauty and the Beast* in the Nederlanders' Palace Theatre, the roughly thirty-four-million-dollar renovation of the New Amsterdam, overseen by a leading architectural firm, Hardy Holtzman Pfeiffer, proceeded apace. By the time the theatre opened in spring 1997 with the limited run of the Menken-Rice oratorio *King David*, it was apparent that a remarkable transformation had occurred in the New Amsterdam.

Disney's success motivated Garth Drabinsky to lease the two theatres across the street from the New Amsterdam and turn them into the Ford Center. It was this kind of competition that the state and city hoped for when it signed Disney to its ninety-nine-year lease. Soon, chain stores like the Gap, Chevy's, and Old Navy Clothing Company were signing leases on Forty-second Street. But Disney was the key. According to Cora

Cahan, "Before Disney came in, just about the only expressions of interest in the theatres were mud wrestling clubs. . . . Now the street has been reinvented."[3]

The reason for Disney's aggressive pursuit of a presence on Forty-second Street may be found in a statement that Eisner made to *Business Week* in 1995. "People have a need to get out of their homes and find live entertainment . . . and if they venture out, we intend to be there." Accordingly, Disney expanded its portfolio by venturing into professional hockey and baseball with its acquisitions of the Mighty Ducks and Anaheim Angels.[4] Real estate in Manhattan is so prohibitively expensive, however, that currently Disney has no announced plans to take over other existing spaces and convert them to legitimate theatres, although the company admits that such moves might be necessary for future productions.

It was not only Forty-second Street that was given a new look. Up and down Seventh Avenue and Broadway itself, changes were rampant. Several high-rise hotels, a Virgin Records store, the headquarters for MTV and the World Wrestling Federation, new movie theatres, office and retail skyscrapers, and a plethora of tourist-friendly but largely interchangeable eateries abounded. Impressive signage, always intended as part of the grand renovation scheme, could be seen in all its newly minted glory, a fin de siècle reinvention of the mid-century Camel cigarette sign that puffed out circles of smoke over billboards touting Coca Cola, Chevrolet, and Planters Peanuts. The area is ablaze with a crazy quilt of signs and lights—stock and news tickers, enormous billboards, neon come-ons for every conceivable product, live video feeds—that transforms the theatre district at night into a twenty-first-century corporate assault on the senses. In earlier decades, the commodities advertised on the twinkling signage bore little relationship to the bustling activities on the streets below. The current incarnation features a much higher degree of connectivity between the global corporate culture hawked electronically and the theme park and shopping mall motif of the newly configured neighborhood. The current theatre district is now the pride of urban planners and corporate moguls, a family-friendly, middle-class entertainment oasis in Midtown.

If the changes were limited to cosmetics alone, most Broadway theatre people would likely applaud the exile of the street hustlers and the abolition of the sex shows, enjoy the diversions offered by the new tenants, and continue about their business. But the makeover has attracted so many tourists that the sidewalks on the main thoroughfares cannot easily accommodate the increased pedestrian traffic. The crush of bodies, especially near the MTV studios and other large-draw attractions, is sti-fling. When all the office towers are eventually functioning at full capac-ity, the streets will be plagued by an even greater number of pedestrians, especially at midday and evening rush hour.

As Nancy Coyne said, "The place is filled with families, not just couples going to Broadway shows. It's a whole new part of town ... and as such, it's crowded with tourists at all times of the year. The percentage of tour-ists in every Broadway theatre is much higher than it's ever been before, and shows run longer than they ever ran before." Richard Frankel con-curred. "We're much more a tourist-driven business than the theatre was thirty years ago. The great New York middle class that supported the theatre for so many years is not as large anymore." More tourists can result in longer runs, but then, fewer new works can be produced. In the early decades of the twentieth century, hundreds of plays opened in a season, and while most of them were unmemorable, the sheer volume of new productions invested Broadway with a continued self-reinvention that is largely absent today.

The Broadway community is divided about the evolution of the dis-trict. Some, like actress Randy Graff, are enthusiastic about the pragmatic upgrades. "I know a lot of people think that the character is gone. But I didn't like walking down Forty-second Street amidst all the porn. They have new rehearsal spaces on Forty-second Street that are great, with gigantic windows that overlook the street; it's really fun to rehearse there. And there's a food court across the street, and if you've got a big break [during rehearsals], you can catch a movie. It's very convenient." Direc-tor Robert Longbottom acknowledged the critical contributions made by Disney and applauded the renovation of the New Amsterdam. But he admitted that "there's a lot of the rest of Forty-second Street that looks a little too much like Las Vegas for my taste. And I think that the street's lost some of its charm." Producer Hank Unger admitted that the make-over "does Las Vegas-ize Times Square more than ever before, and it makes it safe for large masses of people, but we need large masses of people to be here. The cash injected into Times Square is not a bad thing. It's like Vegas, which has changed drastically. Everything is bigger, big-ger, bigger. It's a cultural trend that I can't fight. I have to make my deci-sions in its context. But I don't have a personal crusade that this shouldn't happen. At the end of the day, I think it's good."

Many of the renovation's advocates within the theatre community are "front-of-house" people—producers, advertising and marketing executives, theatre owners—whose need for increased revenue is linked directly to a more inviting ambiance. Theatre owners are enormously pleased that their properties have appreciated in value as a result of the changes. Clear Channel's Scott Zeiger, a longtime New Yorker, enthused that the neighborhood "is not a threatening place anymore. . . . The streets are full during the tourist times of the year, and they're coming to see the shows." The Roundabout's Todd Haimes commented that "I think a very conscious decision was made—again, for better or for worse, depending on what your opinions are—[about] what they wanted Forty-second Street to represent, or to be reflected in the spirit of Forty-second Street." He added that while the sidewalks are overcrowded, as an artistic director of a theatre with a presence just off the intersection of Seventh Avenue and Forty-second Street, "it's good for us in terms of ticket sales."

To others, the main streets of the district reflect the bland chain-store tones found in any suburban shopping mall, family-friendly and corporate. Actor William Parry had returned to New York in 2001 after several months on a national tour. "When I came back and walked down Forty-second Street, I started laughing. I said, 'I could be anywhere, except the buildings are a little taller, and there's a little more density of population. But this really could be anywhere.'" The corporatization of Times Square is not an isolated case in Manhattan, although it is the most visibly blatant and extreme. Many neighborhoods once cherished for their individual personalities and one-of-a-kind shops have yielded to the corporate incursion; the Upper West Side exemplifies the erasure of a once unique neighborhood's distinctive character. Corporate money was the critical ingredient in the Times Square renovation, but the price was the loss of the neighborhood's idiosyncratic aura. A few prostitutes, a slow return of the homeless since Mayor Giuliani's departure, and some petty street crime still remind people of less savory times, but they seem more like an anachronism than a burgeoning threat. No one pines for the return of the bad old days, but the smoke-ring-blowing Camel billboard of years past seems charming in comparison with enormous ads of pouting celebrities hawking underwear and soft drinks. William Parry, raised in Ohio, said that he was struck, during his first years in New York in the early seventies, by the starkly individual nature of the city. "For so many years there were no fast food restaurants here. It was a place that was unique unto itself. It was very proud of that. And I feel to some degree, in terms of Forty-second Street, that that has gone by the board, that in fact, they sold out, to mass culture, common culture." Playwright Arthur

Laurents characterized the new Forty-second Street as "a mall. I don't connect it with theatre. It has one building that has very good rehearsal halls, and a good theatre, the Duke Theatre. The rest of it is kind of up-scale honky-tonk. . . . It's fake vulgarity." Beyond the aesthetic argument, though, lies the fact that Broadway's makeover has to some degree marginalized the theatre business, at least in the public eye. Not too long ago, attending a play or a movie was just about the only legitimate reason to visit the district. Today, the theatres themselves must compete with a host of other entertainment and shopping possibilities.

While no one yearns for the days of vagrants accosting actresses on their way home from the theatre and three-card monte games on every corner, concern about the prospects for Broadway theatre is palpable. For decades, the district represented the apogee of popular entertainment, hospitable to a wide spectrum of offerings from flea circuses to Shakespeare. Now, some fear, the "Disneyfication" of Broadway will render that independent and spirited mosaic of the crass and the enlightened obsolete, to be replaced by ever more comfortable, unthreatening family fare. Disney executives decry the term *Disneyfication* as envious oversimplification that wrongly casts Disney in the role of the mustache-twirling villain whose corporate imperative demands nothing less than the complete homogenization of the American theatre scene. They note that Disney was only one piece in the large renovation puzzle. Rick Elice, now a creative consultant for Disney after years at Serino Coyne, resents the term because he believes that it misses the point of what Disney accomplished. "Disney spent a ton of money to make the New Amsterdam Theatre look just the way it looked in 1903, except with an infrastructure that could support life in the twenty-first century, and it did it meticulously and assiduously and very successfully. . . . It's the rest of the street, of which Disney has no control. The resultant vomiting of neon crap is there. And yes, it is repugnant to look at, but to say it's been Disneyfied, I think, is really, really to miss the point."

Some of the new Times Square amenities are to be applauded, especially in light of the old days, when the concept of "amenity" was largely alien. But although now more revenue is generated throughout the district, the earnestly clean, feel-good neon facade can do little to positively affect the theatrical experience inside the walls of the theatres. While the new district may make the experience of attending a Broadway show more palatable and thus attract more tourists, there is scant evidence that the work itself will enjoy an artistic renaissance. The energy, money, and strident boosterism for the new Times Square do not amount to a profession of faith in the essential experience of theatregoing. Production supervisor Peter Lawrence discussed a possible upcoming extravaganza of *Batman,* to be produced by Warner Brothers, marking the first major incursion by this film studio on Broadway turf. "They want what is essentially an installation project, much like *FX* was in Las Vegas . . . a show that is meant to attract tourists to a safe [place], safe being that there's not going to be overly challenging entertainment here in Times Square, to attract families into the sort of theme park of Times Square. I think we're going to see more and more of that." Lawrence's comment predicts a disconcerting new trend in the programming of Broadway.

Rocco Landesman, who was on the executive board of the Times Square Business Improvement District, was enthusiastic about the positive aspects of the redevelopment, and like every other owner and producer, enjoyed the surge in tourists before September 11. He conceded, however, that audience demographics reflected an increased tourist presence. This change, he said, might drive the nature of the work being produced. "People want to see hits; they tend to want to see a safer show, a revival, or a show that's been certified as a hit. They want a show with a certain reputation. They're not likely to come in and take a chance on something new. . . . I think the tourist audience tends to make safer choices than a traditional New York audience."

Many producers insist, like Barry Weissler, that "I don't try to think of shows to do because tourists are coming into town. I do a show and then I decide on the demographics and I go after them." There is no gainsaying that it is foolhardy not to play to the available audience. Many of the old-guard theatregoing residents of the New York metropolitan area have either decreased or eliminated their attendance at Broadway shows. They perceive them as too expensive as a staple—New Yorkers regard the prices as both an affront and a tourist-oriented marketing ploy ("if it's expensive, it must be good")— and believe that the nature of the work has changed so drastically in the last few decades that there is little of interest offered by commercial Broadway. Off-Broadway and regional theatres offer the more challenging fare that regular theatregoers often demand. Many Broadway cognoscenti point to the English megamusicals of the eighties as the turning point, when producers started to earnestly market shows to a tourist audience. Eventually, barring another catastrophe like the terrorist attacks, tourist numbers will probably revive on Broadway, and as non-English-speaking audiences grow, there will be a similar rise in the number of shows that do not require great facility with the language. One of the greatest assets of *Cats* was its ability to communicate with audiences of every linguistic orientation.

Tourists have amply demonstrated their lack of interest in most straight plays and the more challenging musicals by such composers as Jason Robert Brown, Michael John LaChiusa, and even Sondheim for any number of factors: lack of name recognition of the writers or the title, a reactionary aversion to anything that is perceived as "highbrow," or weighty subject matter that is not leavened by glib irony, a bleating pop score, or sentimental sugarcoating. The perception of a work as challenging does not mean, however, that it is artistically engaging. Some difficult pieces have failed owing to their opaque inaccessibility. When theatre critics pan these shows, it is usually enough to shutter the theatres; when they do the same to pop entertainments prepackaged as instant hits, the shows are sometimes able to build a sustainable presence, the fate of *Seussical* notwithstanding. British cachet was one strong selling point in the eighties, and while even a few Lloyd Webber shows failed, the signal successes were so remarkable that even mixed reviews rendered that juggernaut unstoppable. Former press rep Josh Ellis believes that the renovation of Times Square "will certainly make the material as safe as it can be . . . so that it becomes homogenized." But he did hold out some shred of hope for a resurgence of creativity. If a few audacious producers chose to resist the trend and produce more innovative work, Ellis said, the "pack instinct" could eventually sway other producers to risk similar ventures.

Those gambles have been relatively rare. Playwright John Weidman agreed that today's audience is less sophisticated than twenty years ago.

> I went to see *Thoroughly Modern Millie* quite soon after it opened. And the audience around me—this is not meant to be pejorative, simply descriptive—looked more like the people I was accustomed to seeing a year and a half into the run of a hit musical. I think that the marketing attempt to bring in a new kind of theatregoer has been successful, and that kind of theatregoer is comfortable with the new style of Times Square. I don't think that the theatregoers, when they walk out of *Beauty and the Beast* . . . check the papers to see what's playing at Playwrights Horizon, or even what's coming out of Manhattan Theatre Club.

It has long been the hope of many mainstream Off-Broadway theatres that some crossover between Broadway and Off-Broadway audiences would be engendered by the TKTS booth, the construction of more Off-Broadway theatres in the area, and various marketing schemes, but there is little proof that tourist theatregoers do seek out Off-Broadway works. The major not-for-profits on Broadway are able to succeed during their regular season largely because of subscription audiences and additional income in the event of hit commercial transfers or extended runs. They are able to vary their works so that the more audience-pleasing shows are produced in their Broadway venues, and challenging works in their smaller spaces. Star-studded revivals on a limited run are not generally risky prospects.

There is a feeling, expressed in varying degrees of consternation by many on Broadway, that while production values and artfulness of staging flourish, the content of many shows has been adversely affected by the degradation of mass culture. Glib cynicism, surface irony, and earnest pop-operatic sentimentality are the current lingua franca. The marriage of slick spectacle and pop-rock aural wallpaper has produced a well-honed but soulless wash of sameness. As Todd Haimes noted, Broadway is responding to the cultural vapidity that is being promulgated by the mass entertainment industries, notably television and film. As more film studios have begun to explore opportunities on Broadway, independent producers and artists are anxious about the prospects for work that does not fit the current mold of popular film-to-stage adaptations. Five of the eleven new musicals running on Broadway in 2002–3 were based on films, and projected works indicate that the percentage will grow. The adaptation of commercially successful films offers a producer some initial degree of confidence, because the story and characters have already been proven in a mass market. They are, in a sense, "almost like doing a revival," according to Gerard Alessandrini, the creator and writer of the long-running Off-Broadway hit *Forbidden Broadway,* the musical revue that gleefully skewers Broadway past and present. "Producers want names that are recognizable to the general public. That's why they pick a film. You put it on the stage, and a lot of the general public believes that they are going to see a film, live on stage!"

While nothing inherent in the film medium precludes viable translation to a stage musical, the salient issue is quality. Aside from Disney's works, most film-to-stage adaptations of the past have been mounted without the direct involvement of the studios that produced them. But New Line Cinema was a coproducer of the current hit *Hairspray* and has other works in the planning stage. MGM formed a division in 2002 to explore converting some of its vast holdings into musicals. While some producers view the clout that a studio can offer a production as a boon, others worry that the greater involvement of studios as active producers will spell the end of their own careers. Lindsay Law, a former president of Fox Searchlight, was one of the lead producers of the musical *The Full Monty;* the studio helped finance it. Law commented in a *Variety* article in November 2002, "The greatest advantage of having a corporation behind a project was how swiftly the musical was developed. . . . They told the creative team, 'Here are your deadlines' and provided early financing for workshops. That's not normal. Creative teams tend to disperse while the producers are looking for money and the focus gets lost."[5] The point is valid; time can be of the essence, and the slow pace of independent funding can result in problematic delays. But another statement of Law's is even more critical in the translation of films to the stage. He emphasized that the musical adaptation needs to be a true theatrical expression of the work, not merely a stage version of the film. "*Saturday Night Fever* was problematic because it adhered too closely to the film— and they didn't have . . . John Travolta."[6] Literal-minded adaptations of movies that do not take into account the particular needs and demands of theatre can encounter turbulent waters; the more realistic quality of film can result in a turgid theatrical piece if directly translated to the stage. Contemporary films, especially, often suffer from a prosaic dullness of spirit and content, regardless of how pumped the action and emphatic the visual production. One of the reasons that *The Lion King* translated so effectively to the stage was Julie Taymor's discovery of a compelling theatrical means of expression for the piece. But if studios rush to capitalize on the celebrity of certain films, there is a risk that the gestation process necessary to bear a mature work will be foreshortened. As Clear Channel continues to demand more product to fill its road houses, there might well be an upswing in the number of new works produced. Broadway history teaches us, however, that heightened production does not perforce yield quality. Lyricist Sheldon Harnick made a telling observation about *Saturday Night Fever.* "[The film] was not a musical in the sense that people sang to each other. These songs were on the soundtrack and were germane in one way or the other to what was happening. They took these songs and they had people sing them to one another. And it didn't seem to matter that the lyrics didn't always make sense with one person singing to another." Gerard Alessandrini added, "Since the movies usually don't have ten or twelve songs in them, they interpolate extra songs, and it no longer becomes an organic musical, it becomes a patch-work, and it makes for strange entertainment."

Today there seems little to distinguish one contemporary pop score from another. Some are written in the style of the British pop opera, pioneered by Lloyd Webber and Boublil and Schönberg, featuring over-wrought, unsubtle, on-the-sleeve emotions, while others are rooted in a peppy American faux-rock sensibility, like *Hairspray* and *Seussical.* Composer Frank Wildhorn pointed out, "In the seventies and eighties, the musical vocabulary [on Broadway] had absolutely nothing to do with the musical vocabulary of the rest of the world." Broadway has long endured the accusation that it is typically years behind the times, in part because of the long journey most shows make to the stage. Wildhorn indicated that his passion for working in the theatre involved "trying to be that bridge between the two worlds I love—contemporary, popular, accessible music, and things that involve sitting in a darkened theatre and not knowing what's going to happen when the overture starts."

Regardless of the musical style, these shows often substitute bathos for character development or wink knowingly at the audience as the surface irony drips from the stage. At their best, the works of the British composers successfully mix lush, symphonic orchestrations with pop-inflected melodies. But most new American scores, which tend to rely more on electronic music, suffer from a lack of sparkling clarity that unamplified, acoustic orchestras provide, and elevate the beat to primacy of place over more complex melodies or intelligible lyrics. Sheldon Harnick, whose works include *Fiddler on the Roof,* pointed out that "the clever lyric, that was in vogue ever since the twenties, seems to have faded.... What seems to be important to many audiences, paying the prices that they do, is that what they see is loud and big." A musical like *Rent,* which captured the spirit and concerns of a particular generation of young artists, adheres to a pop-rock style, while riffing on Puccini's themes and employing a few borrowed musical idioms, like the tango. No one quarrels with composer Jonathan Larson's appropriation of a variety of styles, but *Rent* is marred by an apparent lack of trust in the power of sheer emotion. Empathy and sentiment, long the hallmark of musicals, are undermined by an ending that defies both logic and the accretion of events that have transpired and offers instead a forced and ironic coda in strange counterpoint to the more earnestly romantic moments earlier.

Shows that pay scant attention to the organic integration of the songs and story, like some of the more facile movie adaptations, risk eroding the strength of the musical. New forms may be in order, but the current incarnation has failed to find a worthy successor to the integrated musical. Rodgers and Hammerstein discovered sixty years ago that seamlessness of music and libretto was an essential component to the maturation of the musical. Arthur Laurents emphatically criticized a current trend in writing musicals, in which composers and lyricists concoct a score and then seek out a book writer to fill in the blanks. Songs for a book musical, he stated, must derive from the book, from that initial framework for narrative and character, which, even if inadvertently, ensures that the musical will be about something. The strongest musicals, regardless of the genre or style, have adhered to that basic precept, but Laurents fears that it is being increasingly disregarded as professional writing workshops and classes teach young artists to compose songs without a libretto as a point of departure. Gerard Alessandrini wondered whether "we've lost putting the libretto first." Many shows today suffer from a malady in which songs are shoehorned into a show without an organic connection to the rest of the material, or are written without an eye to the precise matching of character, situation, and song style. A unique example of a show that ultimately failed, in part because of its lack of connective tissue, was the revival of Rodgers and Hammerstein's *Flower Drum Song* in 2002. The writers' estate gave permission to Benjamin Mordecai and his producing partners to stage the revival, and all involved realized that one significant obstacle was the dated book. One of the nation's most lauded playwrights, David Henry Hwang, was hired to revise the libretto. Although he retained some vestige of period flavor, the injection of new issues—an escape by the leading character from Mao's Cultural Revolution and the contrast in the aesthetics of performance between Chinese opera and American nightclubs to highlight the generational and cultural gap—painted the work in darker shades than Rodgers and Hammerstein originally intended. The show's jazzy, frothy score seemed out of place in the new book, and the result was a pair of strange bedfellows of song and story.

Gerard Alessandrini pointed to other instances of incongruity, in shows such as *Movin' Out, Mamma Mia!*, and the soon-to-be-produced *We Will Rock You*, hybrid shows that attempt to find a reason to present a rock artist's work in a dramatic context. "They put a book to it, but the book seems to be a very shallow framework, and not at all what the people are really enjoying, which is getting from one song to another. It's like a structured rock concert. I can't even describe it as theatre, and I can't necessarily say that it's bad. It's just different. Somebody needs to coin a new phrase for what type of entertainment this is." In addition to this song-cycle event, dance concerts and revues have also enjoyed popularity on Broadway for a number of years. Alessandrini fears that hybrid works and film adaptations will soon overtake a more traditionally told and sung story, eviscerating the core purpose of theatre by effectively rendering the drama from the production. He contrasted the Kennedy Center presentation of six Sondheim musicals in summer 2002 with the current Broadway offerings. The Sondheim shows

> were very entertaining, but they also made points, they had something to say, and they developed characters, many characters, and told stories. Some of the plots [of current Broadway shows], maybe at best they'll make you understand one character, if that. If you look at some of the musicals that were done a generation ago, and more, they can develop five, six, or seven characters completely. You can see them take journeys, all of them, and do it in song and dance. Unfortunately, it seems like a lost art. The only time you really see it is when somebody revives one of the great musicals and does it well, and then it all comes together.

A Chorus Line has been cited as the apotheosis of song, story, character, dance, and emotion. As Robert Longbottom suggested, the 1975 musical had "a monologue about a gay boy who performed at a drag club that left everybody crying in the audience. It was hugely embraced in this country, and celebrated, and until recently was the longest-running musical in Broadway history. So it can be done. You can have a show with strong emotional narrative and entertainment value that earns the title of must-see blockbuster that's going to bring them in and have them lining up to see it." But *A Chorus Line* was, at its core, a sentimental musical, heartfelt and passionate, and today's works seem to suffer from an overdose of irony that precludes the sort of empathy engendered by *A Chorus Line*. Some Broadway pundits indicated that the show would not be produced today as a new musical precisely because of its emotionality and its lack of spectacle, inexpensive as it may be to mount.

Jack Viertel noted that "the nice thing about spectacle, if you can produce it, is it will paper over myriad other problems. If you aren't going to have spectacle, you'd better deliver the characters, humanity, and the tunes, frankly, of yesteryear. They won't be the same as yesteryear, obviously, because the world has moved on, but you have to find the modern equivalent for that." New shows are at times funny but, geared as they are to attract audiences whose television consumption features a string of reality shows, often lack any deep conviction about the human spirit. A degree of irony can inject dimension and tension into a show. Its use in musicals originally reflected a particular sensibility and worldview of the previous generation of mostly Jewish writers and composers. Today, though, irony seems appliquéd rather than organic. *Hairspray,* based on John Waters's camp film, is set in the swirling retro pastel palette of David Rockwell's design. It presents a determinedly silly, good-versus-evil, "up with family values" story that features the ne plus ultra of ironic postmodern commentary, Harvey Fierstein's over-the-top drag performance as ur-momma Edna Turnblad. *Urinetown* offers a savvy, winking take on the dangers of corporate skullduggery, with music and presentation consciously paying homage to the works of Brecht and Weill and others, but it is ultimately more an exercise in style than substance, devised to delight us with its tongue-in-cheek references to a host of theatrical antecedents.

Many hoped that Baz Luhrmann's bravura staging of *La Bohème* would signal a return to musicals with style, substance, character, and spectacle, but the show closed at a deficit, running well under a year. Despite Luhrmann's huge name recognition for films like *Moulin Rouge,* the show could not bridge the opera-musical theatre divide. *Rent's* telling of the same story resonates more with contemporary audiences who cannot comfortably identify with the unbridled emotionality of a Puccini opera. Stephen Sondheim, who has often stated that he rejects sentimentality in his musicals but embraces true sentiment, has created some of the most enduring and complex works for the musical theatre, and as cynical as some of his characters are—Sweeney Todd views the world as a cosmic dunghill—his shows display a sophisticated rendering of the vagaries of the human condition. In many of today's musicals, irony and cynicism deny us that point of empathy. They also undermine the use of ambiguity, of which Sondheim is a master, that can further yield depth and texture. While Rodgers and Hammerstein and their artistic heirs of the fifties and sixties were not well known for their use of ambiguity, preferring to create rather black-and-white worlds of obvious moral order, the current postmodern shows fall prey to the incessant self-referential deconstruction of emotional, character-driven narrative.

Barry Singer, in a provocative piece in the *New York Times* in August 2001 (published just two weeks before September 11), commented that Broadway musicals are traditionally out of touch with popular values, and generally take time to catch up with the national cultural zeitgeist. In the piece, Singer asked, "Are audiences today—at least the younger members—so inherently embarrassed by musicals that only pre-emptive, reflexive laughter can induce them to listen?" Citing the prevailing postmodern winds, he asked Baz Luhrmann, "Has irony become the chaser audiences require in order to swallow any sort of musical theatre entertainment?" Luhrmann responded, "Well, yes. . . . Irony is one very good way to force an audience's engagement these days." Singer finishes with a quote from writer Larry Gelbart, the coauthor of the book for *A Funny Thing Happened on the Way to the Forum,* the 1961 Sondheim musical that also broke the fourth wall and employed a witty, metatheatrical irony. "You know what? Making fun of yourself is just easier than writing plot. It's easier than creating character. It's easier than creating situations."[7]

One example of irony's success on Broadway was seen in the 2000 revival of *The Rocky Horror Show.* Jordan Roth, son of Daryl Roth, who was in his midtwenties when he presented the show as sole producer at Circle in the Square, was keenly aware of a contemporary young audience's desire for a different type of experience on Broadway, regardless of stylistic orientation. He very carefully created a newly minted theatrical equivalent of the movie version's phenomenon of more than two decades, in which audience members, dressed like cast members and equipped with an arsenal of props, respond to the dialogue with nationally recognized retorts and sing-alongs. Roth believed that there was a place for this sort of engagement between audience and performer on Broadway. Although he initially conceived of the revival as a club event, he learned that the financing would be more readily available if the show was mounted in a Broadway venue. "This is a big show for tourists, because the movie has basically infiltrated every corner of every small town in this entire country." Observing that the unique response to the *Rocky Horror* movie grew out of a teenage audience's need to "create a world in which you are the star," the stage revival, Roth said, attracted an audience that was "tremendously widespread. There are a lot of people who are coming who have never seen a Broadway show. They're in the theatre taking out their cameras, which the normal theatregoer knows is not allowed. And this is tremendously gratifying to me, because people always talk about developing young audiences. Creating something for twenty-year-olds is not a mission for me. Creating things for people for whom Broadway is not on their radar screen, who have never gone to a Broadway show or even thought about it . . . that's a mission."

While it is laudable when producers take the long view, there is a strong feeling that prepackaged consumables are gaining in popularity. Some producers welcomed the musicians' strike in 2003 because they viewed the use of live music as an anachronistic indulgence that bloated their bottom line. Although producers publicly avowed their commitment to the preservation of live music, word was circulated that a few producers would be happy to use synthesizers and eliminate orchestras completely. Musical supervisor Robert Billig passionately argued against this move. "It's all about live music. It's live performance. It's not about virtual orchestras. It's becoming Las Vegas, or it's becoming a theme park, where everything is prerecorded. You go to a theme park now and even the singers are prerecorded. They're out there busting their butts and hustling across the stage, and you're in the thirtieth row and the sound is perfect. Well, that's because it's prerecorded. That's not what Broadway is about."

A few decades ago, most producers gave very little thought to advertising shows as family-oriented fare. Most straight plays were geared toward adult audiences, and many musicals viewed children as an afterthought. *Big River,* the musical version of *Huckleberry Finn,* is usually marketed as a family show today in revivals around the country, but Edward Strong, one of the producers of the original 1985 production, recalled that the marketing approach then was intentionally adult-oriented and avoided touting its family appeal. "I can still remember the marketing meetings where we talked about holding out, 'Don't mention that part of it,' because we had won all the Tony Awards and wanted to be a sophisticated hit." Now it is much more common for shows to be marketed as "four-ticket" attractions, geared toward a family sale. Disney's works, and shows such as *The Secret Garden, Grease, Cats, Tom Sawyer,* and *Seussical* have appealed to families with young children, and other shows have been geared to teenagers. As Strong put it succinctly, "Nothing can run on Broadway unless there is some kind of audience for it." But the audience for these shows must be able to afford the steep prices for four or more tickets, even with discounts. Gerard Alessandrini believes the shows reflect both that change as well as the new ambiance of Times Square. "They're like films onstage, they're like rides. You see the *Lion King* ride or the *42nd Street* ride. Once tickets became one hundred dollars, you don't go to the show because you're looking for intellectual entertainment; you go because it's an event, with your family . . . because you can only afford to go once or twice a year. It is no longer like reading a book or going to a film, something that you do regularly that stretches the mind. . . . Shows have become events."

The irony, as Jack Viertel noted, is that the tourists who attend Broadway for that event hail from a rather narrow strip of the middle and upper middle class. But the exciting sociotheatrical touchstones of some of the newer works, like the African rhythms employed in *The Lion King* and the hip-hop verse of *Def Poetry Jam,* remain largely unavailable to Americans whose culture spawned these phenomena. Frank Wildhorn added, "If you look at the pop charts, you'll see that 70 to 80 percent of those charts are represented by artists of African American or Latin American descent, and yet you see none of that represented on Broadway, so that makes me sad, because Broadway closes itself off in that highbrow attitude they take about what is going on in the rest of the world." Although Wildhorn has, by his own good-natured admission, "taken shots as being the 'pop guy,'" his vision of Broadway as just one piece in the mosaic of a greater production system involving the recording industry and the stage might help reestablish Broadway's connection to popular music, a connection largely absent since the advent of rock music.

While independent producers with a commitment to new straight plays and a flair for producing them still exist, commercial ventures have decreased substantially over the last few decades. Charting the popularity of straight plays on Broadway results in a cyclical graph. Plays took a precipitous drop in popularity in the eighties and nineties; even a new Neil Simon play, long considered a Broadway staple, was staged Off-Broadway in 1995. The only new straight play to open that year was a Broadway Alliance transfer from Manhattan Theatre Club of Terrence McNally's *Love! Valour! Compassion!* While *Angels in America* proved a brilliant coup in its two-part incarnation on Broadway in 1993, very few plays in recent years have enjoyed such visibility on the national cultural radar. In the late nineties, however, there was a brief resurgence of the straight play's popularity on Broadway. Producer Chase Mishkin remembered that "people kept telling us straight plays are dead, you can't make it on Broadway." She credited her production of Martin McDonagh's *The Beauty Queen of Leenane,* in 1998, which ran for almost a year and made back its initial $1.2 million capitalization as well as respectable profits, as "the first one in years that proved a straight play could make it." Soon thereafter, however, new straight works declined again.

It is unthinkable for a straight play to enjoy a life span like those of the blockbuster musicals or to earn such astronomical grosses. If a straight play can eke out a run of a year or more, and if it has relatively low expenses, it can make a reasonable profit. Summer is a time in the theatrical season when the herd has been thinned out after the Tony Awards of early June, and the summer influx of tourists and exodus of native New Yorkers create an environment that is hostile to nonmusicals. In late summer 2003, only one new straight play was running: Richard Greenberg's *Take Me Out.* The play transferred from a successful Off-Broadway run, where it received enthusiastic reviews, and won the Tony for best play, but despite the exuberant reception was playing to only 78 percent capacity at the 920-seat Walter Kerr, earning 66 percent of its gross potential. Richard Frankel, whose straight plays includes *The Weir, Angels in America,* and the recent revival of *Frankie and Johnny,* said, "At the risk of restating the obvious, there are many good plays, great plays, that are not commercial plays." Shakespeare, he volunteered, has not proved a viable commercial playwright in recent decades on Broadway except in limited runs.

The dearth of new straight plays is in part the result of the relationship between the work itself and the contemporary Broadway audience. A younger generation of playwrights has been reared on postmodernism and deconstruction. While many theatregoers who attend plays on Broadway are well educated, they tend to possess middle-of-the-road sensibilities. "They do not always have to be told something comforting," said Jack Viertel, "but they want to be told something that goes directly to their emotional center. And to the degree that playwrights aren't writing those kinds of plays, if that's really the case, that may account to some extent for the diminution of drama being produced on Broadway." Aside from the snob hit or the occasional phenomenon like *Angels in America,* which despite its postmodern trappings has a very passionate and emotionally accessible center, straight plays that succeed on Broadway are fairly straightforward works. A straight play, whether comedy or drama, usually demands greater attention and active listening from its audience. Audiences are attuned to film and television's fast editing, sound bites, instant gratification, and barrage of overlapping dialogue. Straight theatre cannot offer the same sensory experience. The Tony Awards committee has designated a new category for special theatrical events, which reflects the advent of nondramatic productions like *Def Poetry Jam,* developed to attract a new audience. Some members of the theatre community have privately wondered whether this new category may pave the way for a cavalcade of mindless entertainments on Broadway, like stage versions of reality television and other attempts to theatricalize a television or movie experience.

To many in the industry, it is a surprise and a blessing that Broadway continues to operate at its current level of production. The terrorist attacks of 2001 brought New York City to its knees. Shows were closed for days until the industry, government, and police agencies determined that it was appropriate to reopen, and many shows were crippled by the losses. The crisis had the potential to create staggering repercussions for Broadway theatres, given their dependence on the tourist trade and the disruption of New York's daily life and commerce that the terrorism caused. In the week after the attacks, grosses tumbled a disastrous, yet understandable, 70 percent, compared with the same week in the previous season. Yet, in the entire 2001–2 season, which concluded more than eight months after the attacks, Broadway grossed more than $642 million, according to *Variety.* Although a number of shows closed in the wake of the attacks, the annual box office gross was only twenty-three million dollars lower than the previous year's—impressive numbers when considered in the context of September 11. A solid thirty-five productions opened during the season, seven more than in the year before. As Charles Isherwood of *Variety* put it, "Neither the ongoing recession nor the events of the fall seem to have stopped the flow of investment money to Broadway."[8] Of the twenty-seven productions that opened in commercial theatres that season, eight have recouped, nine had not (and closed), and ten were still running but had not recouped by the end of the season: respectable and not atypical numbers. Of the shows that recouped in the course of the season, only one, *Mamma Mia!,* was a musical, but given their size and expense, musicals rarely recoup within a year unless they are runaway hits.

The administrations of Mayor Rudolph Giuliani and Governor George Pataki, which recognized the critical relationship between Broadway and the city's economic and cultural welfare, responded immediately after the attacks, occasioned in part by some very public industry lobbying. The city government bought an enormous block of theatre tickets from the League for $2.5 million, for distribution through various fund-raising and charitable organizations. When box office revenue revived in surprising fashion in the following months, producers returned the unused portion of the proceeds. In return for the city's largesse, producers donated five dollars for every ticket sold to the Twin Towers Fund, raising over $750,000. New York state contributed one million dollars to a Broadway advertising campaign, and the League quickly negotiated for significant emergency salary concessions from the unions for several shows to keep the theatres lit in those crucial weeks after September 11. Internecine squabbling resulted when the Dodgers withdrew from the League in a much-publicized maneuver. They accused the League of failing to include *The Music Man* in the group of musicals the League represented in concession discussions with the unions. There was speculation that the show was at first snubbed to chastise the Dodgers for producing a nonunion tour of the show. The musical eventually received the concessions, but the withdrawal of the Dodgers reinforced the perception that the League's unilateral power had been weakened significantly in recent years.

Predictions of an immediate industry-wide collapse went unrealized, but sequelae of the breakup were still felt two years later. The Iraq war in March 2003 added another layer of anxiety and woe to an industry that relies heavily on a tourist economy. League statistics indicate that in recent years, one in two ticket buyers purchased tickets at least four weeks in advance of the performance date. Producers have always depended on advance sales. They are a reliable indicator of the health and longevity of a production, and allow producers to stockpile funds for anticipated dry spells in the seasonal cycle. At Broadway theaters, however, impulse buying is on the rise and long-range planning on the wane. Arts organizations in general have noted a similar falloff in subscriptions. In a 2002 report, the League acknowledged that a year after the attack, only one in three purchases was long-range. According to Jed Bernstein, "The notion of having an advance and being able to plan with that in mind has been a part of the financial infrastructure for a long time now. If this is a permanent change, it's really going to change the fundamental finances of many shows."[9] Some shows that were living on the financial margins did close in the year after the terrorist attacks, but many of those had already recouped their investment, and it is surprising that more shows did not fold in the aftermath of September 11. The industry's ability to quickly regroup and adjust is testament to Broadway's strength as a New York institution.

But the anxiety about the dearth of tourists continues to plague producers. The rise in gross receipts in the 2002–3 season, much touted by the League as an indication of Broadway's tenacity and renewed vigor, was inflated by the biggest ticket price hike—an average of almost five dollars—in more than twenty years, according to *Variety*, and offers a somewhat distorted picture of the stability of the industry. Nine Broadway shows charged one hundred dollars in 2003; in 2002 only one did.[10] The one statistical ray of hope is the consistency in the number of new productions mounted annually in the two years since the attack, but as ticket prices spiral upward, there is greater likelihood that producers will respond with more spectacular productions, exacerbating the cycle.

An increase in spectacle may well incur the wrath of some members of the press, who have railed against the homogenization of Broadway. In the mid-twentieth century, New York's newspaper critics—or reviewers, since informed criticism was rarely their calling card—were seen as powerful forces that shaped the fate of shows. If they raved, the producers trumpeted the praise in their ads; if they panned, producers tried to cull one or two benign nuggets for padding. But as several of the city's newspapers began to close in the sixties, the power of the *New York Times* became consolidated. The other city and suburban dailies, as well as the national press, can create visibility for a show, but the lead *Times* critic wields the most profound influence within the media. For the decade starting in the mideighties, Frank Rich was referred to as the "Butcher of Broadway" for his uncompromising stance and refusal to serve as an industry shill. His reviews often played a significant hand in determining the future of many shows, although the unpredictability of audience ticket buying would sometimes confound those who used his reviews as barometers of a show's potential. Although many in the community cringed at a bad review, most privately acknowledged that he was the only truly knowledgeable and insightful lead critic on the Broadway beat. Robin Wagner praised Rich several years after he had stopped writing criticism and moved to the paper's op-ed page. "Frank, by the way, is always right about everything in my opinion. I'm really sorry he's not writing for theatre anymore." Many question whether today's *Times* critics enjoy the same power as Rich and his colleagues. This change is less a function of their ability, which is considerable, than it is of the evolution of the role of reviews in the life of a show.

While today's consumers expect to be told in no uncertain terms what they should see and what they should avoid, several shows have received favorable press but failed to find an audience. Robert Longbottom, who directed the musical *Side Show,* noted that Ben Brantley of the *Times* gave it a positive review, but the show could not muster a run of more than a few months. "It used to be if the *New York Times* gave you a nod, that would be enough to get the box office going crazy the next day. And it just simply did not happen." Longbottom attributes that anomaly to the difficulty in successfully selling the subject matter, conjoined twins, to a squeamish public, despite the fact that the show eschewed realism in depicting the Hilton sisters and presented, instead, two stunning actresses merely standing side by side. Juggernaut shows—those productions that have generated tremendous advance sales and word of mouth before opening—can usually survive a critical onslaught, as *Beauty and the Beast* did. Frank Rich found many flaws in *Les Misérables,* yet his review proved no match for the extraordinary preopening marketing campaign and ample positive word of mouth from its London production. When poorly reviewed shows fail to run, producers traditionally aim their bile at the press but rarely acknowledge the flaws in their shows. Although they bemoan the power of the *Times,* they in turn pay more than eighty thousand dollars for a full-page Sunday advertisement.

The prevailing mood of the producers was expressed by Jack Viertel. "I [can't] remember a time when the critics had less power than they have now, which is interesting. I think it has to do with the nature of the audience. It's not that we're doing such great work and they're so stupid; that relationship is probably no different, on average, than it's ever been. [It's] because the audience is so heavily made up of people who don't read the New York press, and who come from another place." Roy Somlyo, who spent five decades managing and producing, said that

> since Frank Rick retired, I think the *Times* has lost a lot of [its clout], and I don't think they're very happy [not] being the arbiter of public taste today. So people pay less attention to reviewers. As a consequence, it hasn't helped the theatre in some ways, because the fact that people pay less attention to reviewers has reduced the number of reviewers, so that you don't have any on television. You don't have the influence of reviewers today. And I think if you walked down the street and asked people who the reviewer was from the *New York Times,* they wouldn't know. . . . [T]hey're not as important as they used to be. I think word of mouth is the key.

Nick Scandalios wryly added that producers typically romanticize practices of years past.

> Now, some of the stuff that is not as good, of sophisticated quality, is running longer in New York. Isn't that what we're all supposed to be striving for? That the critics have less impact on us? So everything we've been working for, we've gotten, and now we're complaining about it. "I long for the days when you could read a smart review and really agree with it." You *long* for those days? Aren't you better off now?

You can do your work. Yes, sometimes the reviews are good and not bad, but a great review doesn't make you automatically, and a bad review doesn't kill you. You're left as a producer to actually produce.

While the power of the press is diminished, it is not inconsequential, and producers still nervously await reviews on opening night. The advertising budget will often be deployed to counter poor press, and the marketing campaign is then adjusted to respond to the realities of postopening box office receipts. Once the reviews are in, and the gloom or euphoria of opening night dissipates, the small army that brought the show to the boards returns to business as usual, enjoying the security of a hit, planning the next project, or paying off debts and filing for unemployment. Frequent failure is an accepted, if unpleasant, fact of life, and the Broadway theatre community is, by necessity, resilient.

Broadway will likely adapt to the exigencies of the moment as it has so many times in the last century, but each adjustment affects, in some measure, the nature of the beast. Absent a catastrophe that outstrips the terrorist attacks of September 11, the Fabulous Invalid will survive in some fashion. But already it scarcely resembles its forebears of just a few decades past. In this environment, the commercial theatre will be hard pressed to support the production of new straight plays, and musicals will probably grow more opulent, more expensive, and less artistically audacious. It is questionable whether the integrity of the work seen onstage will be able to withstand the banality of the theme-park sensibility at play on the street. Broadway resembles Las Vegas more than ever, and a vital and resounding voice in American theatre has been muted. A powerful opposing force is needed to counteract the present momentum and shift the pendulum resolutely in the opposite direction.

Notes

Bibliography

Index

Notes

1. The Terrain

1. A complete list of interviews conducted by the author may be found in the bibliography. To avoid tedious note citations throughout the text, author-subject interviews are not documented in the notes section.

2. Karen Hauser and Catherine Lanier, *Broadway's Economic Contribution to New York City, 2000–2001 Season* (New York: League of American Theatres and Producers, and Alliance for the Arts, 2002), 6.

3. *Regional theatre* is a term largely avoided by the sixty-plus professional not-for-profit theatres that are members of the League of Resident Theatres. *Regional* was banished from the acronym because it suggested that these theatres exist in the geographic and cultural hinterlands and New York City alone is the pulsing heart of theatrical exploration.

4. The workshop production, which *A Chorus Line* birthed, allowed producers to better afford the initial stage in the genesis of a show. It became a staple of Broadway and continues as an important means of developing new work. Some producers use this method in place of the actors-by-the-piano backers audition to raise cash, and spend a significant amount of seed money to conjure some sense of the glories to come in a larger production. Other producers employ the workshop as a low-cost, controlled environment in which to try out the work for the artists.

5. John Willis, *Theatre World, 1975–76* (New York: Crown Publishers, 1977), 6.

6. Karen Hauser, *Who Goes to Broadway? The Demographics of the Audience, 2000-2001 Season* (New York: League of American Theatres and Producers), 11.

7. National Arts Journalism Program, *Wonderful Town: The Future of the Theater in New York* (New York: National Arts Journalism Program, Columbia University, 2002), 19.

8. Hauser, *Who Goes to Broadway?*, 44.

9. *Approximately* is used because theatre buildings occasionally go out of business as theatres. Others have been demolished, and new ones have been built, so that a constant number is difficult to pinpoint.

10. Reputedly one of the most expensive Broadway shows to date was *The Lion King*. Disney Theatrical staff decline to give specific figures for the total costs of their shows, but educated guesses put the figure at a minimum of twenty million dollars.

11. Karen Hauser, *The Audience for Touring Broadway: A Demographic Study, 1999–2000 Season* (New York: League of American Theatres and Producers, 2000), 4.

12. Chris Jones, "'Fever' Pitches a Road Revamp," *Variety,* March 12–18, 2001, 50.

13. Hauser, *Who Goes to Broadway?,* 14.

14. William Goldman, *The Season: A Candid Look at Broadway* (New York: Harcourt, Brace, & World, 1969), 112–13.

2. The Producers

1. Emmanuel Azenberg quoted in Jesse McKinley, comp., "Real Producers Are Nothing Like Bialystock. Right?" *New York Times,* June 3, 2001, Arts and Leisure sec., 9.

2. Ian Parker, "How to Be a Producer," *New Yorker,* November 4, 2002, 62.

3. With only a few exceptions, most commercial houses on Broadway are owned or controlled by three theatre chains: the Shubert Organization, the Nederlander Organization, and Jujamcyn Theatres. The Shuberts control sixteen and a half theatres (the Music Box Theatre being co-owned by the Irving Berlin estate), the Nederlanders, nine; and Jujamcyn, five. A few other theatres are independently owned or leased, including Disney's New Amsterdam and Clear Channel's Ford Center. Three theatre buildings are owned or leased by not-for-profit theatre companies. Lincoln Center Theaters controls the Vivian Beaumont; Manhattan Theatre Club, the Biltmore; and the Roundabout, the American Airlines Theatre.

4. Harold Prince, *Contradictions: Notes on Twenty-Six Years in the Theatre* (New York: Dodd, Mead, 1974), 69.

5. Harold Prince, "In It for the Long Haul," interview by Janet Coleman, in *A Passion for Ideas: How Innovators Create the New and Shape Our World,* ed. Heinrich von Pierer and Bolko von Oetinger (West Lafayette, IN: Purdue University Press, 2002), 202.

6. Actors' Equity Association, which has a membership of about forty thousand, represents both actors and stage managers. Its constitution was drafted in 1913, and it was formally recognized by the American Federation of Labor in 1919.

7. Stephen Farber, *Producing Theatre* (New York: Limelight Editions, 1987), 39–41.

8. Tom Judson, letter to the editor, *Equity News* 87, no. 8 (October–November 2002), 2.

9. Chris Jones, "Union Flap May Spur New Road Map," *Variety,* September 23–29, 2002, 85.

10. Bob Hofler, "These Angels Place Bets on Show," *Variety,* November 18–24, 2002, 60.

11. Parker, "How to Be," 60.

12. Robin Pogrebin, "Broadway Angels, with Smaller Wings," *New York Times,* December 26, 1999, sec. 3, 7.

3. Broadway, Inc.

1. Todd Haimes, panelist, "When Theatre Owners Produce," panel presentation at International Society for the Performing Arts conference, December 12, 1999, untranscribed audiotape.

2. Donald Frantz, panelist, "When Theatre Owners Produce."

3. Bruce Weber, "Gambling on a Trip from 'Ragtime' to Riches," *New York Times,* February 19, 1998, A18.

4. Although the three major theatre owners all have produced shows, they have rarely been sole producer, and their primary function historically has been as real estate owners.

5. Weber, "Gambling," A18.

6. Martin Peers, "Two Sets of Books Unveiled at Livent," *Variety,* August 17, 1998, 2.

7. Peter Marks, "As Giants in Suits Descend on Broadway," *New York Times,* May 19, 2002, sec. 2, 14.

8. broadwayacrossamerica.com Web site, January 1, 2003.

9. Lynn Ahrens quoted in Robin Pogrebin, "Oh, to Keep Horton from Laying an Egg!" *New York Times,* November 14, 2000, B4.

10. Robin Pogrebin, "Who Killed the Cat?" *New York Times,* July 18, 2001, B3.

11. Pogrebin, "Who Killed the Cat?" B3.

12. broadwayacrossamerica.com, January 7, 2003.

13. Ben Brantley, "Cub Comes of Age: A Twice-Told Cosmic Tale," *New York Times,* November 14, 1997, E1.

14. Robin Pogrebin, "Disney Enlists Theater Innovators for Theme Park Shows," *New York Times,* January 6, 2003, B8.

4. When Worlds Collide

1. Jeremy Gerard, *ACT II: Creating Partnerships and Setting Agendas for the Future of the American Theater, A Report on the Second American Congress of Theater, June 16–18, 2000* (New York: League of American Theatres and Producers, and Theatre Communications Group, 2002), 6–7.

2. Tyrone Guthrie, *A New Theatre* (New York: McGraw Hill, 1964), 178.

3. Julius Novick, *Beyond Broadway: The Quest for Permanent Theatres* (New York: Hill and Wang, 1968), 1.

4. To underscore the greater connectivity between the not-for-profit and commercial worlds, the American Theatre Wing, which administers the Tony Awards, bestows an annual award to a distinguished resident theatre. The three

New York theatres listed, however, also enjoy Tony eligibility for the works that they produce, so that *Contact*, for example, a Lincoln Center production, was able to win the Tony for best musical.

5. Ben Cameron, "Broadway: Devil or Angel for Nonprofit Theater? Finding the Right Way to Cross the Divide," *New York Times*, June 4, 2000, archival Web site, n. pag..

6. Bruce Weber, "When the Commercial Theater Moves In on Nonprofits," *New York Times*, October 10, 1999, sec. 2, 1.

7. Zelda Fichandler, "The Profit in Nonprofit," *American Theatre*, December 2000, 31–32.

8. Gerard, ACT II, 19–20.

9. Cameron, "Broadway," n. pag.

10. Rocco Landesman, "Broadway: Devil or Angel for Nonprofit Theater? A Vital Movement Has Lost Its Way," *New York Times*, June 4, 2000, archival Web site, n. pag.

11. Landesman, "Broadway."

12. Robin Pogrebin, "Theatre for Fun or Profit: Producers' Two Camps Remain Uneasy Allies," *New York Times*, June 15, 2000, archival Web site, n. pag.

13. Todd Haimes quoted in Joan Channick, "Turnaround at the Roundabout," *American Theatre*, March 2003, 51–52.

14. Landesman, "Broadway."

15. Landesman, "Broadway."

16. Lincoln Center Theater initially contracts its artists for a scheduled engagement of about sixteen weeks. Should the production be extended, salaries rise from their not-for-profit levels to rates that are closer to those mandated by the commercial production contract.

17. Landesman, "Broadway," n. pag.

18. Gerard, *ACT II*, 42–43.

5. The Money Song

1. Certain costs, such as real estate tax, payroll for essential personnel, electricity, water, insurance, and so forth, continue to accrue regardless of whether a show occupies a theatre.

2. The artistic staff and the actors are employees of, and paid directly by, the producer. The producer employs a small number of salaried stagehands who owe fealty to the production, whereas the theatre owner hires a separate complement of stagehands. Musicians, box office staff, ushers, maintenance staff, and so forth are paid by the theatre. But the distinction is mooted by the fact that the money comes from the same source—the producer's pockets.

3. A typical, large-scale new musical in the 2003–4 season might cost about fourteen million dollars, broken down as follows:

Physical production (sets, costumes, lights, sound, etc.) $3,800,000
Fees (creative artists, staff) 1,600,000
Rehearsal salaries 1,300,000
Casting and rehearsal expenses 180,000
Advertising and promotion 1,000,000
Take-in and rehearsal (salaries and expenses from the
    start of the take-in/load-in at the theatre through
    opening night) 2,000,000
Administrative 700,000
Out-of-town costs (if the show plays in commercial
    arenas) 2,000,000
Advances (writers, director, designers, etc.) 375,000
Reserve or contingency... 1,000,000

The same musical might have weekly operating expenses of about $550,000. These are essentially fixed costs, as they do not include royalties to the creative artists and other percentage royalty earners or the theatre owner's percentage of 5 or 6 percent, which is subtracted from the adjusted gross earnings.

Weekly maintenance of physical production $72,000
Salaries 163,000
Advertising 90,000
Theatre expenses (insurance, utilities, etc.,
    including theatre employee salaries) 190,000
Fixed fees and royalties 8,500
Administrative 29,900

4. The following unions have contracts with the League: Actors' Equity Association, American Federation of Musicians Local 802, Association of Theatrical Press Agents and Managers, Engineers Local 30, International Alliance of Theatrical Stage Employees (for stagehands hired by the producer), IATSE Local One (for stagehands hired by the theatre owner), Makeup and Hair Local 798, Porters and Cleaners Local 32BJ, Society of Stage Directors and Choreographers, Theatrical Wardrobe Union Local 764, Treasurers and Ticket-Sellers Local 751, United Scenic Artists Local 829, and Ushers and Doormen Local 306. Some of these locals work under IATSE umbrella jurisdiction but maintain separate contracts with the League.

6. Page to Stage

1. Peter Marks, "A Happier 'Les Misérables,'" *New York Times,* March 13, 1997, C16.
2. Chris Jones, "Road Shows Seize on Notion of Brand I.D.," *Variety,* September 10–16, 2001, A8–10.
3. Jones, "'Fever,'" 50.

4. Chris Jones, "At Long Last, 'Lion' Slouches Toward Stix," *Variety*, January 15–21, 2001, 97.

5. Miles Wilkin quoted in Rick Lyman, "2 Powerhouses of the Theater Meld Broadway and the Road," *New York Times*, June 9, 1997, A1.

6. Hauser, *Audience for Touring Broadway*, 4.

7. Alan Adamson quoted in Gerard, *ACT II*, 61.

8. Gerard, *ACT II*, 61–62.

9. Howard Kissel, *David Merrick, the Abominable Showman: The Unauthorized Biography* (New York: Applause Books, 1993), 232–33.

10. Jesse McKinley, "For the Asking, a $480 Seat," *New York Times*, October 26, 2001, A1.

7. The Nature of the Beast

1. Ironically, it was a portion of the tax paid by Portman to develop the hotel that was channeled into a fund that supported the New 42, which oversaw the reclamation of several theatres on Forty-second Street.

2. Lynne B. Sagalyn, *Times Square Roulette: Remaking the City Icon* (Cambridge, Mass.: MIT Press, 2001), 341–46.

3. Thomas J. Lueck, "Returning from Decline, 42nd Street Is Now a Magnet for Merchants," *New York Times*, November 15, 1995, B3.

4. Ronald Grover, Suzanne Woolley, and Richard A. Melcher, "Call It the Great Walt Way," *Business Week*, September 25, 1995, 56.

5. Phil Gallo, "Studios Gauge the Stage," *Variety*, November 3, 2002, 65–68.

6. Gallo, "Studios Gauge the Stage," 68.

7. Barry Singer, "Pop Self-Consciousness Finally Infiltrates Broadway," *New York Times*, August 26, 2001, Arts and Leisure sec., 1–10.

8. Charles Isherwood, "Broadway Battles the Blues," *Variety*, June 3–9, 2002, 49.

9. Jesse McKinley, "Broadway Getting the Jitters as Advance Ticket Sales Fall," *New York Times*, August 4, 2002, A21.

10. Charles Isherwood and Robert Hofler, "Broadway Weathers Tough Times: B.O. Sets Record, but War Woes, Economic Slump Raise Fears," *Variety*, June 2–8, 2003, 55.

Bibliography

Books, Contracts, Journals, Periodicals, and Web Sites

"Agreement and Rules Governing Employment under the Equity/League Production Contract." New York: Actors' Equity Association, 2000.

"Approved Production Contract for Musical Plays." New York: Dramatists Guild.

Atkinson, Brooks. *Broadway*. Rev. ed. New York: Limelight Editions, 1985.

Brantley, Ben. "Cub Comes of Age: A Twice-Told Cosmic Tale." *New York Times*, November 14, 1997.

Broadway Across America Web site. broadwayacrossamerica.com. January 1, 2003; January 7, 2003.

Cameron, Ben. "Broadway: Devil or Angel for Nonprofit Theater? Finding the Right Way to Cross the Divide." *New York Times*, June 4, 2000.

Channick, Joan. "Turnaround at the Roundabout." *American Theatre*, March 2003.

"Collective Bargaining Agreement Between the League of American Theatres and Producers, Inc., and Associated Musicians of Greater New York, Local 802, AFM, AFL-CIO, 1998–2003."

"Collective Bargaining Agreement, the League of American Theatres and Producers and the Society of Stage Directors and Choreographers, Inc., 1996–2000."

Farber, Stephen. *Producing Theatre*. New York: Limelight Editions, 1987.

Fichandler, Zelda. "The Profit in Nonprofit." *American Theatre*, December 2000.

Gallo, Phil. "Studios Gauge the Stage." *Variety*, November 3, 2002.

Gerard, Jeremy. *ACT II: Creating Partnerships and Setting Agendas for the Future of the American Theater, A Report on the Second American Congress of Theater, June 16–18, 2000*. New York: League of American Theatres and Producers, and Theatre Communications Group, 2002.

Goldman, William. *The Season: A Candid Look at Broadway*. New York: Harcourt, Brace, & World, 1969.

Grover, Ronald, Suzanne Woolley, and Richard A. Melcher. "Call It the Great Walt Way." *Business Week*, September 25, 1995.

Guthrie, Tyrone. *A New Theatre*. New York: McGraw Hill, 1964.

Hauser, Karen. *The Audience for Touring Broadway: A Demographic Study, 1999–2000 Season*. New York: League of American Theatres and Producers, 2000.

———. *Who Goes to Broadway? The Demographics of the Audience, 2000–2001 Season.* New York: League of American Theatres and Producers, 2001.

Hauser, Karen, and Catherine Lanier. *Broadway's Economic Contribution to New York City, 2000–2001 Season.* New York: League of American Theatres and Producers, Inc., and Alliance for the Arts, 2002.

Hirsch, Foster. *The Boys from Syracuse: The Shuberts' Theatrical Empire.* Carbondale: Southern Illinois University Press, 1998.

Hofler, Bob. "These Angels Place Bets on Show." *Variety,* November 18–24, 2002.

Hoogstraten, Nicholas van. *Lost Broadway Theatres.* New York: Princeton Architectural Press, 1997.

Isherwood, Charles. "Broadway Battles the Blues." *Variety,* June 3–9, 2002.

Isherwood, Charles, and Robert Hofler. "Broadway Weathers Tough Times: B. O. Sets Record, But War Woes, Economic Slump Raise Fears." *Variety,* June 2–8, 2003.

Jones, Chris. "At Long Last, 'Lion' Slouches Toward Stix." *Variety,* January 15–21, 2001.

———. "'Fever' Pitches a Road Revamp." *Variety,* March 12–18, 2001.

———. "Road Shows Seize on Notion of Brand I.D." *Variety,* September 10–16, 2001.

———. "Union Flap May Spur New Road Map." *Variety,* September 23–29, 2002.

Judson, Tom. Letter to the editor. *Equity News* 87, no. 8 (October–November 2002): 2.

Kissel, Howard. *David Merrick, the Abominable Showman: The Unauthorized Biography.* New York: Applause Books, 1993.

Landesman, Rocco. "Broadway: Devil or Angel for Nonprofit Theater? A Vital Movement Has Lost Its Way." *New York Times,* June 4, 2000.

Laurents, Arthur. *Original Story By.* New York: Alfred A. Knopf, 2000.

Lueck, Thomas J. "Returning from Decline, 42nd Street Is Now a Magnet for Merchants." *New York Times,* November 15, 1995.

Lyman, Rick. "2 Powerhouses of the Theater Meld Broadway and the Road." *New York Times,* June 9, 1997.

Marks, Peter. "As Giants in Suits Descend on Broadway." *New York Times,* May 19, 2002, section 2.

———. "A Happier 'Les Misérables.'" *New York Times,* March 13, 1997.

McKinley, Jesse. "Broadway Getting the Jitters as Advance Ticket Sales Fall." *New York Times,* August 4, 2002.

———. "For the Asking, a $480 Seat." *New York Times,* October 26, 2001.

———, comp. "Real Producers Are Nothing Like Bialystock. Right?" *New York Times,* June 3, 2001, Arts and Leisure section.

National Arts Journalism Program. *Wonderful Town: The Future of Theater in*

New York. New York: National Arts Journalism Program, Columbia University, 2002.

Novick, Julius. *Beyond Broadway: The Quest for Permanent Theatres*. New York: Hill and Wang, 1968.

Parker, Ian. "How to Be a Producer." *New Yorker,* November 4, 2002.

Peers, Martin. "Two Sets of Books Unveiled at Livent." *Variety,* August 17, 1998.

Pogrebin, Robin. "Broadway Angels, with Smaller Wings." *New York Times,* December 26, 1999, section 3.

———. "Disney Enlists Theater Innovators for Theme Park Shows." *New York Times,* January 6, 2003.

———. "Oh, to Keep Horton from Laying an Egg!" *New York Times,* November 14, 2000.

———. "Theater for Fun or Profit: Producers' Two Camps Remain Uneasy Allies." *New York Times,* June 15, 2000.

———. "Who Killed the Cat?" *New York Times,* July 18, 2001.

Prince, Harold. *Contradictions: Notes on Twenty-Six Years in the Theatre*. New York: Dodd, Mead, 1974.

———. "In It for the Long Haul." Interview by Janet Coleman. In *A Passion for Ideas: How Innovators Create the New and Shape the World,* edited by Heinrich von Pierer and Bolko von Oetinger. 201–14. West Lafayette, IN: Purdue University Press, 2002.

Sagalyn, Lynne B. *Times Square Roulette: Remaking the City Icon.* Cambridge, MA: MIT Press, 2001.

Singer, Barry. "Pop Self-Consciousness Finally Infiltrates Broadway." *New York Times,* August 26, 2001.

Weber, Bruce. "Gambling on a Trip from 'Ragtime' to Riches." *New York Times,* February 19, 1998.

———. "When the Commercial Theater Moves In on Nonprofits." *New York Times,* October 10, 1999, section 2.

"When Theatre Owners Produce." Panel presentation at International Society for the Performing Arts conference, December 12, 1999. Untranscribed audiotape.

Willis, John. *Theatre World, 1975–76.* New York: Crown Publishers, 1977.

Interviews with Author

Aberger, Tom, Costa Mesa, CA, February 26, 2002.

Alessandrini, Gerard, New York City, by telephone, January 21, 2003.

Bell, Marty, New York City, November 1, 2000.

Bernstein, Jed, New York City, November 1, 2000.

Billig, Robert, New York City, by telephone, February 11, 2003.

Breglio, John, New York City, by telephone, November 1, 2002.

Brown, Barry, New York City, October 26, 2000.

Burstein, Danny, New York City, June 19, 2001.

Bush, Michael, New York City, November 6, 2000.

Coyne, Nancy, New York City, October 26, 2000.

Dennison, Edward, New York City, November 6, 2000.

Dolan, Judith, La Jolla, CA, by telephone, December 19, 2002.

Dwyer, Terrence, La Jolla, CA, October 9, 2002.

Eisenberg, Alan, New York City, November 8, 2000.

Elice, Rick, New York City, by telephone, January 3, 2003.

Ellis, Josh, La Jolla, CA, December 4, 2000.

Frankel, Richard, New York City, October 31, 2000.

Fratti, Valentina, New York City, November 1, 2000.

Gabay, Roy, New York City, by telephone, December 4, 2002.

Gelblum, Seth, New York City, by telephone, October 30, 2001, and June 26, 2003.

Gersten, Bernard, New York City, by telephone, December 12, 2001, and January 15 2002.

Graff, Randy, New York City, by telephone, June 13, 2001.

Grove, Barry, New York City, by telephone, January 4, 2002.

Haimes, Todd, New York City, October 30, 2000.

Harmon, Jane, New York City, November 1, 2000.

Harnick, Sheldon, New York City, October 31, 2000.

Hartenstein, Frank, La Jolla, CA, November 20, 2001.

Hauptman, Barbara, New York City, November 6, 2000.

Keneally, Nina, New York City, November 1, 2000.

Kotis, Gregory A., New York City, by e-mail, November 22, 2002.

Landesman, Rocco, New York City, November 2, 2000.

Laurents, Arthur, New York City, by telephone, January 10, 2002.

Lawrence, Peter, New York City, November 7, 2000.

Lee, Ronald, Pound Ridge, NY, by telephone, January 2, 2002, and January 30, 2002.

Leventer, Wendy, New York City, October 27, 2000.

Levey, Alan, Los Angeles, October 23, 2000, and November 21, 2002.

Longbottom, Robert, New York City, by telephone, January 24, 2002.

Luker, Rebecca, New York City, June 19, 2001.

Markinson, Martin, New York City, October 27, 2000.

McAnuff, Des, La Jolla, CA, November 11, 2001.

Mishkin, Chase, New York City, by telephone, December 21, 2001.

Moriarty, William, New York City, November 6, 2000.

Nederlander, James L., New York City, November 11, 2000.

Parry, William, New York City, June 20, 2001.

Pentecost, James, La Jolla, CA, February 5, 2002.

Rich, Frank, New York City, by telephone, July 9, 2001.

Roth, Daryl, New York City, October 30, 2000.

Roth, Jordan, New York City, November 3, 2000.

Scandalios, Nick, New York City, by telephone, December 26, 2000.

Schneider, Peter, Los Angeles, by telephone, October 4, 2002.

Schumacher, Thomas, Los Angeles, by telephone, November 12 and 27, 2002.

Slaughter, Harriet, New York City, October 31, 2000.

Smith, Philip J., New York City, November 3, 2000.

Somlyo, Roy, New York City, November 7, 2000.

Sondheim, Stephen, New York City, by telephone, February 15, 2002.

Strong, Edward, New York City, November 2, 2000.

Sullivan, James, New York City, October 30, 2000.

Trulock, Dianne, New York City, November 1, 2000.

Unger, Hank, New York City, by telephone, November 22, 2002.

Viertel, Jack, New York City, November 2, 2000.

Wagner, Robin, New York City, by telephone, January 7, 2002.

Weidman, John, New York City, February 14, 2003.

Weissler, Barry, New York City, November 3, 2000.

Wildhorn, Frank, New York City, November 8, 2000.

Wilkin, Miles, New York City, October 31, 2000.

Zeiger, Scott, New York City, New York City, November 2, 2000.

Index

Steven Adler, a professor of theatre at the University of California, San Diego, headed the graduate stage management program from 1987 to 2004. A member of Actors' Equity Association since 1979, he has stage-managed productions on Broadway, Off-Broadway, in regional theatres, and on tour. He is the author of *Rough Magic: Making Theatre at the Royal Shakespeare Company*, published by Southern Illinois University Press. He was appointed provost of Earl Warren College at UCSD in 2004, and continues to teach theatre.